Toward a Feminist

Developmental

Psychology

Toward a Feminist

Developmental

Psychology

*Edited by Patricia H. Miller
and Ellin Kofsky Scholnick*

Routledge
New York • London

Published in 2000 by
Routledge
29 West 35th Street
New York, NY 10001

Published in Great Britain by
Routledge
11 New Fetter Lane
London EC4P 4EE

LIBRARY OF CONGRESS CATALOGING-IN-PUBLICATION DATA

Toward a feminist developmental psychology / Patricia H. Miller
and Ellin Kofsky Scholnick, eds.
    p.   cm.
  Includes bibliographical references and index.
  ISBN 0-415-92178-3 (hb). — ISBN 0-415-92177-5 (pb)
  1. Developmental psychology. 2. Feminist psychology.
I. Miller, Patricia H. II. Scholnick, Ellin Kofsky.
BF713.T66   2000
155'.082—dc21   99-33632
                                       CIP

Designed by Karen Quigley.

Contents

IV. The Other Half of the Partnership: Developmental Psychology Can Inform Feminism

Preface

This book is a developmental project. It emerged from several years of intellectual collaboration, following our independent realization that feminist approaches had something important to say to our discipline of developmental psychology and, conversely, that the field of developmental psychology could enrich and support feminist analyses. We both learned about feminist perspectives during our involvement with the women's studies programs on our campuses. We first expressed our ideas in a symposium at the annual meeting of the Jean Piaget Society in 1994. Our chapters in this volume grew out of those initial attempts to bring feminist approaches to developmental audiences and to introduce aspects of developmental psychology to feminist philosophers. Our talks at each subsequent conference, to different audiences, formed a developmental step in our thinking and led to extending the conversation to several contributors to this volume who shared our perspective or who saw the relevance of developmental feminism to their own research programs. The process of editing the book continued the conversation, collaboration, and learning.

Thus the volume represents the first time a group of active mainstream developmental researchers has turned a feminist lens on their own work. The developmental psychology essays are illuminated by the essays by two women's studies scholars who turn their own lenses on developmental psychology. Together the authors address two issues. What can feminist critiques and feminist epistemology tell us about the methods of developmental psychology and the characterization of development? What can developmental psychology tell us about the nature and process of engenderment? In our attempts to integrate recent research on feminist theories and methods with developmental theorizing and methodology, we address two audiences. One is the set of readers interested in human development who are intrigued by the recent explosion of feminist scholarship in women's studies. For this audience the volume can serve as a tutorial on feminist studies, an illustration of its applications to areas of human development, and, perhaps, an inspiration to use the insights of feminism in their own scholarship. The other audience consists of readers with a women's studies perspective who wish to learn about developmental psychology and the interesting questions it raises for feminist theories. The book may serve as a tutorial on some relevant areas of developmental inquiry. We hope that these scholars will realize that psychology has more to contribute than analyses of the development of gender roles and sex differences. Psychological analyses of the nature of knowledge and the nature of growth may prove a treasure trove for feminist analyses.

The book is intended to create a future for developmental feminism. But we owe much to our past. We would like to thank our colleagues in women's studies at the University of Florida and the University of Maryland, who started us on our path; Rosie Warner and Linda Grahne, who provided the secretarial support; and Heidi Freund at Routledge, who understood what we wanted to accomplish.

Patricia H. Miller
Ellin Kofsky Scholnick

FEMINIST PERSPECTIVES

AND DEVELOPMENTAL PSYCHOLOGY

WHAT ARE THE ISSUES?

1

Introduction

Beyond Gender

as a Variable

Patricia H. Miller and Ellin Kofsky Scholnick

Developmental psychology is inherently interdisciplinary. The complexity of human development requires that those who study it draw on contributions from fields ranging from biology and neuroscience to sociology and anthropology. The discipline has a long history of fruitful assimilation of new ideas from other fields and perspectives. This book represents yet another example of how exciting new scholarship outside of the discipline can contribute in important ways to developmental psychology.

Feminist scholarship, an interdisciplinary field, is one of the most influential perspectives in academia today, and has touched nearly every discipline. The number of women's studies programs has grown from one in 1969 to approximately seven hundred currently, including more than one hundred graduate programs. The top university presses feature feminist books. Ironically, despite its large proportion of women historically compared to most research-oriented disciplines, and despite the large number of articles on gender published annually, developmental psychology has remained almost untouched by this influential intellectual movement (but see, e.g., Belenky, Clinchy, Goldberger, & Tarule, 1986; Burman, 1998; Gilligan, 1982). For example, the chapter that reviews work on gender in the most recent *Handbook of Child Psychology* (Ruble & Martin, 1998) treats gender as an individual difference variable and a social role without attention to the political, cultural, and power structures in which gender is embedded.

Most of the contributors to the volume are mainstream developmental psychologists, often working on gender-related issues. Some have primary or affiliate appointments in women's studies programs. Their chapters express how their assimilation of feminist approaches has informed and transformed their thinking about their own areas of research. We have titled the volume *Toward a Feminist Developmental Psychology* because our rethinking of development is evolving rather than in a final form. The two authors who are not developmentalists—Sue V. Rosser, a biologist, and Lorraine Code, a philosopher—have devoted their careers to feminist scholarship and thus provide useful perspectives on development that are informed by years of feminist thought. All authors share the vision that concepts and tools from feminist scholarship can contribute to broader, more adequate accounts of development. In the final chapter we reverse directions and illustrate what developmental psychology, even in its current form, can contribute to feminist perspectives. Feminists also can learn more about development by reading the various chapters. We hope to inspire developmental psychologists to read feminist literature and feminist scholars to read developmental literature, for we see much of value in each perspective for the other.

Developmentalists and feminists ask some of the same questions—about the effects of social institutions on people, the process of acquiring knowledge, the effects of experience on one's perspective, the reality of social categories, and the causes and consequences of individual differences. But the two fields look through different lenses. Trading lenses alters the vision of each.

The chapters illustrate two parts of a feminist perspective. First, a feminist critique reveals the typically unrecognized masculine assumptions in a discipline. Such critiques have shown that male values, experiences, and beliefs have shaped every discipline examined. Developmental theories usually incorporate definitions of maturity and explanations of the process by which it is reached. Traditionally, male development is the norm with which female development is compared; our stories of development are permeated with masculine content, methods, metaphors, and mechanisms of change. The striving toward autonomy, mastery, analytical thinking, and formal logic and models of change based on differentiation of self from others, conflict, and competition among skills reflects the values and experiences of only one subset of the population. Borrowing from Harding (1991), we ask: *Whose* development? *Whose* behaviors?

The second part of a feminist perspective looks forward in a more positive direction to construct a broader, more inclusive and accurate, nonsexist account for a discipline. Each chapter offers a vision of the form this account might take for one aspect of development.

The Feminist Lens

What is a feminist perspective? Because many developmental psychologists are unfamiliar with the basic tenets of feminist theory and therefore with the applicability of feminist insights, we offer a short tutorial, but encourage further reading of feminist literature (e.g., Alcoff & Potter, 1993; Harding, 1991; Rosser, 1997; Tong, 1998). Developmentalists may also find it useful to examine the small but growing feminist literature within developmental and cognitive psychology (e.g., Adam, 1997; Belenky et al., 1986; Burman, 1998; Goldberger, Tarule, Clinchy, & Belenky, 1996; Wilson, 1998).

Although feminist perspectives are as diverse as developmental perspectives, most tend to focus on three concepts. First, humans, and in fact all phenomena, are interconnected rather than solitary and separated. Second, human experiences and knowledge are situated rather than decontextualized and universal. Third, societies are characterized by institutionalized androcentrism and its accompanying power structure; societies are not simply a collection of gendered individuals. We now elaborate on each concept.

First, regarding connectedness, individuals are relational beings who are embedded in social relationships more than they are separated, autonomous, and distanced from others (e.g., Chodorow, 1978; Dinnerstein, 1977; Keller, 1985). The differentiation and separation of self from others is an ideal derived from the Western/northern cultural heritage, which has heavily influenced theories in the social sciences (Harding, 1998), including developmental psychology. Moreover, feminists tend to emphasize different facets of relations than traditional theorists. Collaboration, reciprocity, and co-construction are as important as dominance, competition, conflict, and hierarchical relations (e.g., Belenky et al., 1986). In addition, a focus on relations challenges traditional dichotomies. The psychological and social world cannot be described in terms of polarities such as reason versus emotion, mind versus body, and public versus private because each term influences and co-occurs with its presumed opposite (e.g., Code, Mullett, & Overall, 1988).

Second, situatedness leads to a distinctive epistemology, philosophy of science, and research agenda. A person's knowledge or a researcher's findings are situated and particular rather than universal (e.g., Harding & Hintikka, 1983). Feminists doubt there is a "view from nowhere," and they critically analyze how research is framed. Knowers are not interchangeable; feminist epistemologists ask *who* knows, in what situation, for what purpose (Code, 1993, 1995b). A knower's perspective is affected by experience, including experiences related to his or her gender, race, social class, culture, sexuality, and so on (e.g., Collins, 1990). Universality and objectivity cannot be assumed, because knowledge, scientific research, development, and so on, are embedded and related within a personal and cultural context. Research is conducted to achieve cultural aims, such as economic development or political dominance. From a feminist perspective, research and theories should be grounded in daily experience and should take into account the perspectives of the participants in the research (Code, 1995b; Harding, 1998). Finally, because gender is situated in a social, political context, it always intersects with race, class, culture, ethnicity, sexuality, and other categories; consequently there is no single, homogeneous, essentialist category of "women" or "girls" (e.g., Collins, 1990).

Third, regarding institutionalized androcentrism, feminist critiques identify the implicit cultural value system, including gender, that underlies and directs the concepts and methods of any discipline, including the sciences (e.g., Keller, 1985). This influence often is subtle and may remain invisible. When revealed, issues of power, control, and self-interest frequently emerge. Feminist scholars view societies as constructed in ways that advantage males over females. The roles of mothers and fathers in the family, the definition of what counts as a family, the lack of accessible quality day care, salary inequities, property laws in certain states, male-oriented pedagogies in science and mathematics classrooms, and portrayals of males and females in the entertainment media might all be examples of ways that societies are constructed that privilege men and boys over women and girls. The outcome of institutionalized biases is differences in the power, status, and opportunities of males versus females, majority versus minority races, and middle versus lower economic classes. In particular, males tend to control economics and politics. Male values, ways of thinking and talking, and ways of conducting science are considered the norm, while others are, indeed, considered "the other," "alternative," "diversity," "different ways of knowing," "gendered," and so on.

Because androcentric cultural values permeate and define the lives of women and men, feminists link the political and the personal. In light of existing inequities, feminists argue that psychological theorizing and research should improve the lives of all people, including women and girls. Consequently, feminists pay attention to global issues such as cross-cultural differences in gender roles and the impact of modernization in developing countries on women and girls (e.g., Harding, 1998). Such variations in political and economic conditions contribute to differences in the experience of girls and women in various societies and thus shape their psychological development and health.

Social-contextual developmental theories incorporate many of these tenets, particularly the concept of the relational self and the importance of cultural context. However, feminist approaches go beyond these theories in several ways. First, feminist theories focus on the power differentials that underlie gender-organized societies. The white male voice often drowns out other voices. The degree of power that a person has determines what experiences are possible for her or him, and thus determines the resulting social and cognitive development. Second, feminist approaches fully explore the implications of being nonwhite and nonmale, of not being in the center. For example, it has been argued (e.g., Collins, 1990), that those situated in the margins have a dual vision—the perspectives of both the dominating and the dominated groups. Third, feminist scholars have shown that gender roles are an overlay in all human endeavors, even scientific investigation, as is evident in, for example, the types of methods permitted, the questions that are asked, and the models of human behavior that are developed (see Scholnick, this volume).

Feminist critiques raise several critical questions that must be addressed by any satisfactory account of development. Does our androcentric cultural heritage favor particular models of development (e.g., conflict as a mechanism of development, increased distancing from others during childhood, dichotomies such as the separation of reason and emotion)? Does this heritage also lead to social structures and practices (e.g., the imbalance of power in relationships between boys and girls, differences in what spaces girls and boys are allowed to explore) that differentially affect the development of males and females? Does this heritage also use males' experiences and values as the norm, consequently making females "the other," when topics of development are chosen for study (e.g., skills generally more valued by males than females) and models of development are constructed? Do developmental theories and research adequately represent girls' and women's experiences? Are accounts or theories of development adequately contextualized in terms of gender, race, culture, class, and sexuality, or is it assumed that developmental processes are universal? Who stands to gain from traditional conceptions of development, families, and social roles?

Beyond Gender as a Variable

Rethinking Gender

A feminist perspective invokes gender in a way that differs greatly from the long history of research on gender in developmental psychology (Huston, 1983; Ruble & Martin, 1998). Developmental psychologists typically have treated gender as an individual difference variable and have searched for its biological and environmental causes. They have also tracked developmental changes in gender roles, including concepts of male and female. Although this work has provided much important information, it differs from feminist approaches. In feminist accounts, gender is not a variable but a social status, and males' position is favored. Instead of starting an account of development with the experiences of males, feminist approaches start with the experiences and values more often associated with females. Moreover, the lesser status and power of females and children in most societies leads to an examination of the impact of oppression and marginalization on people more generally. In short, a feminist approach moves females from the periphery to the center as a basis for reexamining the developmental issues that have formed the core of the discipline. If we take the experiences, interests, needs, values, preferences, and beliefs associated with women and girls as a starting point, our theories of, and research on, the development of boys and girls would look different from our current theories and research.

Rethinking Thinking

An example of feminists going beyond gender as a variable is feminist epistemology. Most developmentalists know, from Piaget's (1970b) work, that epistemology is the branch of philosophy concerned with theories of knowledge—the origin, nature of, and conditions for knowledge, how knowledge claims can be verified or falsified. Research on cognitive development (e.g., Flavell, Miller, & Miller, 1993) examines similar issues about knowledge and its acquisition, though empirically rather than with philosophers' tools. Developmentalists address the origins of knowledge by studying infant cognition or by teasing apart the contributions of biology and experience to the acquisition of knowledge. They address questions about the nature of knowledge by studying whether a newly acquired concept is domain specific or transfers to other domains or contexts. They also examine whether knowledge is represented verbally or in some other way, and whether it resembles a "theory" of reality. Developmentalists explore what causes thinking to change, and whether thinking develops through a sequence of stages or more gradually. The process of cognitive development is examined on multiple levels, ranging from the neuropsychological levels through social-cultural levels.

However, feminist epistemologists use an analytical frame largely absent from developmental psychology (although sometimes found in social psychology; e.g., Fiske & Taylor, 1991). Concerned with the nature and position of knowers within a larger process of knowledge production, feminist epistemologists ask: Who decides what counts as legitimate knowledge? For what purpose? Who stands to gain by these accounts of knowledge, and who stands to lose? How does one's position in society, as defined by one's gender, race, ethnicity, class, and sexuality, affect one's knowledge? What is the relation between power (as influenced by the above characteristics) and knowledge? How does it matter epistemologically whether a knower is at the center or at the margins, is endowed by society with epistemic power and authority or denied these? How do social structures maintain and reinforce social hierarchies and the uneven distribution of power across the population? In contrast, cognitive developmentalists pay little attention to the situated standpoint of a knower except for the child's cognitive level and occasionally gender, race, or class in a global, essentializing way (e.g., "boys tend to ..."). Even developmentalists using social-contextual approaches typically ignore the relative power of the knower in the setting and the ways in which social-political structures constrain the knower. Thus, feminist epistemology can bring to developmental psychology a useful conceptual framework for understanding development.

Rethinking Development

If one makes relationships and connections among aspects of reality primary, one might be led to posit different procedures for acquiring knowledge, different metaphors of development, different research methods, and a different end goal of development. Moreover, if the life course of females were considered the norm and the life course of males the deviation, then the "typical" developmental route would be somewhat different. Feminist theorists are wary of imposing a uniform trajectory on people living very diverse lives. The chapters in this book suggest ways in which development would look different in terms of what is worth developing (content), how it is developed (process), what form the developed knowledge, skills, and behavior take (their organization or structure), and how this set of knowledge, skills, and behavior is used in the child's day-to-day experiences (function).

Bridge Theories

Fortunately, developmentalists have certain theories and concepts that are compatible with feminist approaches and thus can serve as a bridge between these interdisciplinary fields. Examples include Vygotsky's (1978) theory, cultural psychology (Shweder, Goodnow, Hatano, LeVine, Markus, & Miller, 1998), contextual approaches (Lerner, 1991), narrative sense-making accounts of development (Bruner, 1990; K. Nelson, 1996), and social constructionism (e.g., K. J. Gergen, 1994b). These various theories address the social context of development, social-political biases in research, dynamic interconnected systems, and social discourse.

A Road Map to This Book

This book reflects both the uniformity and diversity of feminist scholarship. Although the topics are diverse, the discussions show a metatheoretical awareness of the implicit assumptions underlying each topic and mode of investigation and demonstrate the benefits of a more exclusive frame. We do not attempt to cover all aspects of development, though we do sample a number of areas. Nor do we use all feminist perspectives. The chapters focus on areas for which feminist analyses seem particularly fruitful. Several chapters emphasize autobiographical memory, social context, self, narratives, and interaction between parents and young children. This emphasis is not surprising, given that these areas of research often are studied by the bridge theories as well. Young children are embedded in rich social exchanges with parents and peers, which lead to particular social cognitions.

The chapters reflect developmental psychology's focus on white, middle-class children but also critique that bias, as have many developmentalists. Several authors argue that it is critical to *begin* with the diversity of human experience, with its intersections of gender, race, class, ethnicity, and sexuality, rather than simply to include it as an afterthought. As in feminism, a fully satisfactory developmental psychology will address the rich variety of human values and experiences.

In sum, this book is for developmentalists and those in related disciplines who want to learn what feminism has to offer. It is also for feminists who want to learn what contemporary developmental psychology offers their work.

Feminist Theories

Implications for

Developmental Psychology

Sue V. Rosser and Patricia H. Miller

Individuals unfamiliar with feminist scholarship or women's studies often assume that feminist theory provides a singular and unified framework for analysis. In one sense this is correct; all feminist theories posit gender as a significant characteristic that interacts with other characteristics, such as race and class, to structure relationships between individuals, within groups, and within society as a whole. However, using the lens of gender to view the world results in diverse images or theories, as seen in the following feminisms (Nicholson, 1997; Tong, 1998): liberal, socialist, African-American/ethnic, essentialist, existentialist, psychoanalytic, radical, postmodern, and postcolonial. Their variety and complexity provide a framework through which to explore central issues in developmental psychology, such as the causes of development, the processes underlying developmental change, and variability in developmental pathways and endpoints.

In this chapter we describe each theory, identify the questions that each would raise about psychological development, show how each can serve as a critique of current accounts of development, and suggest fruitful new applications to the study of development. The chapter focuses not on gender differences but on the pervasiveness of masculine views, values, and models of development and on the potential contributions of feminist theories to a broader, richer, and more inclusive view of human development. We present the theories chronologically, in the order in which they tended to emerge and become influential. Most theories identified something that was missing in a prior theory or theories. Thus, the set resembles a development sequence toward a more integrated and complete feminist account. Table 1 provides an overview of the theories' critiques of, and implications for, developmental psychology.

Table 1. The varieties of feminist theories

Feminist Theory	Critique	Developmental Implications
Liberal / equity	Inequities; need to correct bad science	Remove barriers to girls' achievement; more inclusive and less biased samples, topics, methods, practices
Socialist	Neglect of gender/class power structure or social contextualism	Social constructionism; attention to power and social class
African-American/ Ethnic	Neglect of race as source of oppression; critique of dichotomous categories	More inclusive and less biased samples, topics, methods, practices
Essentialist	Biological differences in anatomy and hormones form the basis for social differences	Attention to biological input
Existential	Biology forms the basis of social construction of otherness	Attention to the normalizing role of masculine concepts and language; the social construction of girls' otherness
Psychoanalytic	Reexamination of the origins of gender in early family practices	The early origins of gender
Radical	Gender oppression is deepest, most widespread oppression; make women the focus of analysis	Redefinition of topics in development; models of development based on girls' experiences
Postmodern	Questions possibility of universalizing any knowledge or category, including gender	Deconstructs "development"; questions universality of development
Postcolonial	Neglect of power underlying dominant-subordinate relations; colonizer to colonized parallels male to female; reinforces gender oppression	Places economic and social development in a common framework; attention to power

Liberal Feminism

Beginning in the eighteenth century, political scientists, philosophers, and feminists (Friedan, 1974; Jaggar, 1983; H. T. Mill, 1869/1970; J. S. Mill, 1851/1970; Wollstonecraft, 1891/1975) have described the parameters of liberal feminism. Although liberal feminists today hold varied views, they generally believe that females are suppressed in contemporary society because they suffer unjust discrimination (A. Jaggar, 1983). Liberal feminists seek no special privileges for women and girls; simply, they demand that everyone receive equal consideration and opportunity without discrimination on the basis of sex. However, the implications of liberal feminist theory extend beyond employment, access, and discrimination issues. Liberal feminism shares two fundamental assumptions with the foundations of the traditional scientific method: (1) both assume that human beings are highly autonomous and obtain knowledge in a rational manner that may be separated from their social conditions, and (2) both accept *positivism* as their theory of knowledge. Positivism implies that "all knowledge is constructed by inference from immediate sensory experiences" (Jaggar, 1983, pp. 355-356).

These two assumptions lead to a belief in the possibility of obtaining knowledge that is both objective and value free, concepts that form the cornerstones of the scientific method. Objectivity is contingent on value neutrality, or freedom from the values, interests, and emotions associated with a particular class, race, or sex. Thus, it is assumed, for example, that a substantial increase in the proportion of scientists who are women will be achieved without changes in science itself, except for the removal of barriers. That is, women scientists, like their male counterparts, will perceive the sensations and experiences on which their empirical observations are based separately and individually, while controlling their own values, interests, and emotions.

In the past two decades, feminist historians and philosophers of science (e.g., Fee, 1982; Haraway, 1989; Harding, 1986) and feminist scientists (e.g., Birke, 1986; Bleier, 1984, 1986b; Fausto-Sterling, 1992; Hubbard, 1990; Keller, 1983, 1985; Rosser, 1988, 1997; Spanier, 1982) have pointed out a gender-based bias and absence of value neutrality in science, particularly biology. The exclusion of females as experimental subjects, the focus on problems of primary interest to males, biased experimental designs, and interpretations of data based in language or ideas constricted by patriarchal parameters have caused biased or flawed experimental results in several areas. For example, in biology, when female primates were studied, it was usually only in their interaction (usually reaction) to males or infants.

Female primatologists (Fossey, 1983; Goodall, 1971) and sociobiologists (Hrdy, 1981, 1986) revealed new information that led to the overthrow of previously held theories regarding dominance hierarchies, mate selection (Hrdy, 1984), and female-female competition (Hrdy & Williams, 1983) by focusing on female-female interactions. An example from psychology is Gilligan's (1982) focus on issues of responsibility and care that are ignored by Kohlberg's (1981) moral theory, which was based on research with males.

Feminist critiques presenting these and other examples of flawed research have led to questioning whether science can ever be gender free. Although each scientist strives to be as objective and value free as possible, most scientists, feminists, and philosophers of science recognize that no individual can be completely neutral or value free. Instead, "objectivity is defined to mean independence from the value judgments of any particular individual" (Jaggar, 1983, p. 357). That is, the scientific *community* as a whole, by scrutinizing hypotheses and relevant evidence, corrects for any biases of individual scientists. Liberal feminists argue that lack of objectivity and the presence of bias occur because of human failure to follow properly the scientific method and avoid bias due to situation or condition. They argue that it was through attempts to become more value neutral that the androcentrism in previous scientific research has been revealed. Thus, liberal feminists suggest that now that the bias of gender has been revealed by feminist critiques, scientists can take this into account and make corrections. Both men and women will use this revelation to design experiments, gather and interpret data, and draw conclusions and theories that are more objective and free from bias, including gender bias (Biology and Gender Study Group, 1989).

Most developmental psychology research falls within the positivist framework; some developmental research is consistent with a liberal feminist approach. First, exposing the bias in adults' observations of boys and girls sensitizes developmental researchers to possible biases in their own observations. For example, labeling a baby as male or female elicits different descriptions of the same videotape (Condry & Condry, 1976). A "boy" baby is described as angry when becoming upset after a jack-in-the-box pops out, whereas a "girl" baby is described as fearful in response to the same event. Guarding against such biases would make developmental research more objective, and thus more scientific. Second, a liberal feminist approach would strive toward more equitable development for girls and boys. Differences in the socialization of boys and girls may have, for example, contributed to the greater entrance of males than females into science and math. Projects to attract more girls to science are important because increases in the number of women scientists would alleviate male bias and might lead to a more balanced, and thus impartial, science. Similarly, schools could achieve a more equitable development for boys and girls by eliminating differences in their treatment in the classroom, for example, by eliminating teachers' propensity to call on boys more frequently than girls (Sadker & Sadker, 1994).

The third and perhaps most interesting contribution of liberal feminism in developmental psychology is research focusing on behaviors previously slighted by developmental researchers. Despite the strong representation of women among developmental researchers, certain topics have been slighted, perhaps because of our society's male-oriented value system. Examples from research on females are care-oriented moral reasoning (Gilligan, 1982), "women's ways of knowing" that emphasize connections and relationships (Belenky, Clinchy, Goldberger, & Tarule, 1986; Goldberger, Tarule, Clinchy, & Belenky, 1996), nonphysical relational aggression (Crick & Rose, this volume), and girls' social interaction during games (e.g., Goodwin, 1985).

In contrast to liberal feminism, all other feminist theories call into question some of the fundamental assumptions underlying the scientific method, its corollaries of objectivity and value neutrality, or its implications. They reject individualism for a social constructivist view of knowledge and question positivism and the possibility of objectivity obtained by value neutrality. Many also imply that men and women may conduct scientific research differently, although each theory posits a different cause for the gender distinction. Although developmental psychologists have been receptive to critiques from a liberal feminist perspective, they generally are less familiar with or less receptive to the other theories of feminism, to be described next.

Socialist Feminism

Flowing from Marxism, socialist feminism contrasts with liberal feminism in its rejection of individualism and positivism as approaches to knowledge and in its focus on the oppression of females and lower socioeconomic classes. Just as a capitalist society subordinates the proletariat, so does patriarchy subordinate women. Marxism views all knowledge as socially constructed and thus rejects the notion of a neutral, disinterested, individual observer. Knowledge, even scientific knowledge, cannot be objective and value free because the basic categories of knowledge are shaped by human purposes and values, and ultimately social class. Because the prevailing knowledge and science reflect the interests and values of the dominant class and gender, dominant groups have an interest in concealing, and may in fact not recognize, the way they dominate. For example, under capitalism, the billions of dollars spent on defense-related scientific research and genetic engineering (with potential high profits from patents on genes), and the relatively small amounts of money going into AIDS research and pollution prevention, would be interpreted by Marxists as reflecting the interests of the dominant class. Or, emphasizing the apparent (though small) gender differences in math and science test scores may encourage the channeling of girls into nonmathematical and nonscientific occupations with lower pay and status.

Although strict Marxist feminism emphasizes class over gender, socialist feminism places class and gender on equal ground as factors that determine the position and perspective of a particular individual in society. Thus, women oppressed by both class and gender occupy a position that provides an advantageous and more comprehensive view of reality. Because of their oppression, they see problems with the status quo and the science and knowledge produced by the dominant class and gender. Simultaneously, their position requires them also to understand the science and condition of the dominant group in order to survive. This double vision is more accurate than that of the dominant group, which need only see the world from its own perspective and so has only a single, constrained viewpoint.

Developmental psychologists sometimes examine social class differences, though rarely examine their interaction with gender. But the potential impact of socialist feminism is far greater than this. The socialist-feminist focus on the power of the dominant group raises the question of why, in developmental psychology, certain topics, subject groups, and interpretations of data are privileged over others (see Franks, 1992, for examples). Does this privileging reflect the values and interests of a dominant class of middle-class white males? In the 1960s and 1970s, developmental psychologists' receptivity to Piaget's focus on children's scientific concepts may in part have reflected anxieties about the position of the United States in the cold war, including the space race with the Soviet Union. Concerns about the effects of working mothers (but not working fathers) and "cocaine mothers" (but not "cocaine fathers") on development imply blame on only part of the population. Day care and latchkey children are seen as a problem of working mothers but not working fathers. The conclusion in the fifties and sixties that boys raised only by mothers are less masculine was later shown to indicate only that the boys were less aggressive, which could be seen instead as something positive (Scarr, 1985). These examples suggest that a covert social value system steers developmental psychology. Finally, the bulk of developmental research is on white middle-class children rather than low-income or minority children. Thus, the dominant class is considered the norm and the underclass is "the other," the special case.

With respect to developmental theory, Vygotskian, and certain social-contextual, approaches (e.g., Rogoff, 1990) are consistent with the socialist-feminist view that knowledge is socially constructed. Children develop cognitively as they work or play with adults and peers. More advanced individuals direct and scaffold children's emerging concepts. As children internalize their conversational interaction with others, the social plane creates the psychological plane. Interestingly, however, these approaches give almost no attention to how social class, the masculine values of a society, and the child's gender influence the nature of this scaffolding. The importance of such issues is revealed, for example, in studies showing that parents tend to discuss more of the emotional aspects of past experiences with daughters than with sons (Adams, Kuebli, Boyle, & Fivush, 1995). And middle-class parents consider expressing one's view a natural right for children, but working-class parents consider this something to be earned and defended by children (Wiley, Rose, Burger, & Miller, 1998).

African-American/Womanist and Racial/Ethnic Feminism

Like socialist critiques, African-American critiques reject the individualism and supposed objectivity and value neutrality of the positivist Eurocentric approach and posit social construction as an approach to knowledge. African-American approaches identify the race of the observer/scientist and of the observed/subjects as influences on the resulting knowledge. They also critique the dichotomization of knowledge, or at least the identification of science with the first half and African-American with the latter half of the following dichotomies: culture/nature, rational/feeling, objective/subjective, quantitative/qualitative, active/passive, focused/diffuse, independent/dependent, mind/body, self/others, knowing/being. Whereas Marxism posits class as the organizing principle around which the struggle for power exists, African-American critiques maintain that race is the primary oppression. According to African-American *fem-*

inist approaches (Collins, 1990; Giddings, 1984; hooks, 1983, 1990; Lorde, 1984), for African-American women racism and sexism become intertwining oppressions that provide them with a different perspective and standpoint than those of either white women or African-American men (Collins, 1990).

The fact that African-Americans, especially women, are underrepresented in the population of developmental psychologists while Caucasians are overrepresented relative to their respective percentages in the population as a whole makes it particularly likely that in the choice of problems for study, the methods and theories used, and the conclusions drawn from the data, the profession and its theories do represent and function to further white Eurocentric interests. The more comprehensive view of minority females, one that derives from their race, class, and gender, is rarely represented among researchers or research participants. The vast majority of developmental research involves mainly white participants; relatively few studies focus on African-American or Latino children, and fewer still on girls in these groups. Using the experiences of African-American or Latina girls as a starting point can, however, provide new perspectives (Ginorio & Martinez, 1998; Leaper, this volume). For example, Goodwin (1990) observed how African-American girls engaged in a form of gossip dispute activity in order to create later events of great social importance. And work on African-American girls studying science illustrates complex interactions between gender and race (Clewell & Ginorio, 1996). Finally, recent work on Latino children reveals the effects on development of the importance that Latino culture places on strong family values and family unity, on the extended family as a support system for Latina mothers, and on girls' responsibilities for child care and housekeeping (Ginorio, Gutiérrez, Cauce, & Acosta, 1995). Research on diverse populations not only shows cultural differences, but also clarifies how social processes influence development.

Essentialist Feminism

Essentialism is the notion that every entity has certain inherent, fundamental properties, universal in its kind, that truly define it and make it what it is. This approach emphasizes biology and downplays context and experience. Essentialist feminist theory posits that women are different from men because of their biology, specifically their hormones, secondary sex characteristics, and reproductive systems. Essentialist feminists may attribute gender differences in visuospatial and verbal ability, aggression and other behavior, and other physical and mental traits to prenatal or pubertal hormone exposure. Nineteenth-century essentialist feminists proposed a biologically based gender inferiority of women in some physical (e.g., Blackwell, 1875/1976) and mental (e.g., Hollingsworth, 1914) traits and superiority in other traits. Biological essentialism formed the basis for the supposed moral superiority of women which nineteenth-century suffragettes used as a persuasive argument for giving women the vote (DuBois, Kelly, Kennedy, Korsmeyer, & Robinson, 1985; Hartmann & Banner, 1974).

In the earlier phases of the current wave of feminism, most feminists (Bleier, 1979; Fausto-Sterling, 1985; Hubbard, 1979; Rosser, 1982) fought against certain sociobiological research such as that by Wilson (1975), Trivers (1972), and Dawkins (1976) and some hormone and brain lateralization research (e.g., Buffery & Gray, 1972; Goy & Phoenix, 1971; Sperry, 1974) that seemed to provide biological evidence for gender differences in mental and behavioral characteristics. Essentialism was seen as a tool for conservatives who wished to keep women in the home and out of the workplace. More recently, feminists have reexamined essentialism from perspectives ranging from conservative to radical (Corea, 1985; Dworkin, 1983; MacKinnon, 1982, 1987; O'Brien, 1981; Rich, 1976), with a recognition that biologically based differences between the sexes might imply superiority and power for women in some arenas.

The debate over the relative contributions of nature and nurture to development, including gender differences in child behavior, has a long history in developmental psychology. Currently, essentialist positions often are found in developmental psychobiological, ethological, sociobiological, and neuropsychological work. For example, differences in the magnetic resonance images of brains (MRIs) of males and females, or other brain differences, are sometimes interpreted as reflecting innate differences, though critiques point to experiential influences as well. The debate most often has centered on mathematical, spatial, and verbal abilities (e.g., Halpern, 1992). In developmental psychology, an essentialist orientation may partially account for the explosion of research in the last decade or two on cognitive capacities in young infants, which might show the mind when it is largely "uncontaminated" by experience (Beal, 1995). Essentialist examples not focused on gender differences include work on mental modules, theory of mind in autistic children, temperament, and children's developing concepts of the essence of people and objects (Gelman & Taylor, this volume). Essentialism also supports the work on children's universal cognitive structures, skills, or processes. Similarly, stage theories of development essentialize the child and strip behavior of its contextual influences. As these examples show, there are essentialist tendencies in developmental work generally and work on gender differences more specifically, but there are few examples of feminist essentialism focused on the uniqueness of "women" or female superiority (though work by Gilligan, 1982, and Belenky et al., 1986, sometimes is interpreted this way).

Existentialist Feminism

In contrast to essentialist feminism, existentialist feminism, first elaborated by Simone de Beauvoir (1974), suggests that society's interpretation of bio-logical differences, rather than the actual biological differences themselves, lead to women's "otherness," the social construction of gender, and the devaluing of women and girls. Thus, gender differences in visual-spatial abilities and learning might be the result of the differential treatment and reactions that boys and girls in our society receive based on their biology. Developmental psychologists have provided abundant evidence for the contributions of socialization to gender differences and the subtle interplay of biological and environmental factors. In addition, several chapters in this volume show how girls have become "the other," as described by existen-tialist theory, when masculine metaphors (Scholnick), values (e.g., mas-tery—Code), definitions of behavior (e.g., aggression—Crick & Rose), methods (Nelson), and models of memory (Fivush), the self (Welch-Ross), and cognitive change (Miller) control what is studied, how it is studied, and how development is conceptualized.

Psychoanalytic Feminism

Like existentialist feminism, psychoanalytic feminism draws its focus from biology. Derived from Freudian theory, psychoanalysis posits that girls and boys develop contrasting gender roles because they experience their sexu-ality differently and deal differently with the stages of psychosexual devel-opment. Based on the Freudian assumption that anatomy is destiny, psychoanalytic theory assumes that biological sex will lead to different ways for boys and girls to resolve the Oedipus and castration complexes that arise during the phallic stage of normal sexual development. However, as in existentialism, psychoanalysis recognizes that social influences also operate, as when the child-caretaker interaction differs depending on the sex of the child (and possibly that of the primary caretaker).

In recent years, a number of feminists have become interested again in psychoanalytic theories, after a period of attacking them (Firestone, 1970; Friedan, 1974; Millett, 1970). Rejecting the biological determinism in Freud, Dinnerstein (1977) and Chodorow (1978) in particular have used an aspect of psychoanalytic theory known as object relations theory to examine the construction of gender and sexuality. They argue that male dominance emerges in society because boys are pushed to be independent, distant, and autonomous from their mothers or female caretakers while girls are permitted to be more dependent, intimate, and less individuated from theirs. Thus, males, because they feel comfortable with independence, autonomy, and distance, may be attracted to certain fields, such as science, because they value these masculine characteristics (Keller, 1982, 1985). Consequently, science, in its current socially constructed version, excludes more women and girls from the field, selects topics of interest to males, and uses masculine theoretical models of control, mastery, and separation.

Psychoanalytic approaches have a long history in developmental psychology because of their focus on early socialization experiences, family dynamics, and identification of children with their parents (which results in the internalization of parental values, especially those of the same-sex parent). These approaches often focus on the psychological separation of boys from their mothers and on achieving autonomy, self-control, and mastery more than on the establishment of social bonds. A current psychoanalytically inspired notion of interest to developmental psychologists studying attachment is infants' cognitive "working models" of their interaction with their caretakers (e.g., Bretherton, 1992). It is likely that the different ways that boys and girls interact with their parents lead to different types of working models.

Radical Feminism

Radical feminism, in contrast to psychoanalytic feminism and liberal feminism, rejects the possibility of gender-free knowledge or of a science developed from a neutral, objective perspective. Radical feminism maintains that women's oppression is the first, most widespread, and deepest oppression (A. Jaggar & Rothenberg, 1984). Since men dominate and control most institutions, politics, and knowledge in our society, they reflect a male perspective and are effective in oppressing women. Scientific institutions, practice, and knowledge are particularly male dominated and have been used to control and harm women (Bleier, 1984; Fee, 1982; Griffin, 1978; Haraway, 1989; Hubbard, 1990; Keller, 1985; Merchant, 1980; Rosser, 1990). Radical feminism rejects most scientific theories, data, and experiments not only because they exclude women scientists and participants but also because they are not women centered. Moreover, radical feminism rejects dichotomies such as rational/feeling and mind/body, and supposedly objective Western "logical" linear thinking.

The theory that radical feminism proposes is evolving (Tong, 1989) and is not as well developed as some of the other feminist theories, owing to the nature of radical feminism itself. First, it is radical, and thus rejects most currently accepted ideas about epistemology—what kinds of things can be known, who can be a knower, and how legitimate knowledge can be acquired (i.e., methodology). Second, unlike the feminisms previously discussed, radical feminism does not have its basis in a theory such as Marxism, positivism, psychoanalysis, or existentialism, already developed for decades by men. Since radical feminism is based in women's experience, it rejects feminisms rooted in theories developed by men and based on male experiences and worldviews. Because the oppression of women is the deepest, most widespread, and historically first oppression, women have had few opportunities to come together, understand their experiences collectively, and develop theories based on those experiences.

In an attempt to develop theories of knowledge based on women's experiences, women have met together in women-only groups to examine their personal experiences (MacKinnon, 1987). Radical feminist separatist theory would provide an explanation for the success in some settings of all-girl classrooms, especially for science and math (American Association of University Women, 1992; Rosser, 1997); such classrooms encourage girls to contribute to class discussion and achieve academically. For example, to the extent that interactions among female students in single-sex science classes simulate a consciousness-raising group, which permits them to explore their ideas, attitudes, and beliefs about science and become a scientist in the absence of males, these environments simulate these methods of radical feminism.

Drawing on women's and girls' experiences as a starting point for developmental research and theorizing rarely occurs in developmental psychology, despite the many women in the field. Main exceptions are the work of Gilligan and her colleagues, who have studied women's care-based morality (e.g., Gilligan, 1982) and the impact of girls' preadolescent and adolescent experiences on changes in self-concept (e.g., L. M. Brown & Gilligan, 1992), and the work on women's ways of knowing (Belenky et al., 1986).

Girls and boys engage in different sorts of activities that presumably lead to different learning experiences and views of the social world. Moreover, girls and boys spontaneously segregate in middle childhood, perhaps because of different preferred styles of play and interaction (Maccoby, 1998). Piaget (1932) explicitly omitted the experience of girls (moral reasoning when playing a hopscotch-like game) in favor of the experience of boys (playing marbles). He was perplexed by the fact that girls seemed as interested in the social interaction as in the rules of the game or winning. It seems likely that moral reasoning would look quite different in the two sorts of groups. A focus on girl-only groups would be a starting point for a fresh look at what cognitive skills are developed during childhood play. Several of the chapters in this book describe research that begins by looking at girls' experience as a starting point, for example, in defining aggression (Crick & Rose) and cognition (Miller).

Postmodern Feminism

According to postmodernism, "the values of reason, progress, and human rights endorsed by the Enlightenment have shown their dark side" (Tanesini, 1999, p. 239). In postmodernism, the self is no longer regarded as masterful, universal, integrated, autonomous, and self-constructed; rather, it is socially constructed by "ideology, discourse, the structure of the unconscious, and/or language" (Rothfield, 1990, p. 132). Postmodernism dissolves the universal subject, and postmodern feminism dissolves the possibility that women speak in a unified voice or can be universally addressed. Although one woman may share certain characteristics and experiences with other women because of her biological sex, still, her particular race, class, and sexual differences compared to those of other women, along with the construction of gender that her country and society give to someone living in her historical period, prevent the universalizing of her experiences to women in general. At least some postmodern feminists (e.g., Cixous & Clement, 1986; Kristeva, 1984, 1987) suggest that women, having been marginalized by a dominant male discourse, may be in a privileged position, that of outsider to the discourse, to find the holes in what appears solid, sure, and unified. Otherwise the dominant discourse threatens to rigidify all thought in society along previously established lines.

Within developmental psychology, cultural psychologists most directly explore both the perspectives of those in the margins and the nonuniversal and diverse developmental pathways and end points of development. Cultural psychology examines the processes by which race, class, gender, nationality, and so on, interact to produce diverse "truths" both between and within cultures. Socialization practices are the main mechanisms by which these various markers result in diverse selves and perspectives.

Postmodernism also challenges the assumption of progress in human activity. Developmental psychologists tend to assume that age-related changes reflect progress, and value the growing similarity between child and adult thought during development. Postmodern challenges to concepts of development as progress toward a predefined end state, and a consideration of discontinuities, regressions, multiple developmental pathways, and alternative end points, can be seen in the work of Bradley (1989), Burman (1994), and Morss (1992). A feminist postmodernism might focus on the ways that females' developmental roots tend to differ from those of males and question whether the assumed end point, for example scientific thinking in Piaget's theory, is true for all people. Moreover, life span development may not look linear, especially for women. Development may include detours, temporary regressions, indirect routes, diverse pathways, and rhythmicity. And each "progression" may require the loss of another ability or tendency (Bjorklund & Green, 1992). Finally, postmodern feminism challenges the essentializing tendencies within developmental psychology, specifically, the search for universal aspects of development and the focus on similarities rather than differences among children of a particular stage, age, or category (e.g., "girls" as in middle-class white girls, ignoring diversity in race, social class, or ethnicity).

Postcolonial Feminism

After World War II, many previously colonized countries gained their independence. However, Western colonizers did not fully give up control. They continued their influence, particularly economically but also politically, ideologically, and militarily. Feminists have suggested that just as patriarchy dominated colonial life, so it dominates postcolonial activities. General themes include the underdevelopment of southern continents by Europe and North America historically, ignoring, obscuring, or misappropriating the earlier scientific achievements and history of countries in southern continents, the fascination with (but exploitation of) so-called indigenous science, and, more recently, the recognition that southern countries must become scientifically and technologically literate to join and compete in a global economy (Harding, 1998).

The particular forms and ways that these general themes are expressed vary, depending on the history, culture, geography, and length of colonization of both the colonized and colonizing countries. Thus, the nature of the impact on human development varies from country to country. For example, the issues surrounding postcolonial science vary considerably between India and Kenya (Rosser, in press). Although both India and Kenya were colonized by the British, the differences in indigenous cultures, geographies, and length of time since independence have led to remarkably different problems and uses of modern science and technology. For example, in India, amniocentesis has been used for sex determination to abort undesired female fetuses. The particularities of Indian culture, economics, and religion in which sons are highly valued and the elderly are cared for by sons, and where dowry prices to find a good marriage partner for daughters can be very expensive, encourage this use of amniocentesis. One outcome relevant to developmental psychology may be changes in family structure—boys might be raised with no, or few, sisters with whom to interact, and girls would rarely have older sisters as models. Another outcome with developmental impact might be the scarcity of females when males begin dating in adolescence or seeking marriage partners. Competition for females surely would affect peer interaction during adolescence. In Kenya, in contrast, the indigenous culture, through polygamy and valuing of children and agricultural production, discourages such sex selection and abortion of females.

In both countries, genetically bred agricultural species have been introduced in the context of "green revolutions." Although the effects are positive in the short run, with increased crop yields, in the long run the effects often prove ecologically and economically disastrous, particularly for women (Rosser, in press). For example, the introduction of hybrid corn and high-yielding varieties of wheat necessitates the use of Western farming methods involving, for example, tractors or harvesters. To create fields for agriculture, forests must be cleared. As species are removed, biodiversity is lost. Farm crops also quickly deplete the soil of nutrients, which must be replaced by expensive fertilizers. The accompanying changes in the ecosystem lead to droughts and less water. Women must walk farther each day to obtain water for their families; they must walk particularly far to obtain water unpolluted from agricultural run-off. Thus, mothers must either be away from their children for longer periods of time (with the probable outcome that older daughters take care of the younger children) or take the children with them on these frequent long trips. Both would cause changes in child-rearing practices.

Although developmental psychologists have examined the effects of cultural change on children in various countries, they have given little attention to the impact of postcolonialism on children's development suggested by the above examples. Postcolonial feminist theories could suggest fruitful new research questions for Vygotskian, social contextual, and cultural psychology approaches, especially by considering the following four points. First, the transition from colonialism to postcolonialism has taken different forms in different countries (e.g., war versus peaceful change, the different effects of culture, geography, religion, etc., the length of time taken for the transition). Thus, the effects on children and their development may take different forms in different countries. Second, the lessons of postcolonialism suggest that despite the apparent greater autonomy and freedom of girls and women today, the male-dominated culture may continue to influence their development in subtle ways. Third, the similarities and differences between the process of development of countries in southern continents and of human life span development might reveal interesting parallels and clarify the nature of each of the two developments and assumptions about progress. Technological advances can have both positive and negative effects on a developing country (e.g., amniocentesis, as discussed above) or child (e.g., television). Fourth, the parent-child relationship is in many ways analogous to the colonizer-colonized relationship. Both children and colonized peoples are controlled and socialized.

Summary

Although only psychoanalytic feminism is explicitly developmental, all varieties of feminism, though in somewhat differing ways and to different degrees, encourage a questioning of current (patriarchal) assumptions about what in development should be studied, what processes of change underlie development, and how development should be studied. Liberal feminism, by simply advocating research free of gender bias, provides the least challenge to the questions of what is important in development. At the other extreme, postmodern and radical feminism question the very categories of knowledge or behavior constructed by patriarchal societies. Thus, the contrasts that drive developmental research, such as maturity versus immaturity, are called into question because they reflect prescriptive norms. Similarly, the choice of topic is political. As for mechanisms of developmental change, essentialist and existential feminism may imply that biological characteristics and their interpretation in our society provide important sources of change for males and females. However, other feminist theories suggest that additional factors such as class (socialist feminism) and race (African-American feminism), along with historical-cultural (e.g., postcolonial feminism) change, interact with gender to create oppressions and form more complex sources of change. Postmodern feminism emphasizes that these characteristics and the accompanying power differentials cause the same event to be experienced in different ways by different people, even within the category of "female." Family dynamics and the role of the primary caretaker become powerful determinants in psychoanalytic feminism, while radical feminism looks to the experiences of women and girls for previously unrecognized mechanisms of development and models of development. Finally, regarding methods, liberal feminism calls for research without gender bias, using current scientific methods, while radical and postmodern feminism advocate diverse researchers, using nonpatriarchal methods involving less power of the researcher over the object of study.

In this chapter we have shown that these feminist theories may be identified within developmental theories and research, although these linkages have not been made explicit. More important, these feminist theories suggest new questions about development that would enrich current theories of development. These include questions about the subtle interactions of gender, race, class, and ethnicity, about the limits of science along with the benefits to science of diversity in its researchers and child participants, and about power and marginality. The theories also raise issues about the impact of colonization on children in southern countries, and about the potential for constructing new accounts of development that take the experiences, values, and interests of women and girls as their starting point. The chapters in this book take these themes in particular directions and outline a research agenda for developmental psychology for the twenty-first century.

Although we have focused on the implications of various feminist theories for developmental psychology, we could also look in the opposite direction and ask, How can feminist theories be made more developmental? Certainly age needs to be considered by each theory. Feminist theorists could, for example, address changes in the nature of barriers for females at different ages and age differences in perceptions of bias (liberal feminism) and suggest how theorizing about interactions of race, gender, social class, ethnicity, and sexuality (socialist, African-American, postmodern) must also add age, another social category, as a part of the equation. Moreover, feminist theories should describe an epistemology that takes girls as well as women as its starting point (radical feminism). In addition, essentialist, existentialist, psychoanalytic, and postmodern feminism could be enriched by developmental accounts of the complex interplay of biological and experiential influences (Scholnick & Miller, this volume) and of age differences in the nature of social roles. Finally, cross-cultural work in developmental psychology could clarify how postcolonial oppression of women, children, and families is translated into altered child-rearing practices and, consequently, altered cognitive and social development, which affects the historical course of a country. Thus, a conversation between developmental psychology and feminist theories holds the promise of enriching each.

Engendering Development

Metaphors of Change

Ellin Kofsky Scholnick

> *The intuitive appeal of a scientific theory has to do with how well its metaphors fit one's experience.*
> —George Lakoff and Mark Johnson

> *To the extent that one accepts the view that data are never free of interpretation, it is as necessary to understand the potential bases of interpretation as it is to establish empirical invariance. The core of this interpretive framework is metaphor.*
> —Willis Overton

Feminists often examine cultures to reveal how their descriptive language constructs social categories, such as gender, and ultimately the lives and self-conceptions of persons within each category. Some developmentalists describe the cultural embeddedness of our constructions of the child (Kessen, 1979; Shweder, Goodnow, Hatano, LeVine, Markus, & Miller, 1998). My thesis is that the two constructions are linked.

Whose thought is global, undifferentiated, intuitive, context sensitive, subjective, and concrete? And whose thinking is articulated, logical, abstract, objective, scientific, and hypothetical? Most developmental psychologists would immediately associate the first set of attributes with children and the second set with adults. Feminist philosophers (Code, 1993; Lloyd, 1993b) contend that these descriptors have been used to differentiate the irrational female from the rational male. The parallels are intriguing. If the child is the stereotypical female and the adult is the universal male, does it follow that cognitive development involves acquiring masculine traits (Labouvie-Vief, 1994; P. H. Miller, this volume)? Additionally, because developmental end points and the processes producing them are often related, is the language by which we describe change gendered? One fruitful way to address these questions is to examine metaphors of developmental change.

This analysis of metaphors is based on two assumptions. First, the discursive practices of a culture affect how we view people, objects, and events. Disciplines are cultures with unique linguistic practices that shape the framework within which data are viewed. Hence the metaphors used to describe development mold our understanding of change. Second, there is no unified view of cognitive development, and the focus of study, the developing individual, rarely presents a consistent picture. People of a given age differ along many dimensions, and the factors that produce the variability are also variegated and multidimensional. This variability permits multiple ways of viewing the field, and the choice of salient markers and sources of developmental change reflects the cultural position and ideological stance of the interpreter (Alcoff & Potter, 1993).

Metaphors reflect choices. They organize conceptual domains by highlighting some features while suppressing others (G. Lakoff & Johnson, 1980). The masculine and the feminine, the logical and the intuitive, subjective and objective, and even the child and adult within us are inextricably intertwined. A metaphor singles out certain features and integrates them into a model, such as the depiction of human development as growing into manhood. When masculinity, rationality, and maturity are singled out and correlated, then certain aspects of development are conspicuous, but other facets remain hidden. Even the language that explains developmental change is colored by the metaphorical model. Gendered metaphors exploit one schema, masculine or feminine, at the expense of the other in order to emphasize some facets and sources of developmental change. The choice of metaphor reflects judgments about what is important about cognitive development. Let us examine various developmental metaphors to discern where gender has insinuated itself into our explanations of cognitive change. Whose metaphors are they? Whose values do they reflect? What do they emphasize and suppress? How would switching metaphors change our picture of development? What does a metaphorical analysis tell us about theories of development and development itself?

Masculine Metaphors

The first step for any developmentalist is defining the domain. What is knowledge and how is it acquired? Contemporary Western thought trumpets one source of knowledge, empirical observation of the regularities in physical phenomena, and prizes one way of summarizing these regularities, laws describing a set of mathematical relations among abstract symbols (Code, 1993). Both classical science and traditional epistemology attempt to account for our knowledge of the laws of nature that underlie phenomena like gravity and support, and of medium-sized physical objects with transparent and universally recognized properties. The identity of particular knowers is irrelevant because each follows an identical route to identical knowledge, based on the experimental method and logic.

Many developmental psychologists adopt the same ontology and epistemology. Many standard cognitive tasks require constructing biological taxonomies and solving problems in logic, mathematics, and physics. The child's task is to understand the laws of nature while simultaneously building and using the scientific method and inductive and deductive logic in order to apprehend those laws. Often the young child is characterized as a theoretician whose development formally resembles a series of paradigm shifts (Carey, 1999; Gopnik & Meltzoff, 1997; Wellman & Gelman, 1998). The child starts with a initial theory, encounters anomalies, and develops auxiliary hypotheses to account for counterexamples. As the exceptions and rules to handle them proliferate, the child reorganizes the theory to achieve a better match with the data and better conceptual cohesion. The child's path is lonely. Despite cultural solutions to the task of theory building, these solutions are to be distrusted because they may be erroneous. Instead, the child is driven by a private search for the truth that nature will reveal. Gopnik and Meltzoff (1977) even claim that the early preoccupation with theory building becomes specialized in some individuals, who then call themselves scientists.

Because men are so prevalent in science, and because the tools of science, objective observation and control of variables, draw on stereotypically masculine traits, feminists contend that science is gendered (Keller, 1985). Even the end product of science is hegemonic—control over natural phenomena. Harding (1998) and Lloyd (1993b) have also suggested that Western European societies cultivated and used the scientific enterprise to establish dominance over other cultures and over women and other less privileged groups within the societies. Note how often the end point of development is identified as mastery of a skill or domain. Moreover, when the end point of development is considered to be the emergence of the scientist and technician, masculine imagery of aggression, competition, control, and hierarchical domination is used to characterize developmental trajectories. Four examples of masculine metaphors are development as argument, survival of the fittest, arrow, and building (figure 1).

Figure 1. Masculine metaphors

Argument

The argument metaphor describes how developmental change occurs, through adversarial confrontation. Arguments occur between two clearly defined and exclusive, contradictory positions, categories, or entities. Two debaters or paradigms vie for dominance by marshaling evidence until the force of one position crushes its rival. The winner gains temporary ascendancy until a new challenge arises. The end point of development is a better, broader, or more coherent explanatory theory. For example, Kohlberg (1971) claimed that developmental advances result from engaging in moral disputes. Even K. J. Gergen (1993), a social constructivist , uses the argument metaphor to describe cognitive change. He asserts that any worldview by definition invokes an opposite view or privileges one group at the expense of others. A struggle ensues for domination until the old view is surrendered.

Both dialectical and Piagetian theory (Garcia, 1999; Piaget, 1985), employ another form of the argument metaphor. The child invokes contradictory rules. The schemas collide, resulting in a fusion of common elements into the new, higher-order, more inclusive scheme. But the union is temporary as differences reemerge, collide, and then reunite. Note that these models of developmental change blend masculine imagery with a particular abstract, universal logic form. The direction of progression is the construction of a class inclusion hierarchy.

Survival of the Fittest

Even cognitive theorists who do not emphasize acquisition of logical rules use a combative, evolutionary metaphor, survival of the fittest. Early in brain development, connections between neurons proliferate, but eventually some are pruned. Connectionists describe pruning during the course of learning as cognitive competition among nodes and connections in networks. Similarly, choice of problem-solving strategies has been framed as survival of the fittest (Elman, Bates, Johnson, Karmiloff-Smith, Parisi, & Plunkett, 1996; Siegler, 1996). Children generate many concepts, conceptual associations, and strategies in response to different tasks. Each association or strategy vies for dominance in a hierarchy, and the individual chooses the strongest as the basis for action. If the chosen element solves the task, it gains in potency. Failure and disuse weaken other choices.

Arrow

The preceding metaphors describe how change occurs. The arrow's trajectory and the building metaphor describe the direction of change. G. Lakoff and Johnson (1980) noted that arguments are often described as lines of attack. The arrow metaphor (Overton, 1995) emphasizes linearity. Development is a straight trajectory with a forward thrust. Arrows also map transitive logic to developmental progression. As we proceed from tail to tip through successive points, reaching any point necessarily implies passing through all its predecessors. The metaphor is a graphic translation of the assumption that a later point must follow from an earlier one because the later implies the earlier. The earlier is a prerequisite for the later. This, in turn, focuses attention on the nature of the item, not the nature of the individual who masters the item. Moreover, detection of necessity is easier in mathematics than in the social world.

Travel takes time, and so "time lines" are easily mapped onto arrows
(G. Lakoff & Johnson, 1980). Developmental states or stages are locations
along a path. Arrows have a direction. Development has a fixed end point,
maturity. What causes movement or launches the arrow? Human nature or
logical force. Thus the arrow metaphor expresses three contemporary
explanations of developmental change: (1) biology, which launches movements; (2) an ideal solution to a cognitive task, which serves as the target for
development; and (3) linearity, which ensures continuity of travel. Arrows
describe linear thought and linear development in a universal child. Arrows
are also, of course, typically associated with aggression, domination, imposition of a view, and penetration of an influence. An arrow expresses development as a push toward change, not as a force that simultaneously
transforms and is transformed.

Building

The fourth metaphor has many of the same properties. Cognitive development is likened to a multistory building or its part, such as Case's (1992)
"the mind's staircase." Radically different theories employ the metaphor.
In some, development is characterized as "construction." A building is an
inert entity structured by others who control its design and growth. Its
architecture or ground plan determines its ultimate shape, and the developmental challenge is to scale its heights. At this location the adult peers
out, liberated from his origins, to gain a broader view of the landscape. The
metaphor thus implies upward direction. Buildings and staircases draw
attention to linear progress, with each step or story built on its predeces-
sor. Lower-order functions are the foundation for higher-order ones,
which are superior to the earlier ones. In other theories the completed
building provides more space for processing knowledge and allows for use
of more steps. The building metaphor, like the others, highlights many
stereotypical masculine themes: upward thrust, overcoming obstacles,
inevitable progress and accession of the individual to a superior position.

Feminist Metaphors

Masculine metaphors depict the emergence of scientists in adversarial,
rationalist, and hierarchical terms (Keller, 1995). Because feminist
metaphors are textual and social, they chart the emergence of humanists
and clinical psychologists. Their metaphors highlight social interchange as
both process and end point, the development of relational thought through

Figure 2. Feminist metaphors

a process of relatedness. Social networks provide children with building partners, building tools, and building blocks. These networks also define the child's gender role, social class, historical and cultural context, and ultimately development itself.

Although rationalist theories of cognitive change pervade information-processing, connectionist, neo-Piagetian, and neo-nativist research, these views are disputed by life span psychologists and developmental scientists (Lerner, 1998), who draw on the same marxist and postmodernist theories that have influenced feminists (Tong, 1989). The resulting metaphors are stereotypically feminine. Figure 2 illustrates four metaphors that emphasize the social and interpretive aspects of development: friendship, conversation, apprenticeship, and narrative. Each metaphor is drawn from a content domain in social development, and I would argue that recent increased attention to these sociocognitive domains enables employment of their content as metaphorical models for developmental change. These metaphors cover the same territory as the masculine ones but from a different vantage point. Whereas masculine imagery is aggressive, abstract, and linear, feminist images are relational, concrete, and nonlinear. For example, arguments and conversations are two different kinds of verbal interchange. The environment that challenges survival of the fittest supports growth in an apprenticeship. Narrative and arrows have a different directional structure.

Friendship

Instead of an adversarial relation between the subject and object or between incompatible ideas, feminist epistemologists describe the development of understanding using the metaphor of friendly negotiations among unique individuals who are respectful of each other and of alternative stances (Code, 1991; Harding, 1991). The same metaphor has appeared recently in developmental analyses. A "relational" view contrasts starkly with the view that development is controlled by "master genes" or is prodded and shaped by socializing agents or external stimuli. Growth is not the byproduct of conflict between warring dualities (Gottlieb, 1997; Overton, 1998). Instead, heredity and environment, internal and external, process and product, stability and change—and by extension, masculine and feminine—are two sides of the same coin. The polarities coexist, are highlighted for different purposes, and influence one another during ontogeny. The relational metaphor characterizes the interactions in terms that also apply to the activities that foster and maintain partnerships: bidirectional, cooperative, and reciprocal co-action (Gottlieb, 1997; Thelen & Smith, 1998).

Although relational language has entered developmental psychology, the metaphor could be elaborated further. Cognitive development might be influenced by the same factors that affect friendships: growth in observational skill, direct relational experience, and exposure to cultural lore about human nature. The course of knowledge development is analogous to the development of a friendship. Keller (1983) has described Barbara McClintock's scientific investigation as "gaining a feeling for the organism" or developing an affection for it. During development, understanding of the world, like understanding of friends, becomes deeper, more intimate, and more affect laden. Its culmination is contextual, relational knowledge.

Maintaining a relationship requires flexible reworking based on shifting situational demands, changing purposes, and a past history of interactions. Both the knower and the known are multifaceted and dynamic. The same object is viewed differently and reveals different facets as familiarity with it grows. Like friendship, development is mutual. The child and the teacher are changed by the interchange of knowledge (Bronfenbrenner, 1979). Friendships are built on finding a common ground between partners. Similarly, acquisition of knowledge requires seeking a meeting place between the knower and the object of knowledge.

Building knowledge in a relational structure is not like building knowledge in an architectural structure. The image of a dynamic relationship implies that our representations of information are constantly reconfigured and transformed within the individual. The data are also not fixed building blocks. The object of study may be changed by the course of inquiry. Moreover, the knowledge may refer to adaptive and growing organisms, whose appearance and nature may change. A key facet of cognitive development is, therefore, cognitive flexibility.

The metaphor also lends itself to examination of individual differences in aptitude. Just as people differ in the kinds of relationships they are able to establish, they differ in the modalities of input to which they are attuned (Gardner, 1983). Relationships also take different forms and have different developmental histories. The metaphor invites analysis of the social practices and contexts that define diverse relationships between the knower and the known (Shweder et al., 1998). A feminist analysis focuses on the ways cultures expose boys and girls to different spheres of knowledge, different belief systems about their capacities, and even gendered epistemological stances (Belenky, Clinchy, Goldberger, & Tarule, 1986; Golombok & Fivush, 1994). The analyses also are designed to enable the reader to examine how the problems researchers study and the framework within which they place their analyses have been shaped by various contexts, social practices, and belief systems.

Conversation

The friendship metaphor is closely linked to another one, conversation. Because much of our knowledge of the world is mediated by the discursive practices of the culture, conversation is both a medium for generating cultural meanings and an apt metaphor for developmental change. Knowledge is viewed not as an achievement but as an ongoing conversation with a partner in which both parties discover and recreate the world while coming to terms with each other's perspectives (Seller, 1994). Moreover, conversations are not restricted to scientific knowledge but include indirect knowledge and gossip about the interpretation of the events in daily life. Finally, the goal of a conversation is not to dominate an interchange but to exchange information. Conversations can lead to mutual growth. Arguments are designed to detect vulnerabilities and conquer ignorance. Arguments presume there is an objective, valid knowledge base that needs to be tapped, whereas conversations are based on detecting, appreciating, and building on intersubjectivity.

Obviously, the metaphor appears in descriptions of semantic development where conversation produces psychological change. Conversational partners negotiate, share, and co-construct meaning (K. Nelson, 1985). Valsiner (1998a) asserts that other knowledge is acquired similarly through negotiation and co-construction. Conversational interchanges can lead to insights into the ways differing psychological perspectives on people, physical objects, and events reflect differing attitudes, beliefs, and purposes. Thus the conversational metaphor lends itself to linking acquisition of knowledge of physical objects and psychological subjects to an understanding of goals and purposes achieved when deploying knowledge for different purposes. Just as skilled conversationalists learn how to put a message across by adapting differing genres of expression to different audiences and different goals, cognitive development involves adaptive flexibility, not just acquisition of facts. Milestones of development might also include gaining the authority and space to speak and be heard (Code, 1995b).

Apprenticeship

Developmentalists use another relational metaphor, an idealized apprenticeship or parenting (Bronfenbrenner, 1979; Rogoff, 1990; Vygotsky, 1978). Agents of socialization transmit a constructed reality. The socializer designates salient objects and features and teaches culturally valued skills. During joint activity, the teacher determines the child's zone of receptivity and then scaffolds the child's knowledge and skills. As these skills are perfected, the responsibility for executing them is vested in the child. These teaching practices of the socializer are models for methods of acquiring knowledge.

Cultural psychologists and feminists have used the apprenticeship metaphor to note that societies channel people into epistemic activities by exposing them to specific experts and specific opportunities for exercising their epistemic skills (Code, 1995b; Shweder et al., 1998). Societal beliefs, social hierarchies, and gender roles determine who can know, what they know, and how they know. Children learn what counts as knowledge; they are afforded differential access to knowledge-making opportunities and differential rewards for asserting their knowledge.

Feminists add another layer of understanding to the apprenticeship metaphor, exemplified by research on women's ways of knowing (Belenky et al., 1986). When knowledge is created and transmitted by an epistemic community, the recipient of knowledge must discern whose knowledge is trustworthy and develop criteria for determining credibility. Because knowledge is grounded in interpretation, development moves toward recognition and analysis of the positions that influence knowledge pronouncements. Differences in social positions and in historical location produce variability in awareness of interpretive stances (Code, 1995b; Harding, 1998).

Like the evolutionary metaphor, the apprenticeship metaphor describes how the environment affects development. When the metaphor is survival of the fittest, the survival is due to a match between the individual's propensities and developmental location. The outcome is either triumph or tragedy. In the apprenticeship metaphor, an expert fosters development of the novice, attunes instruction to the child, and attempts to enable success.

Narrative

Another metaphor for cognitive development, constructing a narrative, also reflects the centrality of meaning-making and discursive practices in feminist theory. Bruner (1990) pinpoints three aspects of narrative knowing that fit a feminist framework: sequence, normative explanations, and voice.

One obvious feature of a narrative is temporal sequence. Time is linear, arrows follow a straight course, but narratives rarely depict straightforward progress. Stories tell the attempts of a human agent to attain a goal despite obstacles, detours, and retreats. Similarly the path to knowledge is rarely predictable or solitary. The variegated nature of narrative trajectories has proved to be an apt metaphor for describing adult cognitive changes, but it also fits childhood (Baltes, Lindenberger, & Staudinger, 1998; Fischer & Bidell, 1998; Lerner, 1998).

The meaning of a narrative sequence is supplied by normative or folk knowledge of human motives, actions, and their consequences. Stories account for violations of norms, such as a character in the wrong place or a thwarted expectation. Story plots recount repair processes. An essential part of cognitive development is acquiring the general structure of the grammar as well as stories about ourselves and the structure of the physical and social world. We learn the conventions of narrative and the means to fit our own particular experience into them. Narratives are also gendered (J. K. Conway, 1998). The masculine plot of a hero who overcomes obstacles to prove himself and achieve his goal serves as a model for both male identity and normative theories of cognitive development. One theory of emotions associates each to a particular event narrative (Stein & Levine, 1989). Cognitive development entails revision of those narratives. We even acquire a narrative for learning that relates how knowledge is acquired and tested, and who has the qualifications to master skills. These stories or attributions are the products and producers of cognitive change.

Narratives are situated and personalized. The first node in a story grammar introduces the setting and protagonists (Stein & Glenn, 1979). Thus the narrative metaphor sensitizes researchers to questions like "Who are the knowers? When and where do they acquire and use knowledge?" The narrative metaphor is conducive to delineation of individual and contextual influences on development.

Feminists emphasize another aspect of personalization, the voice of the narrator (Code, 1991, 1995b; Gilligan, 1982; Harding, 1991): "Who tells the story, and why?" The voice metaphor reflects a metacognitive perspective. Knowing one's own voice means monitoring and reflecting on cognitive change. The metaphor also emphasizes the role of interpretation in producing change. Discrepancies between the narrator's voice and the listener's understanding cue the listener to possible biases in the narration or the listener's lack of comprehension.

Implications

An analysis of gendered metaphors of development exposes a layered epistemology. Definitions of knowledge constrain how we study its appearance in the child. The definition of knowledge also determines explanations of direction and causes of change (Overton, 1971). The definition also constrains the methodology for studying development. There is an analytic, objective, empiricist cast to the model of the child as either a scientist or a detector of environmental contingencies. These metaphors lend themselves to the depiction of an abstract, timeless, universal child. In such a portrayal, each child possesses the same processing machinery or innate concepts. This same child may be gendered because the imagery of scientific cognition includes mastery, domination and conflict. Casting the child as an incipient psychologist, however, produces another story. Different metaphors open up different facets of development for study and different kinds of intelligence that deserve more extensive investigation.

This book describes current work in social, narrative, and interpretive understanding.

Much of our knowledge is socially transmitted. We have studied how concepts of social categories like gender are transmitted to the child through social practices and media messages (Golombok & Fivush, 1994), but our concepts of mentality, science, social institutions, and the self are also products of the historical, cultural tradition that surrounds the child. A closer examination is warranted of the form and content of the social practices in which knowledge is constructed and negotiated. We have encoded much of this knowledge in our language and narrative, so a careful examination of the child's exposure to and construction of narrative forms may reveal much about the child's construction of mind in situation and society (Shweder et al., 1998). Moreover, our study of the capacity for transfer of training might be balanced by research on emerging skill in situating knowledge by adapting it to appropriate niches.

Contemporary research on metacognition and theory of mind privileges the abstract and the objective and neglects the child's subjective evaluations of opinion, bias, and the particular self. Research on metacognitive development focuses on knowing what one knows and how one knows in the context of memorization or reading anomalous text. We have not studied as frequently the child's emerging grasp of the fundamentals of interacting minds or appreciation of the ambiguity of events. Our rush to describe an abstract theory of mind has led to a neglect of how we know particular minds and selves.

Once different facets of development are open to consideration, they can be embedded in a more comprehensive developmental theory. Cognition has been studied in two traditions. One postulates a veridical information processor who errs only when resources are strained. This reasoner gradually gains accurate knowledge because there is valid feedback about the true state of affairs. This tradition is countered by the claims of social constructionists that reality is subjective and situated and reasoners are always biased. The approaches are counterweights to each other—rationality and error, objectivity and subjectivity, high-level abstractions and situational sensitivity. Each solves the problem the other extreme generates. The child who masters abstractions has to find a way to apply them. The child concerned with particulars needs a way to generalize from one experience to another. There is a virtue to mixed models. There is also a virtue to metaphorical androgyny. Metaphors are caricatures. Friends can argue. Few designs for buildings are the product of a single architect whose ideas are unchanged during the course of construction. Contrasting metaphors call attention to the intellectual choices we make. Mixed metaphors also reflect the mixed roots of change and the mixture of abstraction and particularity, self-discovery and direct tutoring that arise during the growth process. If we use metaphors as filters to select from the welter of detail certain patterns to study, perhaps the child is doing the same thing. What factors determine their metaphorical choices? Surely gendered practices and imagery influence their selections.

II

COGNITIVE DEVELOPMENT

EMBEDDED, CONNECTED,

AND SITUATED

The Development

of Interconnected Thinking

Patricia H. Miller

Piaget's work on children's thinking sensitized developmental psychologists to interesting questions about knowledge asked by epistemologists within philosophy and demonstrated that developmental research is relevant to these questions. Piaget asked such questions as "What are the origins of knowledge?" "What form does knowledge take at various points in development?" and "What causes changes in knowledge?" Subsequent theorists of cognitive development sought answers to these questions in information-processing, biological, social learning, or theory-change approaches. Feminist epistemological theories provide yet another opportunity for the field of cognitive development to draw on epistemology. Such theories raise new questions, such as "*Who* decides what forms of knowledge are important and which ways of thinking are valid?" and "Does *who* you are influence what you know?" The purpose of this chapter is to outline what cognitive development would look like from a feminist perspective.

As many feminist epistemologists (e.g., Alcoff & Potter, 1993; Harding, 1991) have pointed out, Western culture values stereotypically masculine ways of thinking and therefore has used them to define thinking. Cognitive and emotional distance between the knower and the object of thought and reasoning about the physical world are valued. In contrast, this chapter asks: "What would a model of cognitive development look like if it used activities, experiences, and values associated with girls as its starting point?" Would a focus on nurturing activities, toys and play preferred by girls, and collaborative interaction styles emphasize different concepts or different ways of acquiring knowledge than those emphasized in current views of cognitive development? For example, if Piaget had studied girls engaged in their favorite group games rather than boys playing marbles, he might have constructed a different account of the development of moral reasoning. *Who* you are influences *what* you know because gender (and race, social class, and so on) influences what experiences you have. The universal, interchangeable knower is a fiction.

This paper begins with a description of the nature of cognition implied by feminist theories in both epistemology (e.g., Alcoff & Potter, 1993) and psychology (e.g., Belenky, Clinchy, Goldberger, & Tarule, 1986; Gilligan, 1982). This new perspective is then applied to three topics of current interest to cognitive developmentalists: scientific reasoning, social cognition, and cognitive strategies.

The most basic implication of feminist epistemologies for cognition is that knowledge is *interconnected*. The metaphors of interconnected thinking are a web, fugue, tapestry, dialogue, and perhaps the Internet. Thinking is interconnected in four ways (see 1–4 in figure 1): (1) Thinkers see connections between the phenomenon to be understood (X in figure 1) and its context; all phenomena are situated (2) The knower (person, P) is connected to the phenomenon (3) The knower's mental representations of knowledge are interconnected among themselves and with emotion, the body, and actions (4) The knower is connected to his or her context, including other knowers (P^1–P^4) in the collaborative co-construction of knowledge. These interconnections are not static; rather, they are dynamic and change over time. This view of thinking contrasts with traditional, positivist models of cognition in which the thinker is distanced from a decontextualized object, dominates the object (controls the interaction), ignores emotions, and remains isolated ("autonomous") from other thinkers.

This account must be prefaced by several notes of explanation. This discussion does not address whether females and males think differently. Rather, the focus is on feminist epistemology's alternative perspective on characteristics of thinking in both males and females. In fact, interconnected knowing is valued in both males and females in many non-Western cultures, particularly in Asia (Markus & Kitayama, 1991). Additionally, although this chapter focuses on some of the commonalities among feminist epistemologies, there actually is considerable diversity among feminist epistemologies, and among feminist theories more generally (see Rosser & Miller, this volume). Each feminist theory would stress different aspects of interconnected knowing. Moreover, it is important to keep in mind that gender does not exist in isolation; it intersects with characteristics such as race, social class, education, nationality, and sexual orientation. All of these factors shape people's experiences, which in turn affect their cogni-

Figure 1. Four aspects of interconnected thinking

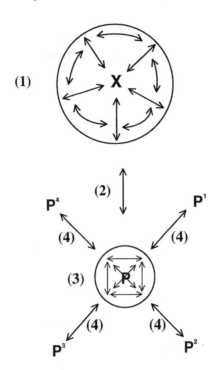

tive development and give them a particular standpoint from which to interpret their world. Interconnected thinking will take a different form in different people.

Finally, some aspects of interconnected knowing are addressed by theoretical approaches other than feminist epistemology—in particular, Vygotskian/contextual/cultural approaches, cybernetics/dynamic systems/chaos theories, some postmodern approaches, and social constructionism. Feminist theorists' main additional contribution is the argument that cultural beliefs and values regarding gender, and their expression in the social power structure, have to some extent led to an androcentric view of reality that values separation and autonomy over connections and that emplaces unequal relations between the knower and the phenomenon to be known. Thus, aspects of thinking that our culture associates with women have received less attention from cognitive psychologists. Feminist epistemologies emphasize the intrinsic connections among values, politics, science, and knowledge. Knowledge is situated; a view is always from somewhere.

Interconnected Knowing

The four aspects of interconnected knowing shown in Figure 1 lead to six characteristics of cognition and cognitive development: (1) contextual-relational, situated reasoning, (2) complex networks of multiple, multi-directional, causal connections, (3) reciprocity, connection, and dialogue between the knower and the known, (4) an emphasis on the social, (5) understanding as a social, negotiated, shared event involving the co-construction of knowledge in a community of knowers, and (6) attention to, and valuing of, diversity. These six characteristics are somewhat overlapping, and a larger, more differentiated set or a smaller, more general set could have been constructed.

These six aspects of interconnected knowing apply, with respect to cognitive development, to questions about the content, processes, and function of development and about appropriate methodology. Regarding *content*, what kinds of concepts are important to study from a feminist perspective? Are some concepts relatively ignored because they are not valued highly by males or generally lie outside of males' experiences? Regarding *processes*, from a feminist perspective, what processes underlie cognitive developmental change? That is, how should cognitive development be conceptualized? What sorts of theoretical models express development? Regarding *function*, what is the function of cognitive acquisition? What do children use concepts for in their daily lives? Finally, regarding *methods*, how do feminist methods change how developmentalists study cognitive development?

1. Contextual-Relational Reasoning

All phenomena are situated rather than decontextualized. A person perceives relations between a phenomenon and its context (physical, social, historical, cultural, etc.). A person understands an object, person, or event by considering its context. Gilligan (1982) describes moral reasoning in which judgments are made in terms of people's relationships with other people in the specific context rather than on the basis of decontextualized universal principles about an autonomous person. Caring and responsibility to others are as important as justice and an individual's rights, emphasized by traditional approaches (i.e., Kohlberg, 1981). As an example of contextual reasoning, Keller (1983, 1985) describes the work of the Nobel Prize–winning geneticist, Barbara McClintock. McClintock examined how the context of a gene (i.e., other genes, the entire cell, the whole organism of which it is a part, and even features of the environment, such as droughts) affects its expression and functioning. As Keller (1985, p. 168) concludes, genes "are organized functional units, whose very function is defined by their position in the organization as a whole." In another example (Sheldon, 1992), cultural norms against girls being directly con-frontational and girls' wanting to maintain their social group lead to self-assertive talk that enmeshes one's needs with those of other people (see also Crick & Rose, this volume). Girls' self-assertion thus is different from, but not less effective than, that of boys. Boys in settings requiring solidarity out-comes also engage in this style of talk. These examples show that relational aspects of the world are "worth knowing" and are mentally represented.

One important cognitive outcome of situated-contextual thinking is that knowledge often is concrete, situation specific, unstable, relative, and tentative rather than abstract, universal, absolute, and certain. What is true for one situation may not be true for another, with its own unique set of circumstances. Partly for this reason, interconnected knowing tends to draw on the knower's own experiences, as in "everyday cognition," rather than on logical abstractions. The most valid knowledge may often come from truth in one's own experience in particular contexts rather than from abstract, decontextualized generalizations based on the perspective of the dominant group in the society. Gilligan's (1982) care-based moral reason-ing stresses the need to attend to the particularities of persons and situations rather than abstract universal moral laws.

In interconnected knowing, people mentally represent an "entity-in-context" and detect patterns in the entire matrix. Although cognitive developmental psychologists recently have given more attention to social context (e.g., Rogoff, 1998), they focus on how the social context stimulates cognitive development rather than on the nature and development of rea-soning about physical and social relations embedded in a network of con-textual forces. Moreover, these contextual accounts in psychology have given little attention to how cultural beliefs about gender, and the resulting social organization of power, organize social contexts and interactions.

2. Complex Networks of Multiple, Multidirectional Causal Connections

Closely related to the first characteristic of interconnected thinking is the second: awareness of a network of multidirectional interconnected causes. From a feminist perspective, to know an entity or event is to perceive its

dynamic causal connections within itself and with the world. One implication of the contextual thinking described above is that a linear, hierarchical, mechanistic causal model does not capture the complexity of the
world. Any event has many causes and in turn affects many other entities
and events with which it is connected.

Feminist biologists would replace the "master molecule" view that
DNA *controls* and *directs* cellular activity with a more interactive, multidirectional model of influences (Hubbard, 1990). And instead of sperm
(active) fertilizing ("attacking") the ovum (passive), the sperm and ovum
are viewed as mutually active partners in a complex system (Schatten &
Schatten, 1983). The egg actively draws in some sperm and keeps out others. Female secretions capacitate the sperm so that it can fertilize the egg
and activate sperm enzymes. Similarly, instead of saying that T-cells "mobi-
lize," "attack," and "destroy" harmful substances that have "invaded" the
body, one could say that T-cells move, enter into chemical interactions, and
facilitate change in other cells. In primatology the prevailing view that male
dominance determines mating with females was challenged by the research
of female primatologists suggesting that females play an active role in
mate selection (e.g., Hrdy, 1986). Finally, cognitive psychologists speak of
"central control" processes. The overall point is that traditional ways of
knowing and interconnected knowing use different language to describe
neutral events. Each language involves metaphors that affect how scientists,
students, and laypersons think about and study the phenomenon. For
example, if one believes that entity 1 "dominates" entity 2, then one is more
likely to study the activities of entity 1 than to look for activities in entity
2 that facilitate the activities of entity 1.

More generally, interconnected knowing in the physical, biological,
and social sciences focuses on relationships, physical or social. This thinking stresses mutual influence over mastery, harmony over domination,
complex models over simple ones, understanding over control, and the
whole organism over the action of one part (Keller, 1985). Interconnected
knowing is not unscientific thinking, it is *different* scientific thinking: it
focuses on function, organization, and development rather than on simple
mechanical causes.

This focus on causal webs, connections, the whole organism, and
complexity is also reflected in a rejection of the dichotomizes that characterize traditional thinking (e.g., Keller, 1985). Some of these dualistic concepts that organize experience into opposites, and often value one element
more than the other, are mind versus body, reason versus emotion, self versus object, inner versus outer world, thinking versus doing, and organism

versus environment (e.g., Harding, 1986). In most feminist epistemologies, these pairs are seen as connected rather than separated, as parts of a whole rather than independent parts, and as equally important and interactive rather than hierarchical. For example, feeling can mix with thinking, science with everyday life, and self with the object.

Although cognitive psychologists use chaos and dynamic systems theories to model complex behavior and cognition, they give little attention to humans' acquisition of representations of such dynamic networks of multiple, multidirectional causal connections. In a rare study of this sort, Chandler and Boutilier (1992) examined the development of "dynamic system reasoning," specifically, understanding ecological systems.

3. Reciprocity, Connecting, and Dialogue between Knower and Known

Knowing is interconnected not only because what is known is interconnected but also because the knower is connected with the known (as depicted in the middle of figure 1). In contrast, most accounts of cognitive development (e.g., Piaget) consider this connection a state to grow out of rather than a procedure for gaining useful knowledge. If a person is interconnected with, rather than separated from, the phenomenon to be known, then there are implications for the process of knowing. That is, certain kinds of knowledge may require the knower to become immersed in that which is to be known, rather than independent of it and distanced from it. One needs to "get inside an idea," "listen to the material, " and develop a "feeling for the organism" (Keller, 1983). In the words of oncological immunologist Anna Brito, "Most importantly you must identify with what you are doing. If you really want to understand about a tumor, you have got to be a tumor" (Goodfield, 1982, p. 226). A friendship metaphor is appropriate (Scholnick, this volume): geneticist Barbara McClintock said, "I know every plant in the field. I know them intimately, and I find it a great pleasure to know them" (Keller, 1983). There are cognitive advantages to entering a reciprocal relationship, a conversation, with that which is to be known, whether it is a person, object, idea, poem, work of art, or phenomenon of nature. Knowledge gradually emerges from the interaction between the knower and the known. Thus, knowing is an active, constructive process in which neither the known nor the knower dominates.

The notion of dialogue is central to interconnected knowing. A dialogue is a verbal or nonverbal exchange involving reciprocity and the negotiation and co-construction of meaning. Regarding the process of knowing, dialogue is a metaphor for the dynamic, changing interchange between the knower and known as knowledge is constructed. Each person accommodates to the prior utterance or actions of another. In this sense, dialogue is an epistemological tool for learning about the self, the other person, and other phenomena. For example, one style of programming on a computer involves a back-and-forth process with the computer (Turkle & Papert, 1991). Formal hierarchical programming techniques involving planning and control are not used in interconnected knowing. Rather, the process is interactive and negotiative, with the programmer starting in a certain direction but making adjustments in response to feedback. The computer is more like a harpsichord than a hammer. Moreover, acquiring dialogic thinking may help children understand, and engage in, collaborative learning situations. Internalized dialogic thinking may serve as a general mental operation that resembles Piaget's notion of mental reversibility or Vygotsky's notion of internalized dialogues. Finally, dialogic knowing, because of the give-and-take it involves, may also function to establish social relationships.

The balance of power between the knower and that which is to be known is equal during immersed cognition, but during distanced cognition the knower is more powerful. By entering the cognitive process with hypotheses to be tested or a set of formal procedures for analyzing the phenomenon, the distanced-knower controls what data will be gathered and how they will be viewed. Hypothesis testing necessarily distorts the phenomenon because it restricts what aspects of the phenomenon the observer considers. In contrast, interconnected knowing advocates initially trying to perceive objects or events in their own right, with no preconceived notions about their nature. In the methods of social science, a dynamic relationship should exist between the researcher and the person studied, as each responds to the behavior of the other. Although even immersed knowers are always situated, and thus bring their own perspectives to the task, they may be more likely to generate plausible hypotheses by listening to what the material (poem, ear of corn, person, chemical compounds, animal) has to say.

One tool of interconnected knowing is "involved understanding," a believing, accepting mode of thought that sometimes precedes a later doubting, critical, judgmental one (i.e., traditional knowing). For example, understanding another person's point of view may require temporarily bracketing one's own (situated) stance in order to experience another's (situated) perspective. This process encourages the knower to take the standpoint of the phenomenon studied and thus clarify how a person, object, or event is influenced by its immediate context, its history of experiences, and the past and present cultural milieu in which it developed. This "subjective" knowing is closely related to the contextual knowledge described earlier.

From a feminist perspective, the self is a reciprocal self, not a defensive self struggling to maintain an emotional distance from others. The self is a self-in-relation-to-others rather than a self-as-separate-from-others (see Welch-Ross, this volume). A person discerns the effect of an event on the self and its meaning for the self. Thus, a person tends to include the self when representing others and to include others when representing the self (Markus & Oyserman, 1988). Experience is personalized and the self concept is defined to a great extent by one's relationships with others. The implications for social information processing are clear: "Those with a connectedness self schema and those with a separateness self schema will have somewhat different strategies for scanning or charting the terrain of the social environment" (Markus & Oyserman, 1988, p. 121). Interconnected knowing directs attention to subtle social cues that are relevant to the self.

Despite Vygotsky's influence, developmental psychologists have given little attention to dialogic cognitive processes. Promising approaches compatible with feminist epistemologies include theoretical work on dialogic thought (Bahktin, 1981; see also Wertsch, 1991), research on certain other cultures (e.g., Markus & Kitayama, 1991) and studies of interactive styles of using a computer (Turkle & Papert, 1991), including navigating the Internet.

4. Emphasis on Social Aspects of Cognition

In interconnected knowing, "social" refers to both literally social (i.e., people) aspects of cognition and to social relationships as the root metaphor and foundation for cognition more generally. The metaphorically social aspect has been more apparent in this chapter thus far—relationships, connecting, equality, conversation, dialogue, cooperation, negotiation, acceptance, and intimacy. These social metaphors apply to thinking about both the social and physical world. Regarding the literally social aspect, there are people and relationships to be understood (content of thought), social processes of acquiring knowledge (e.g., interpersonal and intrapersonal dialogue, perspective taking), and social connections to other knowers—the various senses of interconnection in figure 1.

Cognitive developmentalists have studied children's understanding of other people under the label "social cognition," but tend to study person A's perceptions of, or inferences about, person B as an object separated from person A and from the social context. For example, children learn to use information such as visual and verbal cues to the mental (including emotional) states of another person. From a feminist perspective, social cognition is contextualized. People who value social relationships and develop a morality based on caring may develop a heightened sensitivity to the psychological life of others because they need to understand others and to be understood by others. Considerable experience with inferring the psychological states of others eventually may enable psychological information to be processed automatically and effortlessly (Markus & Oyserman, 1988). The highly elaborated knowledge base about others and relationships would also make this information more easily accessed. In short, the interconnected knower may tend to map out the interpersonal domain in a precise way; the cognitive product may be a detailed social psychological map. In the interconnected knowing model of thinking, then, what is worth knowing is the interpersonal terrain as much as the physical world.

The goal of group interaction differs for traditional and interconnected knowing. The goal for the former is to establish one's dominance in the group and separation from others; the goal of the latter is to strengthen the social bonds in the group or to reach a consensus. To achieve the latter it may be necessary to create and maintain positive mental states in others and seek a solution that will meet everyone's needs. In fact, for the interconnected knower, the social goal may be more important than the particular decision to be made by the group.

In summary, interconnected thinking comes from the social world, both literally and metaphorically. Unlike most models of cognitive development, which begin with reasoning about the physical world and then expand the application of this reasoning to the social world, the interconnected thinking model takes the social world as its starting point. Infants' social cognition (e.g., Flavell & Miller, 1998) acquired in social interaction sets the stage for much of later cognitive development. Metaphorically, the acquisition of knowledge involves a "conversation," a social interaction, a relationship between the knower and the physical or social world.

5. Knowledge as Co-constructed with Other People

With respect to the fourth aspect of interconnected thinking in figure 1, a major way in which interconnected knowing involves social connections with other knowers is that understanding is often a social, negotiated, shared activity involving the co-construction of knowledge. Many feminist epistemologists (e.g., Code, 1991; Jaggar, 1983; L. H. Nelson, 1993) argue that epistemological communities construct knowledge. Knowledge of the world often comes from cognitive interaction with others. Our interpretation of our own experiences may be shaped by discussing these experiences with others or discussing a mutual experience. Children experience and interpret an event through verbal exchange with their parents, siblings, and peers. Valued activities during co-construction include sharing ideas, building on each other's ideas, and nurturing and supporting the ideas of others. Cognitive reciprocity and a narrative discourse are valued over cognitive domination and an adversarial, argumentative discourse (e.g., Tannen, 1993).

Developmentalists have examined collaborative cognition (e.g., Rogoff, 1998), often within a Vygotskian framework (Vygotsky, 1978). Still, Vygotskian/contextualist researchers rarely examine either the cognitive skills that must be developed in order to engage in and to profit from these activities or the way children of different ages conceptualize these collaborative interchanges.

6. Attention to, and Valuing of, Diversity

The theme of diversity runs through the above five characteristics of interconnected knowing but deserves to be addressed separately. One implication of sensitivity to the situated, contextualized nature of objects and events is an awareness of differences and of their importance (e.g., Keller, 1985). Each person (knower) and phenomenon to be known is unique because any entity occupies a particular place in a sociohistorical-physical setting. Understanding other people involves an awareness of how their experiences, formed by gender, race, social class, and so forth, contribute to their attitudes, beliefs, and behaviors. Moreover, these characteristics of the knower place her or him at a particular vantage point. Thus, knowledge is "situated" and therefore diverse. Diverse scientist-knowers can enrich the scientific enterprise. Racial minority and women scientists, who often are low-status outsiders, may bring views of reality to the laboratory that differ from those of white men, who tend to have a more dominant and privileged status (e.g., Harding, 1991; Keller, 1985). In Harding's (1991, p. 124) words, "the stranger can see patterns of belief or behavior that are hard for those immersed in the culture to detect." Girls, women, and minorities may simultaneously process the dominant perspective and their own outsider perspective (e.g., Collins, 1990).

Developmental psychologists have acknowledged individual differences and diverse ways of thinking across cultures and contexts (e.g.,

Shweder, Goodnow, Hatano, LeVine, Markus, & Miller, 1998). Also, a few developmentalists have addressed diverse pathways of cognitive development (e.g., Fischer, Knight, & Van Parys, 1993). However, little attention has been paid to the cognitive basis for people's sensitivity to, conceptualization of, and respect for diversity, or to the development of these skills.

Applications to Cognitive Development

Several brief applications to cognitive development—scientific reasoning, social cognition, and cognitive strategies—provide a flavor of how the above framework might change how we conceptualize and study cognitive development.

Scientific Reasoning

Drawing on the four aspects of the interconnected-knowing model described earlier, we would first emphasize children's growing awareness of a web of causal relations among parts and between parts and whole in the physical world, their awareness of the influence of the physical context of the phenomenon studied, and their understanding of dynamic systems. An example of studying children's understanding of complex interactive systems is Chandler and Boutilier's (1992) examination of children's understanding of ecological systems, mentioned earlier.

Second, we would emphasize close interaction with the material as a source of hypotheses. Most developmental research on scientific reasoning focuses on how skillfully children test hypotheses. In contrast, interconnected knowing emphasizes the hypothesis-generating phase more than the hypothesis-testing phase (e.g., Rosser, 1990). Premature hypothesis testing can distort observations because it restricts which aspects of the phenomenon the observer considers. Advocates of interconnected knowing encourage initially trying to perceive objects in their own right, "listening to the material," while bracketing any preconceived notions about the nature of the object. Interconnected knowing also would advocate teaching children to make a wide search for relevant variables and models, to be open to new definitions of the problem, and to attend to individual differences in organisms and to anomalies. Diversity among children, with the resulting differences in what questions are posed and how they are answered, would be encouraged rather than discouraged.

Third, we would recognize that children's interests and values influence their degree of interest in scientific problems. Scientific problems should be contextualized in social problems or personal experiences (Rosser, 1990). And fourth, the process of collaborative research and thinking would become more important; the traditional metaphor of the child as (isolated) scientist is not appropriate. We know little about the development of the collaborative skills used by scientists in collaborative research. Moreover, much of the current work on children's collaborations focuses on the resolution of conflicting beliefs rather than on the cooperative co-construction of new knowledge.

Social Cognition

From the perspective of the four aspects of the interconnected-knowing model in figure 1, four changes are needed in current models of social cognition (see also Nelson's discussion of theory of mind, this volume). First, we need to study children's perceptions not of an isolated person but of a socially situated person—a person embedded in social relationships. Children not only become aware of mental states but also learn that people have mental representations *of each other* that guide their interpersonal behavior. The developing knowledge of a network of beliefs, desires, feelings, and intentions *among people* leads to a child's "theory-of-mind in society." Children often must reason about the interaction of the minds of people in complex social relationships who have a social history. Second, the interconnected-knowing framework suggests a more dynamic, dialogic process of acquiring social knowledge than is typically examined in research on inferring others' mental states. The processes of reciprocity, empathy, perspective taking, recursive thinking ("She's thinking that I'm thinking that she's thinking... "), and intersubjectivity may be particularly important. Third, thinking about others' mental states and traits is connected to one's self concept (a relational being), emotional state, emotional relationship with others, and current goals. Fourth, a feminist approach would focus more on how the epistemological community influences what mental states or traits children learn to value and thus monitor for in others. Also important are societal-political aspects of "sources of knowledge" from other people—*whose* knowledge can you trust, *whose* knowledge counts, *who* is allowed access to knowledge, *how* social relationships (e.g., friend versus enemy) affect the quality of knowledge. Finally, we would ask what the function of knowledge of mental states and traits is in the child's social world. For example, a theory of mind may help children enter into collaborative problem solving and the co-construction of knowledge and may help establish relationships with others (e.g., Tomasello, Kruger, & Ratner, 1993).

Cognitive Strategies

Several lines of research have documented that a child tends to use multiple strategies during problem solving (e.g., Coyle & Bjorklund, 1997; Miller & Aloise, 1995; Siegler, 1996). Typically, the focus is on how these strategies compete with each other until the best one finally wins out. We also see models of competition and survival in cognitive neuroscience, such as in the favoring of stronger pathways and the trimming back of synapses along weaker pathways. From an interconnected-thinking perspective, however, especially aspect 3 in figure 1, one might see cooperation and collaboration rather than competition (see also Scholnick, this volume). Specifically, the off-and-on reappearance of less mature strategies may serve to support or scaffold the weaker, more advanced strategies until the latter can function on their own. And two strategies working together may be more effective than a single strategy (e.g., Baker-Ward, Ornstein, & Holden, 1984). They may even co-construct a new strategy. Regarding aspect 4, peer support rather than competition can facilitate strategy development. A strategy introduced by one child is more likely to survive if the other child responds in a positive and supportive manner (Ellis, 1995). What is important here is that the differing metaphors of competition and cooperation lead us to look at different developmental mechanisms in our research.

Conclusion

I now return to the four questions about cognitive development—content, mechanisms of development, function, and methods—asked from a feminist perspective near the beginning of this chapter. (1) *Content of thought.* The spotlight would shift to children's concepts of relationships, complex causal interactions, diversity, and mutual facilitation and collaboration. Concepts and skills are situated rather than universal. (2) *Processes of development.* Developmental theories and metaphors would focus on the social, collaborative co-construction of knowledge, on reciprocity between a child and the phenomenon to be understood, on supportive rather than conflictual relations among developing skills or concepts, and on diverse developmental pathways and mechanisms, especially those resulting from the intersections of age, gender, race, social class, culture, and so on. (3) *Functions of cognition.* More attention would be paid to children's use of their cognitive skills to understand others, build social bonds, develop a self connected to others and work cooperatively with others rather than to master and control themselves, others, and nature. Both the content and function of thought vary from person to person, due to the particular situatedness of the knower in developmental time and space. Age, race, gender, class, ethnicity, and sexuality, and their accompanying standpoint and degree of power, carve out particular possible experiences and thus particular possible knowledge. (4) *Research methods.* Researchers would (a) include contextual influences in their designs and interpretations of results; (b) use designs that allow multiple, multidirectional causes to emerge; (c) immerse themselves cognitively in the phenomenon to be studied, establish an egalitarian relationship with the research participant, and consider alternative hypotheses, especially in the early phases of research; (d) give more attention to social cognition, to the functions that cognition serves in everyday life, and to the social origins of thinking about the social and nonsocial world; (e) conduct collaborative research; and (f) give serious attention to anomalies, outliers, and more generally the diversity that comes from varying standpoints.

The feminist interconnected-knowing view expands current perspectives on cognitive development. The gendered aspects of social interaction, such as the focus on imbalance of power, conflict, and separation, on the one hand, and reciprocity, cooperation, and connection on the other, suggest quite different models of cognition and its development. The traditional and feminist models, however, are complementary and together lead us to a richer view of cognitive development. In fact, the ideal end point of cognitive development may be the integration of separated and interconnected thinking (Belenky et al., 1986).

Entering a Community of Minds

"Theory of Mind"

from a Feminist Standpoint

Katherine Nelson, Sarah Henseler, and Daniela Plesa

For almost two decades, researchers in cognitive development have focused extraordinary attention on the problem identified as children's developing "theory of mind." Central to this area of research are questions regarding children's understanding of self and others as "having" and acting on the basis of mental states such as desires, beliefs, and intentions. Developmental psychologists have asked, What are the processes by which young children come to understand people not just as actors, but as thinkers whose actions are affected by what they imagine or believe or know? An understanding of mental life is essential to the young child who seeks to make sense of her social world, and so it is not surprising that cognitive developmentalists have expended enormous effort exploring this topic. Its potential significance, though, extends far beyond their field.

An interest in understanding how children build their knowledge of others out of their social experiences is consonant with feminists' interest in analyzing how knowledge is constructed within specific cultural and historical contexts, founded on particular structures of social and political relationships. Lorraine Code's (1991) claim that "knowing people as well as possible is a worthy epistemological paradigm tout court" (p. 41) emphasizes the relevance of social understanding and its origins to broader issues of epistemology. From this perspective, the topic should be of wide general interest. Although research on children's theory of mind has occupied the attention of many first-rate people in the subfield of cognitive development and has garnered a great deal of support in the way of research grants, conferences, and publications, it has left others with interests in social development, social cognition, and related fields somewhat uncertain about its claims and significance. As a result, many developmentalists interested in social or cognitive development tend to neglect the findings and ignore their implications.

In this chapter, we propose that the reason for this neglect lies in the pretheoretical assumptions underlying the research enterprise in the theory of mind area, assumptions that derive from the parent field of cognitive science. The history and current state of the research and theory on theory on mind reveal the dominance of a universalist, rationalist, objectivist, essentialist framework, metaphysical assumptions that are antithetical to the principles of feminist epistemologies as outlined in the work of such theorists as Bleier (1986a), Code (1991), Harding (1991), and others. In the last section of this chapter we outline an alternative approach to the problem area in terms of psychological understanding grounded in experiential knowledge gained in social-cultural-linguistic contexts and developed further in discourse between people. We view psychological understanding not as a theory in the minds of individuals but as a dynamic knowledge system co-constructed in the context of action, which we call *psychological pragmatics.* We show that this alternative framework is consistent with the principles of feminist epistemologies. We suggest that new lines of research are needed to illuminate the problems that are uncovered in the proposed framework.

History and Current State, and Pretheoretical Assumptions of the Theory of Mind Research Domain

How did the hypothetical construct of a theory of mind enter developmental science as a research question?[1] The concept of "strong objectivity," as formulated by Harding (1991), encourages us to examine the context of discovery as well as the context of justification, and in particular the underlying assumptions, which arise out of specific historical and intellectual contexts. In this case, the history is relatively straightforward and well documented. In 1978 Premack and Woodruff, pursuing their interest in the cognitive abilities of chimpanzees, questioned whether the chimpanzee has a "theory of mind." They wondered, among other things, whether chimpanzees would attribute beliefs to "other minds," and in particular whether they might, in Machiavellian fashion, implant false beliefs into the mind of another to gain a desired end for the self, citing evidence that one of the chimps they observed appeared to do just that, leading a disliked caretaker to the wrong location.

Note the presence at the outset of the following elements that have remained salient in subsequent theories of theory of mind: (1) that understanding others' beliefs and intentions requires a *theory*[2]; (2) that the problem is that of one individual mind attaining knowledge of *other minds*; (3) that the requisite abilities have a basis in evolution, specifically in the theory that the evolution of human intelligence is based on the importance of *social intelligence,* predicting the behavior of others in social groups; (4) that the kind of social intelligence that has evolved is *Machiavellian* (Byrne & Whiten, 1988), designed to win rewards for self by fair means or foul in a basically competitive environment ("red in tooth and claw"); (5) that the critical test for theory of mind is attribution to another of *false belief*; and (6) that the knowledge attained is *culture free* and *language independent.* These elements have continued to form the major constituents of the research program now known as the development of a theory of mind, although some (e.g., items 1and 6) have been contested or substantially qualified in more recent work.

Most of these presuppositions were accepted uncritically by the two initial developmental studies that adapted the problem to the question of whether and when young children might acquire a theory of mind. Bretherton and Beeghly (1982) first reported on uses of mental-state words (e.g., "sad") by children of two years, indicating that they already "had" a theory of mind. More significant to the onslaught of subsequent research was Wimmer and Perner's (1983) experiment in which a paradigmatic task, the "Maxi task," was used for the first time to evaluate whether children of three or four years demonstrated understanding of false belief. In this task, also referred to as an "unexpected transfer task," the child watches as the experimenter uses a pair of dolls to enact the story of a character named Maxi, who puts some chocolate in a cupboard, and then leaves the room. While Maxi is out of the room, his mother (or another character) enters the kitchen, takes the chocolate out of the first cupboard, and moves it to a second cupboard. The observing child is then asked to tell the experimenter where Maxi will look for his chocolate when he returns to the kitchen. Will Maxi act on his false belief that the chocolate is still in the first cupboard and look there, or will he (as most three-year-olds predict) look in the new location where his mother put it? This task has become the litmus test of theory-of-mind acquisition, because children who know that people can have, and will act upon, their own construal of reality, even when that construal is mistaken, are thought to understand the (subjective, private, individual) representational nature of mind.

A second widely used task to evaluate children's understanding of mind is the representational change or "deceptive box task" (Gopnik & Astington, 1988), sometimes called the "Smarties task." Here the child is shown a box designed to hold candy with an appropriate picture visible on the outside. The child is asked to say what is in the box, then the box is opened and she is shown that it actually contains pencils. The box is then closed again and the child is asked what she thought was in the box before it was opened, and what is really in the box. This task enables the researcher to probe for the child's own previous false belief as well as another's by next asking the child to predict what a friend will think is in the box before it is opened. As with the Maxi task, three-year-olds tend to give the "reality" answer—pencils—to all questions, stating that they thought there were pencils, there really are pencils, and someone else will think there are pencils in the box, even though it looks like a candy ("Smarties") box. The Smarties task and the Maxi task, with variations, have come to be regarded as the standard theory-of-mind research tasks.

Findings from Theory-of-Mind Research

Research using these paradigms and their variations have provided results of interest to early social and cognitive development. The false belief task has brought forth the important questions: When, if ever, do children come to understand that some of the perplexities of other people's actions are explainable in terms of their faulty understanding of the way the world is, when the child herself has a presumably veridical view of the way the world is? When can a child estimate another's mental state, based on inferences from the child's own knowledge and perceptual state? By isolating the inferential links between representations and behavior, the experiments in theory-of-mind research paradigms have provided interesting and important information relevant to these questions. Among other things, these experiments have told us the following:

• It is not until about four years of age that children will judge that a person who lacks knowledge of a revised external state will act on the basis of prior knowledge (a false belief).

- Children three years old or younger appear to believe that their own knowledge states are shared by others, regardless of others' informational access.
- Not until five years or so do children seem to associate sources of information reliably with their resulting knowledge states (i.e., that looking leads to knowledge of visual, but not tactual, properties).
- Until well into the school years children remain vague about the meaning of many common mental-state terms, including "think," "guess," "know," and "pretend."
- Children show confusion in attempting to reconcile conflicting information in tasks, for example, by looking at one location and stating another.

These are only some of the many conclusions that can be drawn from this research, which has clearly provided a more elaborate understanding of children's cognitive abilities in the preschool period than was previously available, abilities that are especially relevant to children's social understanding (see Flavell & Miller, 1998, for an extensive, balanced discussion of the contributions of this research). What is most striking from one point of view is the finding of significant lacks and confusion on the part of young children in their inferences about others' intentions and knowledge states. From another point of view, such lapses and confusion are not surprising, given the restricted opportunities of children with limited language capabilities to exchange information with others. Many researchers have now verified that the increased (but still limited) competence seen at age four coincides with increased linguistic competence, enabling greater access to other people's perspectives. That this set of misunderstandings and confusions could have led researchers to the conclusion that children construct coherent logical theories and revise them in the light of new data continues to baffle us, however, and we consider alternative interpretations in what follows.

Theoretical Positions

The theoretical positions that emerged from the standard research enterprise can be summarized in terms of five types of explanations (for summaries see Astington & Gopnik, 1991; C. Lewis & Mitchell, 1994; K. Nelson, 1996; Russell, 1992). These represent variants on what are considered to be the two main theories of theory of mind in the philosophical literature: the theory theory and the simulation theory (Carruthers & Smith, 1996).

- *Theory theory* (Gopnik, 1993; Wellman, 1988). In this conception, what the child is seen as doing is literally constructing and then revising a theory about minds in relation to behavior. The child's theory contains concepts of mental states, both epistemic (e.g., belief, knowing, thinking) and nonepistemic (e.g., dreaming, desiring, liking). The theory applies to both other minds and own mind.
- *Innate module* (Baron-Cohen, 1995; Leslie, 1988). This nativistic explanation assumes that intentionality—understanding mental states in relation to propositions (e.g., "I know that…," "she believes that… ")—is a "built-in" component of the human mind/brain. Various maturational factors determine that it is not expressed until age four years or later.
- *Recursive representation* (Perner, 1991). In this model the child is viewed as developing increasingly recursive (e.g., "I think that you know that…") and metarepresentational (reflection on mental processes themselves) capacities that enable the solution of theory-of-mind tasks at the age of four years, and of more complex tasks later.
- *Folk psychology* based on experience and introspection, the simulation or Cartesian theory (P. L. Harris, 1992). Here the child is viewed as gaining an understanding of his or her own mental states and then coming to simulate others' mental states through imaginative processes.
- *Enculturation* through social interaction or narrative, resulting in the acquisition of a folk psychology (Astington, 1996; C. Lewis, 1994). Although this alternative has been less explicitly claimed by theorists working in the standard paradigm (but see later discussion), it has been argued against by other theorists, and sometimes put forth as a "straw man" (Gopnik, 1993).

With the exception of enculturation models, each of these theories shares to a greater or lesser extent certain metaphysical assumptions, in particular that of a universal, rational mind. Children are viewed as making sense of their own and other people's actions and reactions in a social world by developing a coherent and consistent theory containing mental-state concepts sufficient to explain behavior. The child's theoretical destination is a conception of *mind* construed as a disembodied, autonomous, individually owned information-processing or representational device. The mind so conceived functions primarily as a cognitive mechanism, providing representations that mirror the real world "out there" (see Rosser & Miller, this volume, for ties to logical positivism).

Devising a causal explanation of the mechanisms whereby children come to understand this model, characterized as "folk psychology," has been the goal of empirical research. The model has been described in philosophy in the following terms:

> Folk psychology is a network of principles which characterizes a sort of common-sense theory about how to explain human behavior... if someone desires that p, and this desire is not overridden by other desires, and he believes that an action of kind k will bring it about that p, and he believes that such action is within his power... then *ceteris paribus,* the desire and the beliefs will cause him to perform an action of the kind k... the states it postulates are characterized primarily in terms of their causal relations to each other, to perception and other environmental stimuli, and to behavior. (Horgan & Woodward, 1993, p. 144; quoted in Flavell & Miller, 1998)

The assumption implied is that most relevant explanations for peoples' actions are to be sought in the relationships between the representational contents of their mental states and reality. This assumption privileges epistemic states of belief and knowledge over affect and other nonepistemic states (e.g., pain, empathy), both in research and in development. Nonepistemic states are viewed as more primitive explanatory bases of behavior, representing immature forms of making sense of own and others' actions (Baron-Cohen, 1995; Gopnik, 1993; Leslie, 1988; Perner, 1991; Wellman, 1990).

An additional implicit assumption of these models is that the mind, individually owned, develops primarily through intrapsychic processes of conceptual growth. As the result of conceptual developmental processes, children's theories of the decontexted mind enable universally applicable predictions of the behavior of generalized others. The child who acquires or constructs this domain-specific theory is considered by many theorists (e.g., Gopnik & Meltzoff, 1997) to be a "little scientist" elaborating social concepts by processes of scientific reasoning, revising them in response to confrontation with conflicting "data," and using these concepts to predict people's actions and reactions.

These assumptions of theory of mind are not value neutral. Both the idea that understanding requires a theory and the idea that the theory is about other minds reflect the Cartesian assumption of one individual mind looking out at external reality to represent it as truthfully as possible.

Knowledge of other minds is from this perspective highly problematic. This representation of the problem incorporates the strong northern value of *individualism* as well as of *disembodied minds,* or, in psychological terminology, of cognitive autonomy and the primacy of the individual over the interpersonal.

If these assumptions and values appear to be parallel to those of the scientific method itself, this parallelism is made explicit by those who favor the theory theory and who view children as little scientists constructing and revising theories on the basis of rational considerations of data structures and subsequent tests of theories against new data. Because no one has ever observed a child articulating a theory of mind, the constructs on which the theory theory rests derive solely from the professional terminology of philosophy and psychology. The child's wants become desires, half-formed notions become beliefs, guesses become hypotheses, visual scenes become data for testing theories. The inevitable result of considering the child as a protoscientist is to give the theory theory the look of scientific validity.

One might have expected that when the focus shifted from nonhuman primates to human children, the assumption that knowledge of other minds must be culture free and language independent might be called into question. However, until recently that has not been the case. Rather, such knowledge has been attributed to universalist characteristics of human minds. The very concepts that are held to be essential parts of the attained theory of mind—the concepts of mental states of desire, perception, and belief—are considered as dichotomous, essentialist categories. A person is assumed to either have or not have desire, to perceive or not perceive an object, to believe or not believe a proposition as true or false. Further, minds are assumed to be essentially rational; given information and natural logic, certain inferences follow inevitably. Social, cultural, experiential, linguistic, or communicative conditions have little bearing on the issues at stake; they are not valued in terms of the "scientific" results. Clearly, this is the "view from nowhere" in conventional science (Nagel, 1986), the "culture of no culture" (Harding, 1991).

Developmental Research and Principles of Feminist Epistemology

Many research programs and theories in developmental psychology exhibit pretheoretical assumptions that, unlike the cognitive science–based assumptions of standard theory of mind, are quite consistent with the principles of feminist epistemologies. Versions of cultural psychology, Vygotskian theory, ecological theory, contextual theory, experiential theory, narrative theory, developmental systems, and social interaction theories of language, memory, and cognition all fit this description. Rather than distinguish among these theories and programs or attempt to situate our ideas about the development of psychological understanding within one or another approach, we want to point out the assumptions, common to most of them, that are consistent with the claims of most versions of feminist epistemology.

Relational Knowledge

Taking account of the relational structure of the experimental paradigm requires recognizing the subordinate position and legitimate concerns of the child who serves as subject. The child in our society is in a permanently subordinate role vis-à-vis the adult, who in general exerts control and who in the research context sets up and controls the situation and dictates the rules of the interaction, which may be unfamiliar and strange to the child. The adult may also be unfamiliar, and the child may have only a few strategies for interacting with strange adults; three-year-olds may be at a greater disadvantage than four-year-olds in this respect. Older children may have more familiarity with authority roles and may acquiesce more readily to demands. Thus, issues of power, control, familiarity of persons, and familiarity with rules of interaction must be negotiated with due regard for the child's perspective. The interpersonal knowledge that the child displays may be modulated by his or her understanding of the interpersonal relations apparent in the immediate situation.

Experientially Based Knowledge

Children may have differential experiences that have resulted in different ways of evaluating novel situations or story-tests. For example, some children have had considerable experience with a variety of other children and adults, whereas other children have been exposed to very few. Some children have extensive experience in using language as a semiotic medium through which to receive information, narratives, explanations, rules, and so on, whereas other children may have little experience with some of these uses of language. Children with frequent experiences may have learned more about the mental-state meaning of critical terms such as "think" and "know," which are used pragmatically as interactive directives as well as to refer to mental states. Many other experiential variables might enter into a child's capacity to "play the game," such as number, age, and gender of siblings, gender of self, number of friends, disposition to play alone or with others, and so on. A number of researchers are now tracing the effect of these experiential variables on success on theory-of-mind tasks.

We view the function of experience somewhat differently than theory theorists, who have described it in terms of data structures (Gopnik & Wellman, 1994). We believe that knowledge is a function of an experiencing organism; in this case the organism is a human child with the capacities that we associate with humanness, such as basic cognitive processes, perceptual capacities, and communicative abilities, including an increasing understanding of language forms and structures. These human capacities enable the child to learn about the social world (which is not distinguishable from any other world, although the child is capable of making distinctions between people, animals, and nonanimate objects).

Situated/Contexted

Every action and interaction takes place in a given situation where relevant existing experiential knowledge may or may not be available. Young children rely to a large extent on script-type knowledge to guide their responses in strange as well as everyday situations. It is not surprising, therefore, that children at home in everyday situations may display greater knowledge and interpersonal competence than they do on laboratory tasks (see Dunn, 1988). The context of the laboratory may pose formidable problems of interpretation for the very young child.

Sociocultural

Although a few studies have found similar patterns of responding to theory-of-mind tasks among children from different cultural backgrounds, it is becoming clear that acquisition of understanding of a culture-specific folk psychology also proceeds according to socially and culturally specific time spans (Lillard, 1997). Vinden (1996) showed that children in rural Peru do not understand the theory-of-mind tasks in the same way that American children do. C. Lewis and his colleagues (1996) found that children in a Greek village varied in their psychological understanding, depending on the number of close kin with whom they interacted on a regular basis. People's expectations of children's participation in social life vary in different cultures and among different kin relations; it is not surprising that children's understanding will vary accordingly. Feminist approaches emphasize intersections of gender, ethnicity, social class, and other status variables that determine specific sociocultural contexts and experience.

Discursive/Narrative

Predicting and explaining human actions in the human world is the stuff of literature and drama, involving the complex interweaving of emotions, values, motivations, personalities, politics, agendas, and interests, as well as knowledge. The rational world of costs and benefits tends to be overridden by misapprehensions and miscalculations. Sometimes the outcome is a happy one, sometimes not. Sometimes chance (i.e., nonhuman forces) intervenes to overturn a well-laid plan. In the face of uncertainty, narratives of previous experiences—personal, fictional, culturally shared myths or morality tales—can structure understanding. Young children begin to use narrative resources to understand the complexities of their own experience very early (Bruner, 1990; P. J. Miller, Potts, Fung, Hoogstra, & Mintz, 1990; K. Nelson, 1989), fostered by the practices of caregivers and the general adult discourse that surrounds them. To the extent that narrative suggests alternative interpretations to abstract logic, children, like adults, may prefer the former.

Methodological Critique of Theory-of-Mind Research

In light of the assumptions shared by feminist theories and many contemporary theories and methods in developmental research, it is pertinent to examine more closely the methodological paradigms of standard theory-of-mind research. For example, in the Maxi task described previously, a single child is asked to observe two dolls that are manipulated by an experimenter, the only other person available to the child in this test of the developing understanding of human minds but one who is deliberately muted so as not to affect the child's response in any way. The "people" whose minds are the focus of the experiment are dolls, although the child is not expected to use them in play or to give a playful response to the questions. The only identifiable characteristic of the actor in this paradigmatic experiment is the name, Maxi, and the child is not present in the story as a participant but is an observer of the problem posed before her.

It should also be noted that, although the Maxi task involves three (or more) people, neither the researcher nor the child plays a part in the drama of Maxi's false belief. The child is an observer of the drama, whereas the researcher is an observer of the observer; the child produces "data" but the researcher is almost always treated as invisible, at least as far as the data and their analysis are concerned. The implication is that the researcher is also invisible to the child, as the child is to Maxi. In consequence, the child is not asked to ask Maxi where he will look for the toy, or to tell Maxi where it is. Thus the Maxi situation itself is not interpersonal from the child's point of view.

However, from the child's perspective the experimental situation may well be interpersonal with respect to the child and researcher. For example, the child may be engaged in pondering what the experimenter's game is. What kind of a situation is this? Is it a test? A pretend game? A fictional story? What will happen if he gives the "wrong" answer? These questions invoke "mind reading" of a more personally engaged, even threatening, kind than predicting where Maxi will look next. The fact that the experimental paradigm relies on particular kinds of person-relations, involving issues of power and dominance, is not in focus. As children are always in a dominated position vis-à-vis human adults, the condition is taken for granted, hidden from the research practice. Because the experiment is not conceived of as a social interaction, no account is taken of the roles that child and experimenter play, and of the power imbalance between them.

In actuality the false belief task is not a test of children's understanding of interpersonal action but of the *logic of the conservation of object location,* logic that requires mastery of the conditions for acquiring knowledge, for example, that perception may be a valid source of knowledge. The logic is quite simple when the requisite concepts and words are understood as intended. Further, despite the efforts of researchers to clarify the problem, its representation (i.e., the narrative) is actually ambiguous with respect to the logic of the situation and the conclusions that can be drawn from it (e.g., the child may assume that someone told Maxi about the move).

Although the deceptive box task comes closer than the Maxi task to engaging the child, who herself initially has a false belief about the box content, and although it invokes personal relations (friends), it shares many of the Maxi task's assumptions. Here again, the child is assumed to be a rational, autonomous problem-solver rather than an active participant in a human social interaction that makes sense to her. The data that result from these experiments, based on right and wrong answers, invite single causal explanations of age-related changes rather than reflection on the complex development of social competence derived from lived experience, situated knowledge, and embodied persons existing in groups of men, women, and children. Few investigators have attempted to place the findings from theory-of-mind tasks in the context of earlier developments of interpersonal situations and social understanding (Flavell & Miller, 1998; but see Hobson, 1993; C. Lewis & Mitchell, 1994).

An important question to be asked about both paradigms is this: Does the false belief task reflect anything significant about what young children experience of the social world? In at least one model of the child's world, that of middle-class Britain and America, where most of the research on theory of mind has been carried out, the ideal model is of the nurturing caretaker who attends to the child's needs and desires and who gradually leads the child into a larger world of peers and adults where sharing is a highly valued skill and where aggression, both physical and verbal, is devalued, truth rather than falsehood is expected, and so on. In this model, competition, trickery, and false belief are opposed to cooperation, information sharing, and truth telling. Dunn's (1988) observations, subsequently given support through experimental research (Jenkins & Astington, 1996; Perner, Ruffman, & Leekham, 1994), indicate that siblings may be the source of information about trickery, competition, and false belief, but that these are deviations from valued norms articulated by parents.

Feminist analyses have revealed an androcentric bias in conventional scientific practices of the kind exemplified in much experimental work on theory of mind (and elsewhere in psychology). This bias is reflected in the basic ideas behind the false belief task. Specifically, the hypothesis that human intelligence evolved to solve social problems, a hypothesis first articulated by Humphrey (1976) and later by sociobiologists, evolutionary game theorists, and evolutionary psychologists, rests on the assumption that the social problems to be solved by individual thinkers and actors are competitive ones in a world of potential cheaters. Thus, the value of Machiavellianism, the ability to outwit one's fellows by "mind reading" and trickery, is foremost. This assumption raises the difficult problem of altruism and cooperation, which are treated in sociobiological theory not as alternative values but as costly traits that need special explanations. The alternative possibility, that cooperation and altruism are adaptive traits, implies different expectations of interpretations in the Maxi task.

Theorists of theory of mind emphasize that testing false belief does not rest on a *value* of Machiavellianism but on the inability to discern from evidence of understanding true belief, whether it rests on mental concepts or overt behavioral cues. (Of course, the reverse logic requires testing as well: to what extent do people rely on external cues to others' intentions, and to what extent do they "mind read" in the absence of such cues?) Nonetheless, the stories devised to test false belief seem to focus almost exclusively on trickery (boxes that say one thing and hold another) and mischief (taking a marble from one child's basket and putting it in one's own box).

It is important to point out that, through the nineties, a number of researchers who have explored children's developing psychological understanding from a social development perspective (see Raver & Leadbeater, 1993) have been engaged in the effort to analyze theory-of-mind research and to escape the boundaries of its theoretical and methodological constraints. In addition to Dunn and her colleagues, who have emphasized children's understanding in everyday home situations and with familiar siblings and peers (e.g., Dunn, 1988, 1994), a number of researchers have suggested modifications of theory-of-mind paradigms and have attempted to relate these tasks to memory, language competence, sibling status, parental styles, social competence, and so on, emphasizing the complexity of the developing system of social knowledge in real-world contexts.

Reconceptualizing Theory of Mind in Psychological Pragmatics Terms

Table 1 summarizes the contrasting assumptions of the mechanistic and interpretive—what we call "psychological pragmatics"—views of psychological understanding. The left column lists assumptions consistent with feminist as well as developmental theory; the right column lists assumptions common in cognitive science generally.[3] The assumptions of the alternative feminist/developmental framework imply that the study of children's understanding of own and others' intentionality and belief states in relation to action is of interest primarily from the perspective that human actions ordinarily relate to and coordinate group activities and interpersonal relations, as well as serve personal goals. Thus the interpretation of children's understanding should be undertaken in terms of the context of the activities and persons involved in the task or situation within which a child's response is observed. We assume that interpretation of others' mental states, including their intentions with respect to one's own position in the joint activity, is often difficult and obscure, even (perhaps especially) among adults.

Table 1. Assumptions of psychological pragmatics, in contrast to standard theory-of-mind assumptions

Psychological pragmatics	Theory of mind mechanism
Mind as mental activity	Mind as static analyzer
Mind as embodied: action involved; differentiated by gender, age, and status	Autonomous mind
Mind as enculturated, semiotically mediated	Mind as context free, individually separate
Knowledge as situated	Knowledge mechanisms context independent
Knowledge as experience based	Knowledge as rationally invoked
Persons as active agents and subjective selves	Persons as passive observers of others' actions
Concepts as products of collaborative construction	Concepts individually constructed
Language as mediator of cultural and social theories, conceptual frameworks	Theories not dependent on language or culture
Shared understanding of social realities derived from socially shared semiotic systems	Understanding of social realities by solitary individuals
Human actions and activities interpreted in narrative schemas	Human actions understood in terms of theories

The most important question to ask is, What are the implicit goals of the child's making-sense cognitive activities? When theorists assume that the goal of the child's cognitive effort is to acquire an implicit theory, an objective and abstract framework for interpreting the world is implied, a framework that conforms to criteria of logical consistency, coherence, and universal application. However, if the purpose of making-sense efforts is to relate effectively to others in a particular social world, the criteria of consistency, logical coherence, and universality are less relevant. Rather, individual differences and situational contexts are crucial to one's predictions.

Models of varying social worlds based on experience with different situations and people require a level of complexity in both the information that enters into the models and in the models that result, a complexity that cannot be readily reduced to logical formulas and coherent, noncontradictory structures. This claim is consistent with the view from intellectual history and the history of science and technology that logical formulations, mathematical models, and encompassing theories of phenomena are attained with great intellectual effort *after* much observational and experimental empirical practices in a field. There are persistent claims that the social sciences will never attain the kind of elegant theoretical models that physics and more recently biology have produced. Why then should we expect that young children, working as little social scientists, would come to some such satisfyingly coherent, logical, theoretical propositions about the social world? Is it not enough that we can observe them engaging in socially effective *practices* much (though certainly not all) of the time?

Our psychological pragmatics view is founded on our interest in specifying what resources (experiential, cognitive, affective, linguistic, etc.) are most useful to the child in a social world. What does the child need to know in order to participate effectively in a variety of social contexts? How does children's psychological knowledge emerge out of experience in different pragmatic circumstances? For instance, describing how children come to understand that there are complex routes from belief to action, routes that may involve deception, strategies, problem solving, communication, persuasion, knowledge search, and detailed planning, is essential to an explanation of the development of psychological understanding. Further, it is essential to account for differences among children deriving from their social and cultural contexts, including their different subjective experiences related to gender. Our approach assumes that the abstract knowledge (theory-of-mind) people eventually construct is built *out* of experiential, pragmatic knowledge acquired in an interpreted, social world and is not the *basis* for such knowledge. Therefore our view of the developmental course of psychological understanding reverses the sequence suggested in the standard theory-of-mind theoretical positions.

The methodological consequences of this approach are quite general. Every study concerns a moment in a child's developmental history, and the resources available to the child at that moment must be carefully considered. Does the child bring to the experimental situation familiarity with the routine in which she will participate? What cognitive schemas are available to her to interpret the experimental situation? Is she competent to use the discourse genres required? The interpretation of "performance" should aim at relating the present with the past and future course of development. We need to attend to those particular experiences that support changes in ways of making sense. Key among those is experience with language in social interaction. Although adults share a framework for interpreting action (the folk psychology of their culture), children have limited access to that framework until they develop competence in the use of discourse within and about social environments, particularly competence with narratives about social events.

The elements that go into the construction of folk psychological understanding, although shared within a culture, may vary with specific experiences. For example, male and female social experiences and subjective interpretations of their common experiences vary. Research on gender socialization, construction of self, and autobiographical memory has revealed differences in boys' and girls' conversational experiences with parents (see Fivush, this volume). The consequences of such experientially based differences resulting from the complex intertwining of culture-specific socialization practices and personal/subjective experiences have yet to be specified in relation to the development of psychological understanding. We wish to understand the unique perspectives on social interactions of both boys and girls; but more generally, we share the feminist view that studying diverse populations, cultures, and social groups is important to the understanding of a complex social phenomenon. In this case, study of diversity will yield a better understanding of the psychological pragmatics involved in any person's interpretation of others' minds and actions. Thus, to state that we must understand a particular child's developmental history and specific life experiences does not mean to deny commonality in the developmental process and product. Rather, the expectation is that particular applications of a common process may result in different pathways toward understanding and different constructions of a general model. Commonalities in psychological understanding arise because people, including children at all ages, are engaged in *making sense* of their worlds, and in particular of making sense of self and others in the social milieu in which they find themselves. The job of the researcher is to articulate this process of making sense and apply it to the problems of psychological understanding.

Beyond the View from Nowhere

Essential to a feminist critique is consideration of the perspectives of those whose own subjectivity and voice are often disregarded in experimental research by virtue of their position as the object of scientific investigation.

A new perspective is gained by viewing this problem area from the point of view of the developing child, in contrast to the view from the cognitive science mechanism standpoint. The centrality of the child's point of view is a distinctive principle in the alternative framework proposed here. We believe that it is incumbent upon us to honor the child's perspective in our research, to respect the child's interests and understanding without confusing them with our own. In this sense the child is the Other in developmental research in a way analogous to the subjects of anthropologists' research into different cultures. In one sense, we know the child intimately, both because we have all been children at one time (thus dominated by adults) and because many of us have children of our own or have close child relatives, and have faced the challenge of communicating with and interpreting these Others regarding everyday practical concerns. But the demands of scientific developmental research require that we make the child Strange. The rule is that however well we believe we understand the young mind on an intuitive level, we must not use that belief to interpret our scientifically gathered data. But to bring out the perspective of children's lives in a way analogous to that of privileging the perspective of women (also the Other) in feminist research, we cannot ignore what we know from everyday experience.

Taking the child's perspective requires going beyond giving lip service to the child's assent to participate or providing enjoyable tasks to keep him engaged. Rather, it requires a serious attempt to address the question, What is the child's "theory of the experiment"? To answer this question means at the least attending to all of the child's comments and reactions, rather than focusing only on the child's answers to predetermined data-yielding questions. We must constantly remind ourselves that children may not—do not—interpret research situations in the same terms that adult experimenters do. The total-response situation should be examined for clues to the child's understanding. Anomalous responses should lead to further questions. What appear to be straightforward responses (e.g., "yes" or "no" or a forced choice from a two-choice option) may mask a child's confusion.

The complexity of the obscure targets of our investigation—namely, the hidden mental understanding of the child's understanding of another's hidden mental state—requires that we keep our questions open. Beyond the immediate research situation we should let our interpretations be informed by what we know of children's lived experiences and how these experiences may affect children's understanding of the situation.[4]

Our ongoing research projects concerned with issues related to the theory-of-mind domain have led us to engage in the practice of "listening to the noise," that is, taking account of the extra comments we record and elicit in the course of a study. These comments usually are not mentioned in research reports, or else they are treated as noise in the data and sometimes used to exclude children who apparently do not understand the situation in the way expected of them.

One of the problems that seems clear from our observations is that children do not understand and use language terms in the same way that adult experimenters do. We used a modified version of the deceptive box task, a raisin box filled with crayons, asking children, in addition to the standard question, "What did you think was in the box [before we opened it]?", to answer a second question, "What did you say was in the box?" (Plesa, Goldman, & Edmondson, 1995). Although adults typically assume that the child understands what she said to be a reflection of what she thought, we found that children responded differently to the two questions. Many three-year-olds, as expected, incorrectly answered the "what did you think" question by reporting the real box content ("crayons"), but correctly reported what they had said ("raisins").

There are several possible interpretations of these results. First, the child may not remember a past mental state but may remember a past action, including a verbal action of saying. Second, the child may not have processed the word "think" in the first question "What do you think is in the box?" and rather interpreted the question as "What is in the box?" Then, when later asked "what did you think," the child has no way of accessing a trace of "think" independently of the saying or seeing involved. Third, the child may have no meaning attached to "think" at all, independent of its discursive pragmatic uses referring to real states in the world. "Think" may be a term that ordinarily carries no separate conceptual sense. Then "What did you think was in the box [before we opened it]?" would be interpreted as the equivalent of "What was in the box before we opened it?" In this case only a child who believes magic was involved, that there were raisins in the box when it was closed and crayons after it was opened (and one of the children we interviewed expressed such a belief), would assert the "correct" "think" answer, "raisins."

It is clear from studies of language use that the mental terms in question are commonly used in conversational functions not referring to mental states. Even the alleged evidence for use of "think" as a mental-state term because it is used by the child in a contrastive sense is fallible. For example, the child's statement, "I thought it was a snake, but it's really a stick" (see Bartsch & Wellman, 1995), reflects an appearance-reality contrast: what does perception yield, and how does it relate to world states? It does not entail "thinking" as a mental process. (Of course, this is a common use of "think" by adults as well as children.) This statement is equivalent to "It looks like a snake but it's really a stick." The true contrastive "She *thinks* the cat is in the garage but I *know* the cat is in the house" contrasts two mental states regarding the location-state of an animate object. Kessler Shaw's (1999) study of three- to four-year-olds' uses of the terms indicates that this is a late and rare use by children. Because of the difficulty of testing the child's understanding of "think," we cannot at present decide among the possible interpretations of the think/say results.

It is certainly important that children interpret the language used by researchers in the way that is relevant to the task. The issue of how children interpret the language used in theory-of-mind tasks has been addressed by other researchers, and relations between language measures and task performance beyond relations with age are generally found. But the interpretation of language in experimental situations goes beyond issues of word meaning to the dependence of meaning on interpretation of the larger discourse context. Participants may wonder, Why is the researcher asking this question? What kind of answer (test, imaginative, etc.) is expected? What is the goal of this conversation? The participant's interpretive assumptions and implicit answers to these unarticulated questions may very well influence her or his responses to the experimental tasks. Evidence of the influence of the larger discourse situation on specific responses is seen when researchers are willing to "listen to the noise." The deceptive box task, for example, was taken by some children in our laboratory to be a guessing game rather than a question about mental representations and reality.

Adults as well as children often shape their responses based on their interpretation of the experimental discourse. For instance, when adults were presented with an oral version of the Maxi task, we found that a large number of participants supplemented their correct answers to the questions "Where will Maxi look? Why?" with speculations about where he would continue his search for the chocolate to find it after looking for it where he left it (K. Nelson, Plesa, & Henseler, 1998). We have reason to believe that children as well may interpret the question "Where will Maxi look for the chocolate?" to be a question about where he will find it. Moreover, many of the adult participants went on to provide speculative narratives to explain Maxi's behavior (e.g., "Maxi knows where his mother keeps baking supplies"). In other words, these adults apparently interpreted the question to be a request not for a simple, logical answer (relating perception to action) but for the psychological motivations inherent in the scenario presented.

How do children understand the way that other people narrate and explain the basis for actions, in stories and in real life? What do they make of others' interpretations? Bruner (1990, 1992) has argued that people interpret the social world in terms of narratives that include intentionality as well as action. Adults' linguistically composed explanations and general conversations about people in the world present the child with information that is not available in overt observable actions. Over the course of time, children must abstract from these sources conventional word meanings as well as concepts of mental states, and construct from these abstractions an understanding that fits the conventional theories that adults embody in their everyday gossip, political discourse, and fictional narratives. This is a long, ongoing process. The beginnings are seen in preschoolers, but much lies ahead.

We would like to argue, therefore, not that three- and four-year-olds do or do not have a theory of mind but that they have no coherently organized, systematic understanding about minds. Given the widespread assumption that young children (and even chimpanzees) cogitate about generalized minds, this is a radical claim. But we believe that the study of psychological understanding must derive from a developmental process that relates the child to the social world in an ever-widening circle that permits an increasing accessibility to inferences about actions based on knowledge, belief, and desire states of particular people within specific activities. The derived knowledge becomes increasingly generic, but children's difficulty with many concepts logically and causally related to basic theory-of-mind concepts during and even beyond the school years (Flavell & Miller, 1998) argues, in our view, against the kind of tight conceptual structure implied by many theory-of-mind theorists.

Our goal is to show how psychological understandings are experientially derived. We do not abandon the interest in the cognitive basis of this understanding, but we believe that cognitions in this case are not independent of, indeed are embedded in, a matrix of social, cultural, and linguistic contexts of interactions with specific others. Both the acquisition of psychological understanding and the manifestations of mental activity are culturally contexted, dependent on experiences and activities in which people interact. The mastery of tools enabling reflection on one's own and others' internal states is mediated by a system of cultural symbols, with language acquisition playing a special role, for language allows us to generalize such experiences, leading to the transition from primitive intersubjectivity (seen as emotional connection to others) to personal subjectivity.

Conclusion

The central point that emerges from all of these considerations is the inherently social nature of "mind" and of our understanding of it, throughout development and across cultures. In all human environments, such activities as the establishment of mother-child intersubjectivity in infancy, imitation, role-playing, pretense, participation in everyday routines with others, and peer interactions are the foundation on which psychological understanding is built, and these activities vary with particular social settings and groups. Individual representations are mediated through representations collaboratively constructed in the context of such shared activities. As language interactions come into play, and with growing experience with meaningful narratives, the young child comes to participate in the interpretive practices of her culture, and co-constructs with others her psychological understanding. Thus, the young child's emerging understanding of self and others is not the acquisition of a theory of mind but a complex, developmental process of entering a *community of minds.*

This view is coherent with feminist epistemologies, as is evident from table 1. Entering a community of minds entails entering a shared cultural space of understanding and knowledge making, recognizing the legitimacy of contributions from varying perspectives within that space. As in a developmental analysis, a feminist analysis would reject the notion of one, abstract theory of mind and accept that theories of mind emerge as various rather than hegemonic.

Notes

We acknowledge with appreciation the symposium organized by the editors on this topic at the Piaget Society meetings in Chicago in 1994. Their work raised many of the issues that we review here, and we thank them for their helpful comments and advice on an earlier version of the chapter. We also appreciate the contributions of other graduate students working on these issues, particularly Faye Fried

Walkenfeld, Sylvie Goldman, Nechama Presler, Lea Kessler Shaw, and Reese Heitner, all of whom have contributed to the construction of the ideas articulated here. Work on this project was supported in part by NSF grant No. SBR 9421511 to the first author.

1. In this description we focus on standard theory-of-mind accounts, from the 1980s and early 1990s.
2. The term *theory* has entered cognitive and developmental psychology since the mid-1980s as a mental structure that organizes concepts within a knowledge domain. Theories in this sense are assumed to be coherent assemblies of causally related concepts designed to explain real-world phenomena. Mentalistic theories, especially in developmental work, are usually assumed to be implicit rather than explicit.
3. A caveat in regard to the terms of this table: some theorists may protest that they do not buy the assumptions identified in the right column of the table. Nonetheless, these assumptions appear to underlie the planning, execution, explanation, and theoretical interpretation of most of the laboratory-based research in the area, and it is incumbent on those who wish to reject some or all of the assumptions to make their positions clear. On the other hand, we expect that many will find the terms in the right column to be acceptable mentalistic propositions necessary as a foundation for the establishment of a scientific developmental psychology.
4. By stressing what resources the child brings to an experiment we are not confining the assessment to a "pretest" that aims to assess whether the child has the particular assumed prerequisite skills theoretically predicted for solving the problem at hand. We are interested more in the kinds of clinical interviews pioneered by Piaget to tease out what resources children of different ages use to attempt to solve the same problems.

Accuracy, Authority, and Voice

Feminist Perspectives

on Autobiographical Memory

Robyn Fivush

It is our parents...who not only teach us our family history but who set us straight on our own childhood recollections, telling us that this *cannot have happened the way we think it did and that* that, *on the other hand, did occur just as we remember it.*

—Mary McCarthy

All autobiographical memory is true. It is up to the interpreter to discover in which sense, where, for which purpose.

—Passerini

How we come to understand and represent our experience is a fundamental epistemological question. How can we have knowledge of the world and our experience of it? Who has the authority to determine whether our knowledge is accurate? These questions are at the core of human psychology; without a clear epistemological framework, we cannot hope to explain the process by which individuals develop knowledge about the world and about themselves. In its brief history, psychology has relied, often implicitly, on an epistemology grounded in logical positivism. This epistemology stresses the linear, autonomous, and progressive nature of knowledge development. But recent arguments within critical theory question many of these assumptions. Postmodern and feminist critiques of science have raised troubling concerns about the assumptions of objectivity, of truth, and of authority that underlie much of experimental psychology. Moreover, by bringing gender to the center of epistemological questions, feminist theories have reconceptualized what it means to know.

In this chapter, I explore how feminist epistemologies change the way in which we conceptualize knowledge and its acquisition in the domain of autobiographical memory. Autobiographical memory is the heart of knowledge, as the ways in which we understand and represent our personal experiences are the ground from which all other knowledge grows. Given this, it is perhaps somewhat surprising that there is relatively little psychological research on autobiographical memory. When one examines the assumptions underlying the study of memory, however, the reasons for this deficit become obvious. In the first part of this chapter, I outline the assumptions underlying traditional, logical positivist approaches to psychology and memory. I then turn to a discussion of how feminist epistemologies question these assumptions and lead to a reconceptualization of cognition and its development. In the third section I specifically consider autobiographical memory and discuss the challenges to assumptions of accuracy and authority that feminist epistemologies pose for studying autobiography.

I must stress at the outset that my purpose is not to dismiss or discredit memory research conducted within a logical positivist framework. Rather, my goal is to examine the often unexamined assumptions we make in conducting and interpreting our research. Obviously, I am not the first to do so. Many theorists have written eloquently about the limitations of the scientific method and the bias imposed by our theoretical frameworks (see especially Kuhn, 1970; Pepper, 1946). By critiquing logical positivism, my goal is that we will become more aware of the limits of some of our assumptions and methods, and search for new ways to conceptualize the phenomenon under study. The ultimate goal is to expand the theoretical frameworks available for studying autobiographical memory and to provide alternative conceptualizations that will allow us to investigate autobiographical memory in innovative and productive ways.

Assumptions Underlying Logical Positivism

As psychology emerged as a discipline separate from philosophy in the late 1800s, there was an explicit and concerted effort on the part of these pioneers to create a true science of the mind (see Heidbreder, 1933, for a historical overview). This science was to be modeled on the master science, physics, which relied on reductionistic, cause-and-effect models of real-world phenomena. The hope was to discover a relatively small and simple set of universal principles that would explain complex behavior, whether of atomistic particles or of human beings. Psychologists adhered to the scientific method in the pursuit of generalized laws of human behavior. The methodological tools of psychology included objective observation, in settings that controlled for extraneous variables, by rational experimentalists driven only by a thirst for truth.

Three fundamental assumptions underlie this formulation of psychology. First, the scientist is assumed to be objective, in that he (virtually all the early psychologists were white men) can observe others' behaviors without bias. By virtue of his detached, rational, objective observations of the phenomenon under study, he is in a privileged position to discover true knowledge, untainted by emotions, values, or prior beliefs. Second, events can be reduced to component elements, each of which can be independently studied for cause-and-effect relations. Once these lower-level cause-and-effect relations are discovered, the component elements can be reassembled to explain the larger whole. The whole is no more than the sum of the parts; emergent properties of the whole are not seriously considered.

Third, the psychological subject is assumed to be an independent knower. Knowledge is represented in the minds of individuals; the particular social-cultural worlds in which individuals live are not relevant. Reality can be objectively defined without recourse to history, culture, or context. Accuracy can be assessed objectively as a comparison between the material as the experimenter presents it (operationally defined as the stimulus) and the material as the subject represents it (operationally defined as the dependent variable). Within this framework, the experimental subject in the psychology laboratory is assumed to behave according to universal principles of cognitive functioning. Differences between experimental subjects are attributed to extraneous variables (or noise or error variance), which is of little use in explaining "true" systematic variance accounted for by the manipulations under the control of the scientist. It is the way in which subjects in the same experimental group perform similarly that is of interest, not the way in which they perform differently.

Although this is an extreme characterization of the logical positivist approach, most psychological research rests at least partly on the assumption that human behavior can be studied adequately in this kind of objective, reductionistic framework, without consideration of the individual's history, beliefs, values, or culture (see Harding, 1986; Morakowski & Agronik, 1991; Parlee, 1992; Riger, 1992; Sherif, 1987, for further discussions).[1] In Susan Bordo's (1990) apt phrase, this epistemological stance is "the view from nowhere."

Feminist Perspectives

In contrast to the assumptions underlying logical positivism, feminist epistemologies assume that knowledge is relational and contexted. Knowledge does not exist in an individual's head but in patterns of social interactions. Thus, knowledge is not abstracted from experience but is always embedded within it. Knowledge must be considered in terms of who knows, in what situation, and for what purpose. Although there are various feminist theories (see Rosser & Miller, this volume), a particularly important distinction is that between postmodern feminist epistemologies, which argue for relativity of knowledge, and feminist standpoint theories, which claim that objective knowledge is possible but under different conditions than logical positivist frameworks claim (see Alcoff & Potter, 1993; Harding, 1990, for overviews).

In brief, postmodern feminism argues that science is not possible because all that can exist is the multiple stories we tell about multiple ways of knowing (Flax, 1990; Irigaray, 1989). Postmodern feminism challenges any notion of rationality, claiming that there are no criteria for determining which version of reality is "better" or more objective than any other. In this way, postmodernism derails the whole notion of "doing science." Because we can never determine whether one way of knowing is better than any other way of knowing, or whether one version of reality is better than another version of reality, we are left with competing knowledge claims and no way to decide among them. This form of feminist epistemology leads to complete relativism of knowledge.

Feminist standpoint theory, in contrast, assumes there is a basis for evaluating empirical claims about reality. Moreover, feminists are in a privileged position to evaluate knowledge claims (Code, 1993; Haraway, 1988; Harding, 1993). Adapting Hegel's master/slave analysis of knowledge, feminist standpoint theorists argue that the struggles of oppressed peoples yield truth. Masters, or oppressors, need only see the world from their privileged vantage point, but oppressed peoples, or slaves, must see the world both from their own vantage point and that of their oppressors in order to behave in ways that the oppressors believe are appropriate, and thus avoid sanction.

Owing to current social and political structures, females are oppressed and males are oppressors. As oppressors, males have access only to their own viewpoint, but as the oppressed, females have access to both their own viewpoint and the viewpoint of the oppressors, the males. Females thus have "double consciousness." They have knowledge viewed both from the center (i.e., the oppressors' viewpoint) and from the margins (i.e., the oppressed's viewpoint) of cultural power structures. Obviously there are multiple oppressed groups, and therefore multiple viewpoints from the margins (Bar On, 1993). Objectivity is achieved through coordinating multiple perspectives, perspectives both from the center and from the margins (Code, 1993). Whereas objectivity in logical positivist episte-mologies is defined as knowledge from an "unbiased" viewpoint, objec-tivity in feminist standpoint theory is defined as knowledge from multiple viewpoints, each of which alone may be biased but all of which together, when coordinated, lead to more objective knowledge. Rather than the view from nowhere, feminist standpoint theorists argue that objective knowledge is the view from everywhere (Bordo, 1990). Objectivity is the coordination of multiple subjectivities.

It is important to note that feminist standpoint theory accepts the sci-entific method as a valuable tool for gaining knowledge. However, the way is which this tool is used must be reevaluated in terms of the underlying epistemological assumptions. First, feminist theory does not assume inde-pendence of subject from object; the scientist is not in a privileged position to know (M. M. Gergen, 1988; Keller, 1990). Rather, the scientist is a par-ticipant in her culture and is as prone to seeing the world from a particu-lar perspective as is the experimental subject. Thus, the scientist cannot define experience or reality a priori. Related to this, the experimental sub-ject is not simply an object to be studied but is an integral part of the con-struction of knowledge gained from any investigation. More objective knowledge will be garnered from the scientist and subject participating together in constructing knowledge than from either viewpoint alone. Methodologically, this means that we, as scientists, should work toward involving our research participants as informants. How they conceptual-ize the tasks we set for them and how they construe their performance on these tasks are important components of the data we gather and analyze.

Second, knowledge is always relational (H. E. Longino, 1993; L. H. Nelson, 1993). What we know is always known in a particular context. This context can be defined at multiple levels. The macro level comprises the particular historical time and cultural place in which we are situated. At an intermediate level are more or less enduring individual differences, such as race, class, and gender, that provide us with a particular perspective on our cultural-historical moment. And at the micro level are specific situational variables, such as whom we are interacting with and what our current goals are. These levels interact with each other, such that our current goals are influenced by our situated position as a person of a particular race, class, and gender living in a particular cultural-historical place. Moreover, the way in which we conceptualize ourselves as persons of a particular race, class, and gender will be influenced by the specific situation in which we are interacting at any given moment.

In this way, knowledge must be conceptualized as dynamic and fluid. Knowledge is not just "in our heads" but also in the situation in which we are participating. Who we are and what we know at any given moment is as much a function of whom we are with and what we are doing right now as it is a function of knowledge we have stored from previous interactions. Universal laws of behavior will not take the form of what individuals do in general, but rather will specify the conditions under which different individuals will display different kinds of behaviors. From this perspective, behavior cannot be conceptualized in linear, cause-and-effect chains. Instead, feminist theories posit a transactional, relational causality among events. Because knowledge emerges from situated interactions in the world, and because situated interactions create new knowledge, knowledge development is not necessarily linear but emergent. Finally, feminist standpoint theory assumes that knowledge is always value laden (Bar On, 1993; Keller, 1990; H. E. Longino, 1993). Logical positivist claims that knowledge is rational—divorced from emotion, meaning, and value—simply do not hold. Knowledge is always used to achieve some goal or purpose.

Because feminist theorists are particularly concerned with gender as an epistemological category, feminist theories have focused on the ways in which gender is an integral part of knowledge. From birth onward, females and males are subject to different social worlds and different kinds of interactions (see Golombok & Fivush, 1994, for a review). Because knowledge is created in and emerges from social interactions, the kinds of interactions in which one participates critically determine the kind of knowledge one constructs. In fact, the logical positivist model of an autonomous knower is very much a male model of knowledge, as males are socialized to be independent, autonomous, and focused on individual achievement. Females, in contrast, are socialized to be more relationally oriented, more attuned to social and emotional interaction; the kinds of interactions in which they participate are more embedded and contexted (N. J. Chodorow, 1978; Gilligan, 1982). Consequently, females value relational, cooperative learning to a greater extent than do males (Belenky, Clinchy, Goldberger, & Tarule, 1986). Moreover, the kinds of knowledge gleaned from social interactions will be different, as females coordinate multiple perspectives in a transactional fashion, whereas males defend their perspective in an autonomous fashion. Thus, females construct knowledge *with* other people, whereas males construct knowledge *against* other people.

Implications for Cognitive Development

Clearly, feminist epistemologies change the way we view cognitive development. Traditional approaches, such as Piagetian and information-processing models, assume that development is progressive (see P. H. Miller, 1993, for a full discussion of assumptions underlying developmental theories). Whether it is postulated that children develop in small increments or large leaps, the direction is always forward, toward more and better-integrated knowledge. Cognitive development is conceptualized as a linear, autonomous, progression. The mechanisms underlying this progression are internal reorganizations of knowledge, constructed through logical, hypothetical deductive inferences performed on internal mental representations. Both the child and the developing knowledge structures are devoid of gender, race, class, and context. Moreover, once children display knowledge in one domain, it is assumed that they have some underlying competence that should be displayed again, at least within that same domain, if not across domains. Unevenness in performance across similar tasks and so-called regressions in cognitive development are seen as problematic. Although the role of the environment in cognitive development is often acknowledged, it is usually in the form of facilitation of skills that would emerge in time regardless of environmental input.

Feminist epistemologies lead to a very different conceptualization of cognitive development. Because it is assumed that knowledge is relational and situated, different performances in different situations are predicted. They are not a problem to be explained away but the core of what we need to understand in order to explain development. Analysis of development must include a consideration of the world as the child experiences it, in terms of culture, place (i.e., gender, race, and class), and situational goals. The environment is not a facilitator of epigenetically emergent skills but the very ground in which knowledge is embedded. There can be no knowledge independent of the environment in which it is used.

Many of the assumptions underlying feminist epistemologies are reflected in Vygotsky's (1978) dialectical theory of development. This similarity is not surprising, as, historically, both Vygotsky and feminist theories owe a large intellectual debt to Hegelian and marxist analyses of power and knowledge. Arguing from Hegel's law of the dialectic, Vygotsky posited that all cognitive skills develop first in social interaction and that the true measure of knowledge is what a child can accomplish with the intellectual support of others, as opposed to what the child can accomplish independently. Thus, for Vygotsky, as for feminist epistemologists, knowledge emerges from social interaction and is expressed in social interaction as participants engage in meaningful behaviors organized around mutual goals; the kinds of supporting social and cultural structures available to the developing child are seen as integral to the specific performances displayed and skills developed over time. Several current models of human development are based on Vygotsky's social-cultural theory of human development in context (Laboratory for Comparative Human Cognition, 1983; Rogoff, 1990), and research generated from this perspective has yielded rich information about the development of memory, language, and cognition. Still, even within developmental psychology, this approach remains somewhat marginalized.

Clearly, many of the key assumptions underlying logical positivism and feminist standpoint theories lead to different conceptualizations of knowledge and its development. How do these differences inform our understanding of autobiographical memory?

The Study of Autobiographical Memory

Largely as a result of positivist assumptions about methodological rigor and experimental control, historically little research has examined autobiographical memory. Cognitive psychologists sought to discover the fundamental principles of memory regardless of the material to be remembered, by whom, for what purpose. Guided by the assumption that basic memory processes could be studied only by stripping material of context and meaning, psychologists devised lists of words (or nonsense syllables) that psychological subjects memorized and recalled, and the accuracy and exhaustiveness of recall were measured in order to derive mathematical functions of forgetting and error (see B. Schwartz & Reisberg, 1991, for an overview). Within this paradigm, critical questions concerned the ability to recall material in the form in which it was presented by the experimenter.

Although memory research has been dominated by these kinds of list-learning paradigms, occasional studies of more personally meaningful events have appeared in the literature. Most of this work has concerned adults' memories of early childhood experiences, partly to examine Freud's (1905/1953) theories of "infantile amnesia," in which he claimed that adults have difficulty recalling events of their early childhood (Dudychea & Dudychea, 1941; Waldfogel, 1948). This research remained on the margins of cognitive psychology, however. Because the accuracy of autobiographical recall could not be reliably established, the research lacked the experimental rigor deemed necessary for scientific inquiry.

In 1977, Brown and Kulik published a seminal paper that brought autobiographical memory into mainstream cognitive psychology. They asked individuals to recall the circumstances under which they learned of the assassination of John F. Kennedy. Surprisingly, even many years after the event, participants were able to recall details of where they were, whom they were with, and how they heard the news. Brown and Kulik argued that, because some events are so surprising and meaningful, there may be a special mechanism that essentially "prints" a veridical memory that is retained in pure form over extended periods of time. Since the publication of this study, studies of "flashbulb memories" have become a cottage industry in cognitive psychology (see M. A. Conway, 1995, and Neisser & Winograd, 1992, for reviews).

It is particularly telling that when autobiographical memory was accepted in cognitive psychology as an important, tractable question, it was in the form of flashbulb memories. Several things should be noted about this methodology and the epistemological assumptions underlying it. First, all individuals are ostensibly asked to recall the "same" event. Thus the scientist presumably maintains control of the material to be remembered. One of the major criticisms of the study of autobiographical memory has been (and continues to be) that we, as scientists, do not have privileged information about the event being recalled, and we are therefore unable to measure memory objectively. Accuracy with respect to some predefined criteria is seen as the core question; if this cannot be addressed, then we essentially cannot study autobiographical memory. Further, Brown and Kulik not only asked all subjects to recall the same event, they also asked them the same set of questions. They predetermined the important information to be recalled about Kennedy's assassination, based on notions of canonical narrative forms (e.g., Labov & Waletzky, 1967). All subjects were asked the same seven questions about whom they were with, where they were, what they were doing, and how they felt. In this way, again, the scientist determines a priori what is important to remember and has a metric for quantification and analysis that is consistent across individuals.

In contrast to studies in which participants are asked to recall individual events in their lives, psychologists assumed that flashbulb memories can be studied scientifically because the experimenter has control of the material to be remembered. But this, of course, is an illusion. First of all, although everyone was asked about the same event (Kennedy's assassination), the data were not what people recalled about the assassination itself (the facts of which may be the same for everyone) but, rather, the personal circumstances under which they heard the news (where they were, whom they were with, etc.). Clearly, these circumstances were different for every individual, and thus the participants were not being asked to recall the same information. Further, the researchers had no "objective" information with which to judge the "accuracy" of an individual's responses. Moreover, although each person was asked the same set of questions, the way in which those questions were answered varied from person to person. Not only was the actual amount of information recalled different for each individual (e.g., how many people were you with when you heard the news? alone? with one other person? in a group?), but individuals could choose to give a great deal of detail about their personal circumstances, essentially giving a well-constructed, coherent, elaborated account, or they could give a one- or two-word answer. In Brown and Kulik's methodology, any answer to a specific question counted. Although, on the surface, this method allows the experimenter to predetermine what information can be recalled, in fact it distorts what individuals are doing in this situation. Whether one recalls bits and pieces or a full-blown narrative certainly should matter in evaluating the claim that an individual has a flashbulb memory. Moreover, information recalled that does not fit into one of the predetermined categories is ignored.

With the burgeoning interest in flashbulb memories, researchers also began examining memories for other real-life experiences as well. Although this work still represents a small fraction of research on memory, there is a growing literature examining adults' autobiographical memory (see M. A. Conway, 1990, and Rubin, 1989, 1996, for overviews). Yet the basic questions still revolve around accuracy and retention. Most studies of autobiographical memory rely on diary methods, in which the psychological subject records a specified set of events as they occur and memory for these events is assessed at specified retention intervals (e.g., Brewer, 1988; Linton, 1982; Wagenaar, 1986). It is assumed that the way in which the subject initially records the event is more or less veridical; that is, reality is assumed to be transparent and the immediate memory of that reality is assumed to be accurate. Thus the scientist obtains a "true" record of what occurred to

compare subsequent memory of the event against. At the specified retention interval, the subject is given a cue, and any memory generated is
matched to the original report. Accuracy and errors are quantified, and
analyses focus on how well individuals recall specific aspects of past events
over time. The issue of personal significance and meaning is operational-
ized as the individual's rating of the emotionality of the event at time of
experience. How this event fits into the individual's larger social-cultural
life history is largely ignored. Autobiographical memory is conceptualized
as the way in which an isolated individual cognitively organizes and represents specific experienced events. Thus, although the study of flashbulb
and autobiographical memories represents a move toward studying more
meaningful events in people's ongoing socially and culturally imbued lives,
the research still shares the basic epistemological assumptions of logical
positivism.

Feminist Perspectives on Autobiographical Memory

From the perspective of feminist epistemologies, many of the questions
about autobiographical memory change. If knowledge is relational, we
need to examine how autobiographical memories are constructed in social
interactions. How are memories shared with others, and how does sharing
memories influence how and what is remembered of one's own personal
experience? If knowledge is situated, we need to explore the ways in which
the particular interaction shapes the memory. Who is talking about what
past event, for what reason? Finally, if there are multiple perspectives, we
need to consider issues of authority in how memories are constructed.
Experience is not given in a pure form but is always interpreted and evaluated, both in the moment and in retrospect. Who judges the "accuracy"
of what "really" happened?

Although these issues have not been seriously considered in the literature on adult's autobiographical memories, within the developmental literature there has been more emphasis on studying autobiographical
memory in context, at least partly as a result of the growing influence of
Vygotsky. Whereas early research on memory development was predominantly conducted within a positivistic, information-processing paradigm
(see Kail & Hagen, 1977, for an overview), in 1981 K. Nelson and Gruendel published a paper that fundamentally changed conceptualizations of
early memory. If we are interested in understanding the early development
of memory, they argued, then we must ask children to recall meaningful

events in which they have participated in the real world. Rather than asking children to repeat back material just presented by the experimenter, Nelson and Gruendel asked children to report what happens when they engage in familiar and meaningful activities, such as going to McDonald's or to the grocery store. In these interviews, children as young as three years of age readily and eagerly told researchers about their experiences. Moreover, even very young children reported events in an accurate and organized manner. Clearly, young children represent and remember meaningful experiences in coherent ways. Nelson and Gruendel argue that this kind of event knowledge is culturally mediated; they speculated that children learn this knowledge both through participating in events deemed culturally appropriate and structured by adults and through discussing events with more knowledgeable partners, especially parents (see also K. Nelson, 1986, 1996).

This research was the ground from which more detailed work on children's autobiographical memory grew. Several researchers began to investigate how young children and their parents spontaneously discuss past experiences together and how the structure of these conversations influences children's developing autobiographical memory abilities (Engel, 1986; Fivush & Fromhoff, 1988; Fivush, Haden, & Reese, 1996; Hudson, 1990; McCabe & Peterson, 1991; Reese, Haden, & Fivush, 1993). This approach to understanding the development of autobiographical memory led to a detailed examination of how cognition emerges from and is expressed in social interactions. It is now generally accepted within the literature on the development of autobiographical memory that the ways in which parents structure conversations about past events with their young children influence children's developing autobiographical memory skills. Although not explicitly informed by feminist theories, this research reflects some of the assumptions underlying feminist epistemologies. The fact that the research has also generated a wealth of new information about how autobiographical memory develops indicates that feminist theory has much to offer to developmental psychology. Three issues central to the study of autobiographical memory emerge from feminist perspectives: the situated nature of autobiography, the relations among objectivity, authority, and accuracy, and the question of autobiographical voice and silence.

The Situated Nature of Autobiographical Memory

If we take the assumption of situated knowledge seriously, what implications does it have for understanding the development of autobiographical memory? First and foremost, it means that we cannot assume a coherent underlying representation of a past event that is accessed, given an appropriate cue, and reported in more or less the same way whenever we recall that event. Rather, the act of autobiography must be seen as a social process. As Braham (1995) has argued, autobiography is always the result of a conversation. Even when one recalls the past to oneself, or writes the past in a diary or memoir, a listener is always assumed. A report of a personally experienced event must be conceptualized as a process in which information represented by the individual is coordinated with the perceived listener and reported in such a way as to conform to current goals and values.

This view contrasts with dominant models of autobiography both in psychology and in literature. "The dominant current in autobiography provides readers with exemplary lives...it inscribes what a 'life' should look like, the form in which (written and spoken) tales of lives should be told and actual lives should be lived. These lives are linear, chronological, progressive, cumulative, and individualist, and follow highly particular narrative conventions" (Stanley, 1992, p. 12). In contrast, "women's autobiography has always understood the need to compose a life from bits and pieces of the past marinated in memory, resurrected by the imagination and imbued with meaning" (Braham, 1995, p. 2). From this perspective, autobiography must be understood as a creative work in process; what is remembered and reported emerges from the interactions during the experience of the event (Haden, Didow, Ornstein, & Eckerman, 1997; Tessler & Nelson, 1994), as well as during subsequent reminiscing about the event (Fivush et al., 1996).

Autobiographical memory, then, is not something we *have* but something we *do* in interaction. It matters whom we are reporting the past to or with. What individuals may report to a "strange" experimenter in a laboratory situation is very different from what they report to a friend or family member. This is not just a matter of disclosure, although disclosure plays a part as well. It is fundamentally a matter of what material is brought to the situation by each of the participants in order to achieve ongoing, mutually negotiated goals. Because most studies of autobiographical memory in the psychological literature are studies in which an individual is asked to report past experiences to an experimenter, the ways in which autobiography is created in the moment are virtually ignored. However, a few studies attest to the power of this approach. When individuals are asked to recall a story or movie (Hyman, 1994; Middleton & Edwards, 1990) in the context of a memory experiment, they report the story in chronological order. But when asked to discuss the same movie or story with others, they jump from scene to scene, focusing on their interpretations and emotional reactions. The first performance would lead one to conclude that memories of personally experienced events are linear and chronological, the second that memories are haphazard and emotional. Neither conclusion is right or wrong. Rather, autobiographical memories are both chronologically organized and haphazard, both rational and emotional, depending on the context and goals of the individual recalling the event. No one conversational interchange gives us privileged information about what is in memory or how it is organized. Rather, following from feminist epistemological assumptions, we need to coordinate multiple perspectives to obtain a truer, more objective picture of what autobiographical memory is; we have multiple kinds of information organized in multiple ways about our experiences, and the question is how we come to report a particular event given the situation we are in.

Developmentally, we need to consider how the kinds of interactions in which children participate shape their understanding of their world and of themselves. My students and I have been examining the development of autobiographical memory in family contexts over the past several years, and one of the intriguing findings is that preschool children recall different information each time they recall the same event (Fivush, 1994b; Fivush, Hamond, Harsch, Singer, & Wolf, 1991; Fivush & Shukat, 1995). We have puzzled over this finding for a long time because, from traditional approaches to autobiographical memory, it is not clear why children should report radically different information about a family visit to SeaWorld, for example, each time they recall this experience. Moreover, children are inconsistent regardless of whether they are recalling the event at intervals of a few weeks or a few years. These findings become interpretable within a feminist perspective. Indeed, whereas this level of inconsistency is a difficult problem to explain from traditional approaches to autobiographical memory, it is actually predicted from a feminist perspective. Children are responding to the immediacy of the conversational context, and therefore the information they bring into the context is a function of the context itself. Different conversational partners will elicit different information, not simply because they ask different questions, but also because the meaning and the goals of recalling this particular event are different with different people.

Moreover, children not only recall the past differently with mothers versus unfamiliar adults; they also recall the past differently with their fathers than with their mothers. Preschool children recall more information when talking about past events with their fathers than with their mothers, and in particular they recall more evaluative and more emotional information (Adams, Kuebli, Boyle, & Fivush, 1995; Reese, Haden, & Fivush, 1996), even though fathers do not elicit this kind of information more frequently or more explicitly than do mothers. So there is something about conversing with dad versus mom that changes the conversational context so that children perform differently. We have speculated on several reasons for this (see Reese et al., 1996), but the point is that the context matters. If we are interested in the question of "how much" children can remember, which data would we take as representative? If instead we are interested in how autobiographical memories are constructed in a social context, this difference becomes an interesting piece of data in its own right.

Similarly, mothers and fathers discuss the past differently with daughters than with sons. Parents talk about the past more frequently and more elaboratively with daughters than with sons (Reese et al., 1996), and they discuss more of the emotional aspects of past experiences with daughters than with sons (Adams et al., 1995). More detailed examination of the conversations reveals subtle ways in which the gender composition of the dyad makes a difference in how the conversation proceeds. Even when the same event is discussed, it will be discussed differently, depending on the gender of the parent and gender of the child. Thus, reminiscing is a gendered activity. From feminist perspectives, this is, of course, not surprising. Gender is a critical component of where one is situated in the world and will have clear consequences for how one constructs knowledge. What we are seeing in these parent-child conversations about the past is one of the ways in which this situated being is expressed. The fact that gender differences between mothers and fathers or between girls and boys depend on whether the other partner is the same or other gender indicates that gender is not a causal factor per se. Rather, gender must be conceptualized as a process of interaction rather than as a categorical variable. The ways in which gendered performances will be expressed in any given situation will be as much a function of whom one is with and what one is doing as of one's actual gender.

Thus, even the way in which we define variables to be studied and the data to be interpreted changes as a function of the epistemological assumptions we make (Code, 1993; M. M. Gergen, 1988). From a situated knowledge assumption, we must take seriously the idea that children's skills must be assessed in multiple contexts and that any understanding of their knowledge or competency must be based on a coordination of these performances. No one context is any more "real" or "objective" than any other; rather, each provides unique information about the phenomenon under study. Moreover, because performances are as much a function of the context as individual ability, the ways in which contexts modulate performances become the critical data for understanding skill development. Variables to be studied are not only the enduring characteristics of the individual, but also the contextual factors that facilitate the expression of particular performances. Even gender, which has been a categorical variable par excellence from traditional perspectives, must be reconsidered as an emergent process of the ongoing interaction.

Objectivity, Authority, and Accuracy

The idea of situated knowledge has already been a thread in developmental theory, reflecting the influence of Vygotsky. Most developmental researchers consider the interrelations among context, performance, and ability to at least some extent. A more radical reconceptualization of autobiographical memory comes from the assumptions about objectivity intrinsic in feminist epistemology. Logical positivist approaches assume a transparently real world and that accuracy of memory for events occurring in the world can be objectively measured. From this perspective, accuracy is defined as a comparison between what the individual reports and what the experimenter has defined as the material to be remembered. Thus the experimenter has the authority to define what reality is and how well the psychological subject represents and remembers it. In sharp contrast to this notion of objective knowledge, feminist standpoint theories assume that, although there is a real world, the scientist is not in a privileged position to define that reality. In terms of autobiographical memory, this issue becomes the question of who has the right to say what "really" happened. "The past, like the present, is a result of competing negotiated versions of what happened, why it happened, with what consequences" (Stanley, 1992, p. 7). In essence, who has the *authority* to *author* the autobiography?

This conceptualization adds an intriguing dimension to the way in which we study autobiographical memory. It may not always be the case that the individual is the authority on his or her own experience. Certainly the individual is not the authority in traditional laboratory studies of memory, where the scientist decides what counts as memory by specifying the to-be-remembered material. But given the previous discussion about the situated nature of autobiographical recall, this assumption extends to any study of autobiographical memory. When individuals discuss their past experiences with others, who defines what the "truth" is? For example,

Ross and Holmberg (1990) studied spouses' reports of shared personal experiences. When they disagreed about what occurred, husbands generally deferred to their wives' memories. Moreover, this was not simple compliance in the service of marital peace; men claimed that they believed their wives' versions more than their own, even in private conversation with the experimenter. Why would this be so? Ross and Holmberg speculate that women are assumed to be the keepers of social history, and therefore are assumed to have better memories of life events. Thus, accuracy cannot be defined as a simple relation between some objective measure of what happened and the individual's report of it. Accuracy must be placed in a social-cultural context that gives credibility to particular people over others or to particular versions of reality over others.

In thinking about the development of autobiographical memory, the question of who has the authority to say what occurred is particularly intriguing. Obviously, in parent-child interactions, there is a power differential; moreover, most adults assume that they have better cognitive skills than their young children. Thus parents may believe that they are in a privileged position to say what occurred. However, parents may also believe that their young children are competent and capable of noticing or remembering things that the parent might not. In such cases, they would give credence to what their child recalls. Individual differences in the ways in which parents and children resolve memory disagreements provide a way of studying how children come to understand their own experience, as the following examples illustrate (from Fivush & Fromhoff, 1988). The first excerpt is from a conversation between a mother and her 32-month-old son, in which they are discussing playing at a friend's house (M stands for mother and C stands for child):

M: What toy did you play with that you liked a real lot?
C: The sandbox.
M: She didn't have a sandbox. Remember in that playroom, she had lots of toys. What was your favorite toy that you kept wanting to play with, do you remember?
C: The airplane.
M: No, not the airplane. Do you remember?
C: What.

In this example, the mother asks her child what he enjoyed about this event, yet when he responds, she negates his experience. Although the mother engages the child in sharing his experience with her, she then dismisses what he says. After two attempts, the child gives up and asks the mother which toy he himself most enjoyed. In this way the child's experience is defined by the mother's reality, not his own. In contrast, here is another mother with her 32-month-old son, discussing a walk on the beach:

M: What did Mommy find for you that you brought home?
C: Rocks.
M: Yeah, we got some rocks, didn't we?
C: And fire hats.
M: And fire hats? Yeah that's right. Those little tiny fire hats. I forgot about those. Where did you get those?
C: Grandma and Grandpa.
M: Grandma and Grandpa gave you those.

In this example, the child responds to the topic the mother initiates by recalling what they collected on the beach, but he then switches to something else he got on the same outing. The mother immediately follows in on what the child says, and pursues this topic. Moreover, although she had forgotten about the fire hats, she accepts the child's memory as veridical. In this way the experience is truly co-constructed, with both mother and child contributing to the account of what happened.

In these brief exchanges we see a very important process occurring. In the latter example, the child is learning to own his experience; he has the authority to say what happens. In the former example, it is just the opposite: the child is learning that he does not have the authority to say what happened. Children who learn to trust their own version of what occurred may be able to create an autobiographical self, a self grounded in personally meaningful experiences. These children may come to have authority over who they are and what they have experienced. Children who do not come to trust their own version of what happened, who do not trust their memories, will be considerably more adrift in their lives; they may not have a sense of authority and control over their experiences. In essence, some children may develop a "voice" whereas others may not (Belenky et al., 1986).

Moreover, it is not only authorship over what actually occurred, but also authorship over the evaluation of that experience. For example, in this excerpt a mother and her 32-month-old daughter are discussing seeing bears at a carnival:

M: They were big bears. Did they scare you?
C: Um-umm.
M: A little bit? Just a little bit?
C: Oh, I'm not scared of bears.
M: You're not scared of bears. Well, that's good.
   (There are several intervening comments, and then the child says:)
C: Bears scare me.
M: They scare you. I thought they didn't scare you.
C: I'm scary (i.e., "I'm scared").

Was the child scared of bears or not? There is no way to tell what the child's experience was at the time of occurrence, but we can see in this excerpt that the mother and child jointly reconstruct this event to be one in which the child was scared. By negotiating these kinds of evaluative perspectives, parents are informing their children how to feel about their past experiences, what kind of sense to make of them. Through reminiscing with parents (and others) children learn how to interpret their own experiences; they learn whether or not to trust their own recollections and how to evaluate their past. The way in which authority is negotiated in these conversations becomes an important part of the process of understanding one's own experiences and placing these experiences in the evolving construction of an autobiographical self.

Voice and Silence

A final aspect of parent-child reminiscing is who decides what is talked about, and, perhaps more important, what is *not* talked about. "We see the past, in female autobiography, in something of the same way we see a Henry Moore sculpture. The 'holes' define the 'shape.' What is left repressed, or what cannot be uttered, is often as significant to the whole shape of the life as what is said" (Braham, 1995, p. 37). By emphasizing certain aspects of experience over others, parents are informing their children what is important to remember about their experiences. This extends beyond focusing on particular details (as in identifying the favorite toy in the example above) to include more overarching aspects of experience, such as what events are reportable or not reportable and what aspects of experience are open for discussion. In turn, what is not talked about, what is not emphasized, is equally informative about how experience should be constituted. In this regard, it is particularly interesting that parents talk a great deal less about emotional aspects of the past with sons than with daughters (Adams et al., 1995). By emphasizing emotions with daughters, parents are placing emotions at the center of autobiographical experience for females; in contrast, by not talking about emotions much with sons, parents are indicating that this is not a critical part of male experience.

In light of the situated nature of autobiography and the larger feminist critiques of linear, reductionistic models, we must be careful about drawing causal connections from parent to child. It is also the case that girls discuss emotions more frequently and more elaboratively that do boys from a very early age, and so the emphasis on emotion that we see in parent-daughter conversations is most likely a complex interaction of what both members of the dyad are bringing to the conversations. It is also noteworthy that in conversing about the past with their young children, fathers often discuss emotions as elaboratively as mothers do, despite the large experimental literature indicating adult females disclose more emotionally than do adult males (see Brody & Hall, 1993, for a review). Again, this finding highlights the need to think about performances in specific contexts. When discussing meaningful personal experiences with their own children, fathers may be as emotionally open as mothers. However, both mothers and fathers discuss emotions differently with daughters than with sons.

The ways in which events are discussed and not discussed is critical in the formation of an autobiographical voice. As the novelist Isabelle Allende writes, "if we kept silent, it would be as if nothing had happened—what is not voiced scarcely exists; silence would gradually erase everything and the memory would fade" (1989, pp. 165–166). Acceptance and denial of experience set the parameters of what is real; accuracy and authority can only be understood in the context of what is allowed to be spoken of and what is prohibited.

Summary and Future Directions

In this chapter, I have highlighted the epistemological assumptions underlying much of the psychological research on human memory and discussed ways in which feminist epistemologies change the way we approach the study of memory, especially autobiographical memory. I want to end by emphasizing two points. First, there is no doubt that the scientific method, which has traditionally been driven by logical empiricist assumptions, has generated a great deal of valuable knowledge about human behavior and will continue to do so. However, many interesting questions about human memory have gone unexamined because of some of these assumptions. Feminist epistemologies provide intriguing alternatives for approaching autobiographical memory. By drawing attention to the situated nature of knowledge, feminist epistemologies push us to consider the ways in which autobiographical memories are constructed in dialogue and how these dialogues shape individual autobiography. By emphasizing authority over accuracy, feminist epistemologies focus on the ways in which individuals come to understand and own their experience, how they create an autobiographical self. These are important questions about human experience that need to be integrated into our scientific conceptualization of autobiography.

Second, the construction of knowledge and the construction of autobiography may follow very similar courses. From a feminist perspective, "scientific knowledge is constructed not by individuals applying a method to the material to be known but by individuals in interaction with one another in ways that modify their observations, theories and hypotheses, and patterns of reasoning" (Longino, 1993, p. 111). Exactly the same statement can be made about the construction of autobiographical memory. Memories of our own personal experiences are not constructed in isolation but are constituted in ongoing meaningful interaction with others, in which our versions of reality are negotiated and modified. The way in which we construct knowledge, whether it is scientific or personal, is always social, situated, and value laden.

Note

1. Although the description I have given of mainstream cognitive psychology is reasonably accurate, it must be noted that several movements within the field have been critical of this approach. Best known is, of course, Bartlett's (1932) work on remembering and the contextual approaches to cognition by such researchers as Bransford (e.g., Bransford, Barclay, & Franks, 1972). However, cognitive psychology has been dominated by a more reductionistic approach to thinking and memory.

A Feminist Perspective on the

Development of Self-Knowledge

Melissa K. Welch-Ross

The development of self-knowledge is a classic topic of research that focuses on the emergence of self-awareness and the development of the psychological self-concept (Damon & Hart, 1982, 1988; Harter, 1986, 1990; M. Lewis, 1991; M. Lewis & Brooks-Gunn, 1979; Rochat, 1995). However, much of this work is based on traditional philosophies that are inconsistent with how women understand the world and themselves, according to principles of feminist epistemology. The first part of this chapter reviews theories and methods that characterize traditional research on the development of self-knowledge and explains why these approaches may be considered androcentric (Baier, 1985; Bordo, 1987; Code, 1991, 1998a; Duran, 1991; Gatens, 1998; Haraway, 1989; Harding, 1986, 1991; Jaggar, 1983, 1989; Keller, 1985; Longino, 1993; L. H. Nelson, 1990). The second part of the chapter outlines a feminist model of self-knowing and suggests research questions and methods that would be useful for studying the development of self-knowledge within this framework. The final section describes research programs that approach the study of self-knowledge in ways that are consistent with feminist epistemological principles and offers directions for future research.

Traditional Research on Self-Awareness and the Psychological Self-Concept

Self-Awareness

William James's (1890) distinction between the subjective "I" and the objective "me" provides the conceptual foundation for most current empirical and theoretical work on the development of self-knowing (e.g., M. Lewis, 1991; M. Lewis & Brooks-Gunn, 1979). According to this traditional view, a subjective self-awareness emerges at about eight or nine months of age that involves knowing how to act within one's social and physical world. M. Lewis (1991, 1995) describes this quality of self-knowing as mechanical self-regulation. That is, self-knowledge consists of a first-person perspective on actions the child has learned she can perform during everyday interactions with people and objects. However, this type of self-knowledge is immature because the child is acting in the world rather than thinking about herself acting in the world. Therefore, she does not know about her existence as an individual being with unique physical and psychological characteristics.

A qualitative transition in cognition occurs between the ages of eighteen and twenty-four months that causes the emergence of the objective self. The mechanism of objective-self development is a series of primarily endogenous, organismic transformations of cognitive structures, consistent with Piaget's theory of cognitive development (M. Lewis, 1991). Cognitive structures are organized patterns of interacting with the environment. These action patterns evolve into more abstract ways of thinking. Old cognitive structures give rise to new structures as a result of maturation and interactions with the environment. The child becomes the object of her own thinking and an increasingly distanced observer of the subjective self during solitary acts of reflection. The child's new perspective on her own everyday activity advances self-knowledge. Now the child knows that the subjective self exists as an individual, distinct being in the world. From this point forward, the objective self and the subjective self exist simultaneously. Knowledge about the subjective self becomes increasingly elaborated and organized throughout childhood as the objective self begins to observe, reflect on, and thereby acquire knowledge about the activities of the subjective self, using more advanced cognitive structures.

M. Lewis and Brooks-Gunn (1979) adapted the well-known visual self-recognition task from Gallup (1970) and Amsterdam (1972) to measure the emergence of the objective self. In this procedure, an adult marks the child's body, say, on the nose, with a spot of rouge. Then the child looks at a mirror. If the child touches the mirror, she is unaware of her subjective self. Thus, mirror-directed touching indicates that the objective self has not yet emerged. However, if the child reaches to touch the mark on her own body, she is aware of the subjective self reflected in the mirror. Therefore, self-directed touching indicates the emergence of the objective self. Most children begin to engage in self-directed touching between eighteen and twenty-four months of age. At approximately the same time, children begin to recognize the self in photographs and video images.

This model of self-knowledge provides the conceptual basis for studies of temporally extended self-representation (Povinelli, 1995; Povinelli, Landau, & Perilloux, 1996). In a prototypical study of the temporally extended self, an experimenter unobtrusively places a sticker on the child's head, and the child watches a videotape of the action a few minutes later. Only 25 percent of children reach for the sticker at age three, but most children reach for the sticker by age four. According to Povinelli's model, a child is motivated to remove the sticker only if she understands that the self that existed in the past is the same self that exists presently, and that experiences of the past self (e.g., receiving a sticker then) cause the condition of the present self (e.g., wearing the sticker now). Higher-order, abstract thinking is a cognitive prerequisite for integrating multiple memories of events involving the self and creating a continuous, linear, representation of temporal self-continuity.

The Psychological Self-Concept

Researchers have also focused on the development of knowledge about the personal and psychological qualities of the self (Damon & Hart, 1988) and on the development of personal evaluations about the self, or self-esteem (Harter, 1986, 1990, 1996a). Damon and Hart's model builds on James's distinction between the subjective and objective self and on Piaget's organismic theory of cognitive development. Damon and Hart (1988) propose that changes in cognitive structures result in more complex representations of information about the self. At about age four, the child begins to organize information into a multidimensional, cognitive concept, and by late adolescence she constructs an elaborated self-theory. In turn, the self-concept and self-theory organize and give meaning to personal experience.

The Self-Understanding Interview used to study the claims of the model assume universal qualities of the subjective experience of self on which the objective self observes and reflects. These qualities measured include temporal continuity (e.g., "Do you change at all from year to year? If so, how do you change?"), distinctness (e.g., "What makes you different from anyone you know?"), and agency (e.g., "How did you get to be the way you are?"). In addition, self-knowledge becomes increasingly multidimensional with development. Objective self-representation primarily includes physical characteristics initially, and then active, social, and psychological characteristics in turn as the child moves through the stages of development. Changes in cognitive structures lead to qualiative changes in processing information about the self. These processes include making categorical identifications (early childhood), making comparative assessments (middle and late childhood), considering interpersonal implications of the self (early adolescence), and developing systematic beliefs and plans (late adolescence).

Comparing Traditional and Feminist Views on Knowing about the Self

Most research on the development of self-knowledge has focused on the problem of how children know that the self (1) exists in space and time and (2) is a distinct being with unique qualities. The emphasis has been on how the child discovers these facts through independent observations and reflections on subjective experiences, which evolve into increasingly abstract knowledge about the self. This view of self-development is based on traditional philosophical assumptions about what true knowledge is and how it must be acquired. For example, the process of knowing involves solitary, rational thinking about abstract propositions divorced from the concrete and specific experiences of everyday living. According to some feminist perspectives (Bordo, 1987; Lloyd, 1998), these ways of knowing are ideals of the white upper-class male experience, which historically included devoting time to solitary thinking about abstract ideas relating to men's own interests.

Another traditional assumption has been that one obtains accurate knowledge through acquiring information that is uncontaminated by the biases of individual perspective and emotion. Therefore, a distanced and neutral perspective from which to observe and reflect results in knowing the objective facts. However, feminist critics of the concept of objectivity in science suggest that valuing these forms of knowing creates an imbalance of power, which results in a need to enlighten laypersons about the content and meaning of their own subjective experiences and behaviors (Hawkesworth, 1998; L. H. Nelson, 1998). These traditional values concerning how knowledge can be achieved have filtered into current theories of self-development. Children become aware of the qualities of their own subjective experiences, including knowing about their existence, their pasts, and their personal characteristics, through engaging in individual, distanced, and neutral acts of observation and reflection.

The traditional philosophical values underlying this model of knowledge acquisition—objectivity, distancing, and rationality—differ from the values of many women whose primary, traditional roles have consisted of satisfying the practical needs of home and family. The experiences of women have included participating in routine social activities of everyday living and knowing about the emotions, wants, and perspectives of others with whom they share significant interpersonal relationships. From this perspective on the world, understanding and knowing (1) emerge in specific, concrete, and often routine personal experiences, (2) occur in and through social relationships, and (3) include considering emotional evaluations and multiple perspectives on experience. Specifically, feminist theorists suggest that knowledge emerges in epistemological communities in which the meaning of experience is negotiated and constructed within the regular, everyday patterns of activity that are typical of a particular group (Code, 1991; L. H. Nelson, 1993). One acquires knowledge through establishing a shared intersubjectivity about the meaning of experience within networks of interpersonal relationships. Therefore, the process of knowing is a dialogic, interactive, culturally embedded social activity and not an independently acquired, private property of isolated, individual minds (Code, 1987b, 1993; L. H. Nelson, 1993).

Clearly, some theories emphasize the importance of social information, including the perspectives of others, for acquiring self-knowledge. For instance, Damon and Hart (1988) specify social processes through which the individual may gather information about the self, using as a conceptual foundation Mead's (1934) theory of the social construction of self and Cooley's (1902) concept of the looking-glass self. For example, in early childhood, children include social information in their self-descriptions, such as labeling their social roles or group memberships. In middle and late childhood, children begin to compare their personal characteristics with the characteristics of others in order to make judgments about the quality of their own abilities and achievements. Moreover, in middle and late childhood, the perspectives that others have about the child's own characteristics become part of the child's self-representation.

However, the proposed role of social factors in the development of self-knowledge remains inconsistent with a feminist approach to self-knowing. First, the focus of study remains on the cognitive processes of the individual child and not on the social interactions themselves. The child alone collects and organizes information into a self-concept and uses this information to interpret experience. Second, in earlier models invoking social factors children organize social information into abstract traits and elaborated theories that are removed from particular situations, times, places, and people. Although Harter (1986) assumes that self-evaluation differs across contexts (see also Hart & Fegely, 1997, for a discussion of cultural diversity), a feminist approach would focus on routine social interactions that more directly frame subjective interpretations of specific experiences in particular contexts of a child's everyday activity. Studies would target the social interactions that establish intersubjective understandings between the child and others concerning the meaning specific personal experiences have for the self.

The fact that most human social interaction consists of spoken language highlights another divergence between traditional and feminist approaches to self-knowing. Traditional models consider self-representations to be mental objects of individuals that eventually become accessible to awareness. This awareness does not depend on sociocultural mediation through language. Rather, the child discovers categorical realities through independent observation and reflection, and uses language to express the content of this self-discovery to others. Linguistic expressions that indicate the child is capable of thinking about the existence and distinctiveness of the self include using the pronoun "me," using one's proper name to label the self, and distinguishing among the pronouns "I," "me," and "you." In addition, in traditional models, self-descriptions that consist of abstract traits and concepts provide evidence that the child has acquired the complex representational skills necessary for constructing such explicit and organized self-concepts. In sum, language serves only expressive and descriptive functions, according to traditional theories of self-development.

Many feminist theories of knowing, however, claim that language constructs thinking, imposes structure onto experience, and thereby asserts what is real (Lacan, 1968). This claim arose in part because feminist theorists noted that the discourse of a dominant group has the power to construct the identities of women and make the views of a particular group seem universal and natural. One example of the normative and constitutive function of language is the assumption shared by many that biological sex is the cause of specific behaviors associated with traditional gender roles, which are socially prescribed. Discourse constructs ways of thinking that can ultimately become typical of a particular group or society (for related discussions, see R. Lakoff, 1975; Tirrell, 1998).

Thus, feminist theories of self-development would recognize the power of language to create a subjective sense of self-awareness and qualities of the self-concept. Humans use language to select particular objects and events for another's attention and to evaluate these aspects of experience. This process leads subjectivity to take particular forms and not others. In this way, the meaning and apprehension of experience become transformed from the time one enters into the symbolic communicative system of a culture. From this point forward the "structures of our discourses establish norms that govern what can and cannot be said, and with that what can and cannot *be*" (Tirrell, 1998, p. 141). The child's experience of self emerges in and is inseparable from the mutual ways of interpreting experience that the child's immediate social network and larger culture construct through language and recognize as legitimate.

With respect to the development of self-knowing, self-awareness emerges through language others use to address or refer directly to the child, providing the child with evidence of her existence. Language specifies the child's subjective connections to particular people, environments, and activities and connects the child's present subjective experiences to those of the past and future. Thus, self-representations that include a subjective sense that one is an individual, temporally extended being with particular personal and psychological qualities emerge in linguistic interactions that motivate us or invite us to act and think consistently in particular ways and not others (see K. J. Gergen, 1994a; C. Lutz, 1992; Shotter, 1989, for related discussions).

Note that current-traditional theories have conceptualized the development of self-knowing as a neutral, cognitive process. This neglect of the relation between emotional evaluations of personal experience and the development of self-knowledge is consistent with the traditional view that emotion contaminates rational, logical thinking. Past research has focused on the link between self-development and emotional experience. However, the goal of these studies has been to determine whether the development of the objective self enables the child to experience mature forms of emotion, such as guilt, shame, and embarrassment (e.g., M. Lewis, Sullivan, Stanger, & Weiss, 1989; Sroufe, 1979). A feminist perspective on self-development would focus on the role that emotional evaluations of experience play in constructing self-knowledge. More specifically, studying the ways in which everyday interactions with significant others construct these evaluations would be important for understanding how self-knowledge develops.

Another traditional assumption of research on self-development is that of universality. Particular subjective experiences are considered natural realities that everyone experiences and discovers through universal processes of knowing (e.g., understanding the self as a physically and psychologically distinct being whose natural history consists of temporally linear, causally connected episodes; see Gatens, 1998; Lloyd, 1998; Schott, 1998). In traditional models, the development of the self-concept proceeds in the same way for everyone, regardless of gender, ethnicity, culture, race, and socioeconomic background. Broughton (1987) states that traditional models of self-development that propose universal, endogenous change and rational, independent reflection on cognitive structures offer a system in which people have "no biography; they are not only genderless and generationless, but also lacking in personhood" (pp. 289–290). Feminist approaches reject these notions of absolute, universal realities and ways of knowing the self in favor of illuminating the specific, lived experiences of particular groups. Thus, differences in everyday experience lead to differences in mature self-representation and to diverse processes of self-development. Consistent with this feminist perspective, H. R. Markus and Kitayama (1993) emphasize that qualities of mature self-representation (autonomous versus interconnected) differ as a function of culture and gender, and they discuss specific sociocultural values and practices that might lead to these differences (see also Markus, Mullally, & Kitayama, 1997).

However, a related concern more specific to feminists has been that a society's power structure leads to biased, universalist views. Feminist theorists contend that the perspectives and ideals of powerful groups become accepted as the standard for people who are powerless and marginalized. In addition, a biased, universalist perspective leads to interpreting individual differences in development as deviations from the majority standard (Bar On, 1993; Harding, 1991, 1993; Jaggar, 1983). In contrast to a traditional perspective, most feminists attempt to make normative claims that take into account how individuals adapt their thinking to meet the goals of everyday life in their specific circumstances (Code, 1991, 1993). Therefore, a feminist claim about the typical development of self-knowledge is mindful that self-development occurs in routine social activities situated within the power structure of a particular society. Ways of thinking about the self that develop among the powerless in their particular circumstance may differ from those that develop among the powerful. A feminist approach focuses on the perspectives and experiences of relatively powerless, marginalized groups and foregrounds these in models of typical self-development. In this way, diversity and variability become *integral and fundamental* to explaining the development of self-knowledge (Lloyd, 1998).

New Directions in Research on the Development of Self-Knowing

What is self-knowledge? What processes are involved in the development of this knowledge? Which methods would be useful for studying these processes? Traditional metaphors that have guided research on the process of self-knowing invoke images of selves as static, separated, bounded, assembled entities with a physical, tangible mass and a stable structure into which things can be added (for related discussion, see Markus & Kitayama, 1993). Sometimes the language used to describe the process of self-knowing is quite literal:

> Concepts and knowledge about oneself are stored in referent bins.... Self bins contain information that has been acquired and thought about with reference to oneself as object. There may be different self bins, each pertaining to a different domain of experience. Each self bin is identified by a header whose features circumscribe the domain of self knowledge that is contained in it.... (Wyer & Srull, 1983, pp. 410–422)

In contrast to thinking of self-representation in this way, Jordan (1992) offers a feminist conceptual model in which self-knowing is a subjective experience of "relational being," which developmentalists may find helpful as they consider what self-knowing is and how to study its development. According to Jordan, a child's connections to others and to situational contexts is critical for the development of self-representation. In addition, self-knowing is a fluid process of experiencing an ever-changing, "interacting sense of self" that emerges in an "ongoing relational context." This conceptualization invokes images of flexible patterns of changing coherence that emerge and develop in the process of interacting with particular others. Therefore, it focuses our attention on how the "deepest sense of one's being is continuously formed in connection with others and is inextricably tied to relational movement" (p. 141). This dynamic perspective is especially appropriate for conceptualizing development because it allows for the continual reconstruction of the self across times, places, and interpersonal contexts.

According to a feminist framework, one knows the self through participating in an empathic relationship rather than through a private, neutral process of separating the self from others. The assumption is that humans experience a need to establish emotional connection in their relationships with others. Engaging in an empathic understanding of another person's subjective experiences helps to construct one's own evaluations of personal experience. Therefore, Jordan proposes that "studying the development of empathy, then, may provide a route to the delineation of relational development and intersubjective processes, slighted for so long in Western psychology" (p. 142).

The concept of relational being seems similar to postmodern views of the self in which a new self is created and known differently in each physical and social setting. However, Jordan emphasizes, "If we posit a model of contextual, dialogic movement, the constancies and patterns of interpersonal interactions and the ways they shape our sense of ourselves become the focus for understanding personal integration. Study of relationality is needed to supplement intrapsychic investigation" (p. 146). Jordan appeals here for an integrative approach to understanding the process of self-knowing that would include studying internal, psychological self-representations *and* patterns of social activity, linguistic regularity, and empathic engagement with others. Postmodern perspectives assume also that the process of self-knowing is embedded in specific physical and social contexts. However, Jordan's model does not preclude that one knows the self as an individual being with particular psychological traits that are organized into an internally consistent core identity, as many postmodern perspectives do. A feminist perspective would allow for this situated reality of self-conception but would acknowledge that this possibility is only one among other, diverse possibilities.

Traditionally, research has not incorporated individual and cultural differences into explanations of the development of self-knowledge. Instead, the types of self-knowledge studied and the kinds of mechanisms proposed have tended to treat individual and cultural differences as minor derivatives of a normal developmental pathway. However, diversity in the process and content of self-knowing would be expected according to the relational-being perspective on development. Differences in the qualities of a child's interpersonal relationships, the typical forms and functions of social and linguistic communications, and aspects of the broader social and cultural context would all be critical to study in order to understand the development of self-knowing. Thus, diversity and variability would be integrated fundamentally into the proposed mechanism of development.

Specific research questions that would be important to ask from this feminist perspective of relational being might include the following: Through what processes do children construct the personal meaning of specific experiences in their relationships with parents, siblings, and peers? Do these communications become part of the child's subjective experience of self? What aspects of these communications play critical roles in constructing the child's self-knowledge? Does the sharing of emotional experience play a role in constructing self-knowledge? How does the ability to engage in an empathic understanding of others relate to the development of self-knowledge? Do the content and process of self-knowing differ depending on the quality of one's interpersonal relationships? Are these differences in self-knowing mediated through diverse routine patterns of communication that occur within these relationships? Do some children come to know about the self earlier or later than other children do, depending on the patterns of communication experienced in routine social activities?

A general guideline for selecting procedures for answering these questions would be to observe routine social activities and forms of communication with significant others in which the participants construct and evaluate specific, everyday experiences. Thus, one procedure would involve studying the stories of personal experience that children and others share together. Examining the co-construction of personal stories differs from traditional methods in several ways. First, unlike traditional methods, the proposed causes of change may be examined directly through observing regularities in social activity and the relation these have to changes in particular qualities of self-knowing. Second, the researcher can use this method to show how self-knowledge is created and represented during routine social activities, and therefore the narratives themselves are sufficient for assessing self-knowledge, without requiring independent measures of self-knowledge. Third, in comparison to clinical interviewing techniques or controlled experimental settings, studying co-constructed narratives is more consistent with the feminist ideology of fostering compassionate, empathic, unauthoritarian views of the other because the procedure gives experiencing persons the power to define their own subjective experiences (Lieblich, 1994).

Focusing on narratives about past experiences may be particularly useful for understanding the development of self-knowledge. The self becomes remembered according to the agreements reached with others about the meaning of past experiences (K. J. Gergen, 1994a). Recently, others have specified how self-knowledge and the development of personal memory might relate to one another, but not in ways that are consistent with feminist perspectives on knowing. For example, Povinelli (1995; Povinelli et al., 1996) proposes that the development of abstract, representational thinking leads to integrating memories of personally experienced events into a linear, continuous time line, giving memories the potential to become autobiographical. Also, Howe and Courage (1993,

1997) propose that autobiographical memories emerge when a "cognitive sense of self" develops between eighteen and twenty-four months of age, as indicated by performance on the visual self-recognition task. The endogenous unfolding of abstract cognitive structures causes an objective awareness of unique physical and mental attributes. These accumulate into a critical mass that enables children to organize experiences "with respect to me" and to create long-term personal memories. In this model, language serves an expressive and descriptive function. The development of language allows children to copy ways of speaking about independently constructed memories that make those memories intelligible to others.

   Both of these hypotheses build on traditional assumptions of the subjective/objective model of self-development, and therefore neither incorporates the values of a feminist approach. Rational self-reflection, which is indicated in the ability of children to recognize their physical bodies, is the sole basis for developing personally meaningful recollections about the self. The conceptualizations and methods minimize, if not denounce, the importance of the particular social, cultural, emotional, and linguistic contexts of a child's everyday experiences. Finally, neither model addresses issues of diversity and variability in remembering and knowing about the self.

Studies of Self-Knowing That Are Consistent with Relational Being

Several researchers have studied self-development in a manner that is at least partially consistent with feminist perspectives on knowing. For example, Peggy Miller's research (P. J. Miller, 1994; P. J. Miller, Mintz, Hoogstra, Fung, & Potts, 1992; P. J. Miller, Potts, Fung, Hoogstra, & Mintz, 1990) works toward explicating an interactionist, discourse model of the socialization of the self-concept that considers the novice (e.g., the child), the institution of socialization (e.g., the family), the member of the institution (a parent or sibling), and typical forms of discourse. The assumption is that the organization of institutions brings novices and members together repeatedly for particular activities that are mediated through language and result in specific developmental achievements for the novice. For example, Miller examines naturally occurring stories of personal experience that are told within families, and asks questions such as, "Is personal storytelling routinely practiced in everyday family life? If so, what forms does it take? How is it practiced with respect to situating young children in the act of storytelling? What are the implications of this practice for self-construction?" Storytelling is a routine practice that consists of recurring patterns of discourse that mediate mutual participation in social activity. This practice is thought to socialize young children into systems of meaning that construct self-knowledge. This research is consistent with a feminist perspective on self-knowing in that (1) people come to know about the self in a social process that is mediated through language and occurs in close interpersonal relationships, (2) people use stories to evaluate the concrete experiences of everyday life and to construct personal meanings of events (i.e., their standpoints), (3) variability in the particular forms of discourse used when reconstructing experiences in stories characterizes the process of self-knowing, and (4) self-knowledge is fluid and changes with changes in context.

Miller finds that children experience a rich, narrative environment that consists of stories that significant others tell around children, about children, and with children, although differences exist in the degree to which children are invited to participate actively in the storytelling. Some stories are told consistently and others are not. The mere selection of a story guides attention to the experiences that should have personal meaning for the child, and retelling those stories establishes the actions, people, things, feelings, and so on, that were most important. Thus, personal stories reflect one's standpoint and may become evaluative frameworks for developing self-knowledge through the simple act of telling the story repeatedly.

In this research, children heard significant others tell personal stories that were rich with subjective evaluations of specific experiences in their own lives. Miller assumes that self-understanding grows in the empathic understanding of others' subjective experiences in a variety of contexts with particular people, although research has not shown directly how or if these stories become part of the child's self-knowledge. However, the fact that children retold these stories and sometimes even appropriated another person's experiences as their own indicates that these stories may become important for constructing self-knowledge. Notably, particular forms of discourse that could ultimately contribute to the construction of self-knowing would have been overlooked if these observations had been limited to co-constructions between dyads, such as between a parent and child. Instead, discourse processes were studied as they occurred in the natural, social composition of the child's interpersonal relationships. Using this procedure in future research could lead to a more complete understanding of how self-knowledge develops.

In other research, Miller and colleagues showed that self-representation is fundamentally an interpersonal process. Miller et al. (1992) examined the orienting frameworks that children used to tell about past experiences. Interpersonal frameworks included information about how the child was situated with respect to other people. For example, children remembered sharing an activity with others ("We went way down in the pool"), remembered being set apart from others ("No one was holding my hand"), or compared themselves with others. In noninterpersonal frameworks, other people were never mentioned. Children rarely used noninterpersonal frameworks in their storytelling, indicating that children routinely represent the self as embedded within a network of social relationships.

Importantly, the qualities of self-representation differed depending on who participated in the event and in the storytelling. For example, social comparisons between the self and others occurred when a sibling or a peer participated in the narrated event or in the process of narration. Thus, this study showed that social comparisons may or may not matter for self-knowing, in contrast to other theories that assume social comparison to be a universal quality of self-knowing that emerges with particular cognitive advances. Specifically, the finding suggests that making social comparisons may play a minimal role in the construction of self-knowledge for some children, depending on the typical interpersonal contexts of each child's everyday experiences and co-narrations.

Consistent with Jordan's concept of relational being, Miller emphasizes that self-knowledge should be conceptualized in future research as a more dynamic construct than it has been previously. For example, when children retell personal stories they often produce different versions of events. Initially, a narrative of personal experience may be sparse, but in the process of co-narration others select and elaborate on incidents that they believe the child should tell about and remember. Children may use episodes that others highlight to structure their own stories when they next tell about the experience, and may even insert additional details. However, children may omit some or all of these episodes and details in favor of their original perspective during subsequent retellings. How the story changes may depend on how the child has made sense of the event during previous tellings and on what the child believes is important to tell about the event in a given context. Miller (1994) suggests that qualitative transformations occur in self-construction when children begin to narrate their own personal experiences in different social and physical contexts and for a variety of purposes. Therefore, one must examine the content and structure of the child's personal stories not only within a single interpersonal context, but also continually in the child's subsequent narrations of events, in order to understand the development of self-knowledge.

Other researchers have proposed that talking with significant others about the emotional aspects of subjective experience may play a role in constructing self-knowledge. For example, Fivush (1994a) found that mothers use different ways of talking about emotions with daughters and sons that may lead to different qualities of self-understanding for girls and boys. Mothers used a social-relational framework most often when referring to emotions with girls, in which the child's emotional experiences were linked to other people as causes of emotion and regulators of emotion. However, when referring to emotions with boys, mothers most often used an autonomous framework that did not include references to people. Rather, mothers suggested that objects or activities, such as losing a toy, caused emotional experiences. Fivush suggests that parents teach girls to value relationships and to be responsive to others. This socialization process may establish a remembered self that is interpersonally oriented. In contrast, boys may learn to conceptualize the self as an autonomous being.

Yet, a critical question that must be addressed in future research is whether or not various qualities of discourse, including references to emotional experience, actually predict children's self-knowledge. Very little research has been conducted on this issue. In one study, Welch-Ross, Fasig, and Farrar (1999) proposed that mother-child conversations that focus on the emotional evaluations of past events construct frameworks for interpreting the personal meaning of experience, which lead to self-knowledge (see also Fivush, 1994a). For example, a recognition that "I am a person who is sad a lot" or "I am a person who has fun around people" develops as mothers and children negotiate how children should and typically do evaluate and respond to particular people and situations. The procedure involved recording conversations about four past events between four-year-olds and their mothers and coding the conversations for references to emotional experience, including initial references to emotion and subsequent elaborations on the emotional experience. Elaborations provided an explanation for the emotion, requested an explanation for the emotion, provided a resolution for the emotion, described how others responded to the emotion, confirmed or denied the emotion, or other.

Self-knowledge was defined in this study as a coherent representation of information about the self that enabled children to determine consistently whether behaviors associated with a particular personal quality described them or not. R. A. Eder's (1990) Children's Self-View Questionnaire was used to measure self-knowledge. Each item consists of a pair of statements, such as "I like to tease people" and "I don't like to tease people." One of two puppets endorses each statement. For each pair of statements, children choose the puppet they believe is most similar to themselves. The scale consists of three factors of self-knowing—Self-Control, Self-Acceptance via Affiliation, and Self-Acceptance via Achievement. The consistency with which children endorsed behaviors for each factor was the measure of self-knowledge. For example, both the child who endorsed many statements that were indicative of a factor, such as Self-Control, and the child who endorsed few statements that were indicative of the factor would be credited with a consistent self-view.

The amount that mothers and children talked about emotional experiences predicted the consistency of children's self-views, after controlling for a measure of language ability and references to other types of subjective experiences, such as wanting and believing. In addition, mothers' initiations of talk about emotion accounted for 75 percent of the total initiations, indicating that mothers played the primary role in using emotional evaluation to frame the meaning of personal experience.

Consistent with a feminist perspective on self-knowledge, the assumption of this research is that self-knowledge develops in the routine social activity of talking with significant others about subjective evaluations of specific experiences from everyday life. The method targets particular qualities of this social interaction for study but focuses in particular on the role that emotional evaluations may play in constructing meaningful representations of personal experience. Thus, the development self-knowing is not viewed as a neutral, purely cognitive process. Rather, it emerges in felt emotional experience and evaluation. Although not examined directly in this study, the assumption was that talking together about emotional evaluations establishes a shared representation of personal experience from which the child constructs self-knowledge. Moreover, the expectation was that self-knowing is fluid and changes with time and context, similar to a postmodern perspective (e.g., Sampson, 1989), yet self-knowledge becomes "fixed" at a particular point in time as a result of specific forms of discourse in relationships that define the personal meaning that experiences have for the self. Consistent with traditional views of self-knowing, this temporary fixedness can take the form of a consistent, psychological representation of one's personal qualities. Thus, in accordance with Jordan's feminist model of self-knowing, "intrapsychic investigation" of a specific quality of self-organization was complemented through studying patterns of discourse during a routine activity performed in a close interpersonal relationship. Integrating procedures in this way may be useful for understanding the culturally mediated, sociolinguistic processes through which particular individuals organize self-knowledge.

In addtion, feminist theorists are concerned with how diverse experiences lead to diverse selves with diverse epistemological standpoints. Several studies of the structure and content of personal narratives have shown intriguing patterns of gender and cross-cultural differences that have implications for understanding the development of self-knowledge from a feminist perspective. However, these variations probably would not be important for understanding the development of self-knowledge according to traditional views. For example, with respect to gender differences, mothers and fathers talk in more elaborated detail about past experiences with daughters than they do with sons (Reese & Fivush, 1993). Moreover, Mullen (1994) found that girls tended to have earlier memories than boys do. Regarding cross-cultural differences, Mullen found that Caucasian students had earlier memories than Asian students, particularly when compared with students who had spent their childhood years in Korea. These results converge with other research findings in which Caucasian American mothers elaborated on shared experiences in conversation and focused on their child's perspective on these experiences more than Korean mothers did (Mullen & Yi, 1995). This pattern of results suggests that a relation exists between the qualities of discourse children experience about past events and the development of personal memories. One implication of these findings is that self-knowledge begins to develop at different ages, depending on one's gender and culture.

Feminist models may build on current models of self-development by foregrounding the experiences of marginalized groups to offer a less biased perspective on development than universalist views do. For example, in most traditional models of self-development perspective taking plays a role in developing self-knowledge and an evaluative self-concept. One feminist claim is that marginalized, powerless members of society hone their perspective-taking skills more than powerful groups do (e.g., Harding, 1993). The rationale is that only the views of particular people have personal relevance for powerful persons, but the views of many more people have personal relevance from the circumstance of powerless persons, who must be aware of the perspectives of more powerful others.

An implication of this claim for studying self-development is that relatively powerless groups, such as girls or women, learn to incorporate the perspectives of others into their self-concepts, whereas members of powerful groups do not. Alternatively, a more likely possibility is that powerful and powerless groups use the perspectives of others differently in constructing their self-views. For example, powerful members of U.S. society (e.g., males, adults, Caucasians) may learn to discount the attitudes that most others have about them and learn to incorporate the perspectives of only a significant and powerful few into their self-view. However, relatively powerless groups (e.g., females, adolescents, racial and ethnic minorities) may learn to incorporate the perspectives of many others into their self-concepts.

Research supporting this argument shows that people who incorporate the perspectives of many people who are not significant others into their self-views have lower self-evaluations than people who discount those views (Harter, 1986, 1990). In addition, children and adults who identify with characteristics typical of the feminine role (dependent, agreeable, emotional), which is associated with less power in U.S. culture, make more negative self-evaluations than individuals who identify with characteristics typical of the masculine role (independent, aggressive, rational), which is associated with power (Alpert-Gillis & Connell, 1989; Boldizar, 1991). Individuals with feminine characteristics also have lower self-evaluations than do androgynous individuals. Thus, a direction for research consistent with a feminist perspective is to determine if the typical self-development of those who experience powerlessness in a society involves learning to incorporate many more perspectives into self-knowledge and self-evaluations than does the typical self-development of those who experience power.

Conclusion

A goal of this analysis has been to suggest how research on self-development might be conducted using theoretical models and methods that include feminist views of knowing. A feminist analysis often offers "a sharper articulation of the different strands—intellectual, imaginative and affective—involved in human ways of thinking" (Lloyd, 1998, p. 172). Thus, a starting point for regendering self-development research is to integrate traditional concepts and procedures with feminist ones in order to construct a more complete model of how self-knowledge develops.

REVISIONING SOCIAL

AND COGNITIVE DEVELOPMENT

The Social Construction

and Socialization of Gender

during Development

Campbell Leaper

A feminist approach to psychology is distinguished by two underlying assumptions. First, equal value is placed on the study of women and men (or girls and boys). In this regard, feminists have criticized many of the theories and research approaches in psychology for emphasizing males as the norm and either ignoring females or considering them somehow deficient in comparison to males (Gilligan, 1982; Tavris, 1992; Weisstein, 1993). Second, a feminist analysis stresses power and status in interpersonal relationships and societal institutions as fundamental sources of gender inequities.[1] A related goal of feminism is to identify directions for social change (Unger & Crawford, 1992; Wilkinson, 1997). Consequently, feminist psychology is "avowedly political" in its approach (Wilkinson, 1997, p. 248).

To date, most feminist psychology has occurred within the area of social psychology (see Lott, 1991; Nicolson, 1997; White, 1993, for reviews). Several researchers have pointed out ways in which gender-related variations in social behavior are derived from people's expectations and the demand characteristics in the immediate setting, as opposed to being a result of inherent sex differences in abilities (e.g., Deaux & Major, 1987). Social psychologists' emphasis on the power of the situation reflects what some social theorists refer to as a *constructionist* perspective on gender. Social constructionists locate the source of gender in social transactions (e.g., West & Zimmerman, 1987). Gender is something that people "do" rather than an aspect of individuals' personalities or predispositions. The constructionist perspective has been compatible with the feminist argument that gender inequities are due to sexist practices rather than to inherent biological differences between women and men.

What remains largely unexplained in a social-psychological or a constructionist analysis, however, is why people enter situations with gender-stereotyped expectations and preferences. Also, what accounts for variations within gender? For example, one woman may conform to gender-typed situational pressures whereas another woman may actively resist the same type of pressure. These are largely ontogenetic questions pertaining to variations in people's developmental histories. Thus, understanding people's pasts may additionally help explain their present behavior.

In this chapter I argue for a feminist developmental psychology that integrates feminist, constructionist, and socialization perspectives. First, a feminist analysis provides a conceptual model of society that stresses the existence of gender inequities in power and status. Second, a social constructionist approach offers a useful way of examining how gender is constructed in everyday social interactions. For example, Deaux and Major's (1987) interpersonal model of gender highlights how people's expectations and situational demands account for gender-related variations in behavior.[2] Finally, a developmental analysis further addresses the cumulative impact of social constructions on children's and adults' lives. Consistent exposure to one set of contexts influences the kinds of expectations, preferences, knowledge, and competencies that a person develops (Bandura, 1986; Lott & Maluso, 1993). Thus, understanding people's pasts may help explain their present behavior. Moreover, a better understanding of how gender develops in children can be used to devise intervention strategies aimed at reducing sexist biases (e.g., see Carpenter, Huston, & Holt, 1986; Katz, 1996; Leaper, 1994; Lockheed & Klein, 1985).

Three points will be emphasized in this chapter. First, the initial step in any feminist analysis should be a consideration of the broader cultural context that shapes and defines gender imbalances in status and power. Second, these analyses need to take into account relevant cultural practices that give gender its meaning. Finally, researchers need to investigate the social and cognitive processes within particular social interactions that reflect as well as create gender divisions during children's development.

The Macrosystem and the Individual's Development

A feminist developmental psychology should begin with the premise that gender inequities in power and status exist in society (Wilkinson, 1997). Thus, we need a conceptual model that addresses the link between society and the child's development. To this end, we can borrow from already existing models and theories in developmental psychology. Various researchers have emphasized the need to recognize different levels of analysis when examining children's development. Among them is Bronfenbrenner (1977), who has proposed an ecological model of human development. Bronfenbrenner's levels of analysis range from the macrosystem to the microsystem. The macrosystem refers to the broader cultural values and practices that make up a society, such as its form of economy, political structure, traditions, and laws. The microsystem refers to specific environments in which the child may be found in a given moment. Some microsystems include the family, the neighborhood, the classroom, the school playground, television, and the Internet.

Ogbu (1981) applied an ecological model to interpret variations in child rearing. In his analysis, a fundamental feature at the macrosystem level (what Ogbu calls "the effective environment") is the economic opportunity structure of a particular community. Child-rearing strategies reflect adaptations by parents or other caregivers to help prepare children for success in the local economy. Accordingly, Ogbu argued that the typical child-rearing practices in a middle-class suburb are not necessarily adaptive in a poor inner-city neighborhood. The same model can be extended to understanding gender development. Specifically, the type of socialization practices directed toward girls and boys may reflect the existing opportunity structures for women and men in a particular community at a particular time in history. For example, if women are expected to be primarily responsible for raising their children, childhood practices would be more apt to emphasize the practice of nurturant behaviors in girls than in boys. If men are expected to be primarily responsible for economic subsistence outside of the home, childhood practices would be more apt to emphasize the practice of independent behaviors in boys than in girls. Indeed, cross-cultural studies do reveal that the division of labor according to gender is correlated with child-rearing practices in societies (e.g., Hewlett, 1991; Weisner, 1979; Whiting, 1986).

Given the link between cultural practices and child outcomes, Weisner (1996) has argued that the child's "cultural place" (cultural beliefs, practices, meanings, and ecological setting) should be in the foreground of any developmental inquiry. For a *feminist* developmental psychology, we need to recognize how patriarchal structures in society shape the nature of children's and adults' microsystems. Furthermore, to the extent that children's development is largely an adaptation to their existing opportunities, we also need to consider how changing aspects of children's macrosystems and microsystems can lead to greater gender equality. Toward the latter goal, a feminist analysis necessarily involves evaluating the desirability of certain cultural practices. Researchers studying racial and ethnic discrimination and other forms of social injustice must make similar judgments about existing institutions (e.g., Clayton & Crosby, 1992; Haney & Zimbardo, 1998; Pettigrew, 1991).

By placing emphasis on the larger sociocultural context, many feminist social scientists downplay the importance of biological sex differences in the creation and maintenance of gender divisions and inequities. In order to highlight this point, some researchers have begun to make a distinction in their writing between the terms *sex* and *gender*. For these writers, the term sex is used to refer to any hypothesized or known biological differences between females and males, whereas the term gender is used to refer more broadly to the social assignment of people in a sex category. The distinction in terminology underscores the idea that male-female differences may be due as much or more to social expectations (i.e., gender assignment) than to biological predispositions (i.e., sex). Many researchers, however, still argue for a strong biological basis for gender divisions. Therefore, before addressing sociocultural contexts and psychological processes in more depth, I shall briefly address the issue of biology in gender development.

Biology and Evolution: Constraints or Adaptive Flexibility?

> *All biological phenomena come in a complex range rather than tidy, isomorphic polarities; it is culture that constructs the dichotomous sex categories, "woman-man."... Just as the biological dimension of skin color has been evoked in the social process of creating and subordinating racial minorities, so have biological differences been evoked in the social process of creating gender and subordinating women.*
> —Marie Withers Osmond and Barrie Thorne

As previously noted, an underlying goal for feminist social science is to identify the sources of gender inequities and the corresponding subordination of women (Osmond & Thorne, 1993; Unger & Crawford, 1992; Wilkinson, 1997). Therefore, many feminists criticize biologically deterministic research agendas as rationalizations of the status quo. Although evolutionary theory is often invoked to argue for the existence of biological constraints on women's and men's behavior (e.g., Buss, 1995), evolutionary theory can be used to advance the idea that what has evolved in humans is the brain's capacity to *adapt* and modify behavior across a range of different environments (e.g., Gould, 1991). The evolution of human intelligence has permitted us to invent tools and technologies that regularly transcend biological limitations. For instance, the invention of contraceptive devices has allowed women to increase control of their bodies and their sexuality. Additionally, technological advances make the average physical differences between women and men increasingly irrelevant for economic subsistence in most Western societies. Increasing gender equity in labor force participation and pay in the United States and other Western nations has meant that fewer women are economically dependent on men. In these ways, we see how humans have the capacity to adapt and change. Thus, instead of stressing biological constraints, we can emphasize the human capacity for behavioral *plasticity* in relation to whatever *environmental constraints* may exist (Nisbett, 1990; Silverstein, 1996). Accordingly, the view presented in this chapter is that sociocultural contexts and the opportunities they provide are largely responsible for the construction and development of gender. In the next section of the chapter, some of the possible ways of investigating the impact of the sociocultural context are explored.

Testing for Macrosystem-Microsystem Relationships

Gender, ethnicity (or race), and economic class are intertwined aspects of the macrosystem that partly define a person's status in society and can limit one's access to opportunities (see Chow, Wilkinson, & Baca Zinn, 1996; Collins, 1986; Hurtado, 1996; Peplau, Veniegas, Taylor, & DeBro, 1999; Reid & Comas-Diaz, 1990). According to feminist standpoint theory (e.g., Collins, 1986; Harding, 1991), people occupy overlapping and interacting positions in the social hierarchy because of these factors. For example, a poor African-American woman has a different standing than either a poor African-American man, a poor European-American (white) woman, or an upper-class African-American woman.

In order to test possible links between aspects of macrosystems and children's development, researchers may take two approaches. One is to examine variations across different cultures. Comparisons of how societies vary from one another can be used to infer how features of the macrosystem—such as the economic subsistence patterns and cultural values—are related to gender and children's development. A second approach is to examine variations within a particular culture. The researcher investigates how gender is constructed according to particular sociocultural contexts within a given society. This includes studying variations in people's opportunities to practice culturally meaningful tasks and their relative standings within the society. Examples of these two approaches are offered below.

Variations across Cultures

Hewlett's (1991) study of Aka culture in central Africa illustrates the link between the socioeconomic structure of a society and child development. The Aka people are a highly egalitarian, foraging society living in the central African rain forest. The typical Aka wife and husband spend much of their day mutually engaged in subsistence and child-rearing tasks. Aka fathers' active involvement in early child care is especially notable in contrast to Western norms:

> The Aka father's role can be characterized by its intimate, affectionate, helping-out nature.... Aka fathers spend 47 percent of their day holding or within an arm's reach of their infants, and while holding the infant, father is more likely than mother to hug and kiss the infant. The father's caregiving often takes place while the mother is carrying a heavy load, collecting firewood, or preparing a meal.... When adolescents were asked who played with them when they were children, just as many said father as said mother. (p. 168)

The active involvement of fathers in caregiving has a corresponding impact on the development of the children. Given that fathers are readily observed being active in caregiving and other domestic tasks, Aka boys do not appear to reject what mainstream American culture generally considers feminine-stereotyped attributes and activities. Specifically, infant care and food preparation are not viewed as "feminine" activities but rather as adult tasks for men as well as women. Hewlett also observed that Aka fathers "demonstrate intrinsic satisfaction with caregiving" (p. 174). Thus, Aka families reveal, first, that egalitarian gender roles are possible in human societies, and, second, ways in which gender arrangements in adulthood may influence children's construction of gender.

Variations within Cultures

Another strategy for examining macrosystem-microsystem links is to examine variations within societies. Cultures are not monolithic entities. Although women in a given society may generally experience social and economic discrimination, typically there are variations in the degree to which these biases occur. For instance, within the United States, gender may be constructed differently depending on *socioeconomic factors* such as income level, education level, race, and ethnicity (e.g., Bardwell, Cochran, & Walker, 1986; Chow et al., 1996; Collins, 1986; Hurtado, 1996; Peplau et al., 1999; Leaper & Valin, 1996; Reid & Comas-Diaz, 1990) as well as *structural variables* such as marital status or maternal employment (e.g., Etaugh, 1993; Leaper, Leve, Strasser, & Schwartz, 1995; Risman, 1987; Stevenson & Black, 1988). As previously noted, feminist standpoint theory emphasizes the intersection of gender, ethnicity, and class.

To illustrate with an example of within-culture variation, researchers have found that gender differences in attitudes and behaviors may be less prevalent among African-American children than among other ethnic groups. Among preschool-age children, gender stereotyping may be less likely among African-American children than among European-American children (Albert & Porter, 1988; Bardwell et al., 1986). Similarly, among adults, African-American women may be more likely than women from other ethnic groups to reject culturally dominant, gender-stereotyped beliefs (Binion, 1990; Dugger, 1988) and behaviors (N. M. Henley, 1995; Stanback, 1985). In contrast, studies suggest that African-American men generally adopt traditional gender attitudes (P. A. Smith & Midlarsky, 1985) and behaviors (Stanback, 1985).

The greater likelihood of nontraditional gender attitudes and behavior among African-American girls and women may be related to prevalent patterns of family structure. Most African-American children are raised by a mother who is a single parent and employed outside the home (Brookins, 1985; Cauce, Hiraga, Graves, & Gonzales, 1996; Reid, 1985). Acting as both economic providers and caregivers, single-parent African-American mothers may thereby provide their daughters with nontraditional, egalitarian gender-role models. In support of the hypothesis that family structure may be an important mediator in the gender-typing process, studies based on European-Americans and other ethnic groups indicate that nontraditional gender-typing patterns are more likely for children raised in single-parent mother-headed households (Leaper et al., 1995; Stevenson & Black, 1988). Thus, social, cultural, and economic contexts collectively influence children's development.

Another example of an investigation looking at variations within a culture is Ember's (1973) study of the Luo culture in Kenya. Ember observed that in many instances Luo boys were assigned domestic work, including housework and child care. However, in other instances boys were not assigned domestic tasks because either a daughter or an older brother was available to do the tasks. Boys who did and did not do domestic tasks were compared for types of social behaviors they demonstrated outside the home. Boys with greater responsibility for domestic tasks demonstrated significantly more prosocial and altruistic behaviors and less aggression than boys with less responsibility for domestic tasks. Thus, we see a link between cultural practices (assignment of tasks) and child outcomes (prosocial or aggressive behavior) (also see Goodnow, 1988; Grusec, Goodnow, & Cohen, 1996). The role of activity structure in the construction and socialization of gender is addressed further in the next section.

Opportunities for Practice: The Beginnings of Gender Discrimination

> *Different situations provide differential opportunities to practice particular behaviors and also present demand characteristics that make some responses more probable than others.*
>
> —Bernice Lott and Diane Maluso

According to sociocultural theory, children learn culture in the context of their social interactions and daily activities. The idea of contextualized learning of culture is expressed in Vygotsky's general genetic law of cultural development:

> Any function in the child's cultural development appears twice, or on two planes. First it appears on the social plane, and then on the psychological plane. First it appears between people as an inter-psychological category, and then within the child as an intra-psychological category.... Social relations or relations among people genetically underlie all higher functions and their relationships. (Vygotsky, cited in Wertsch & Tulviste, 1992, p. 548)

Contemporary proponents of sociocultural theory make similar points. For example, Rogoff (1990) argues that "the particular skills and orientations that children develop are rooted in the specific historical and cultural activities of the community in which children and their companions interact" (p. vii).

Although sociocultural theorists' analysis focuses on particular microsystems, social interactions are interpreted in relation to the macrosystem. In other words, the activities of children in particular settings are cultural practices that integrate the children into the larger society. For example, Leaper, Anderson, and Sanders's (1998) meta-analysis of gender effects on parents' speech to their children underscored the role of activity settings in the social construction and socialization of gender. Across a variety of speech act measures (e.g., total talking, directive speech, supportive speech, informing speech), effect sizes were negligible when studies used assigned tasks but were medium to large when studies were based on unstructured observations. Thus, gender effects (mother-father differences as well as differences in the treatment of daughters and sons) were mediated by the task or activity that was selected. Similar findings have been reported regarding the relative effects of activity structure and gender on children's behavior (Leaper & Gleason, 1996; Leaper et al., 1995). The studies indicate that when placed in similar situations, women and men—as well as girls and boys—tend to demonstrate similar behaviors. However, in several ways, girls and boys generally are *not* provided similar opportunities to practice certain behaviors. The gender-typing process traditionally prescribes different sets of activities for girls and for boys.

From a developmental perspective, it is helpful to examine children's early play activities to understand the etiology of gender discrimination in people's lives. In their meta-analysis, Lytton and Romney (1991) found that the most likely way in which parents differentially treat daughters and sons is in the encouragement of gender-typed toy play and activities. Boys' and girls' gender-typed toys and play activities tend to provide different opportunity structures. Most masculine-stereotyped forms of play—such as toy guns, construction sets, and team sports—emphasize instrumental or competitive behaviors. Conversely, most feminine-stereotyped forms of play—such as dolls, food sets, and playing house—emphasize cooperative and nurturant behaviors. Hence, boys are being groomed to compete for dominance while girls are being prepared to compromise and offer emotional support (see Leaper, 1994, for a review). By considering ways in which members of different groups within a society are systematically exposed to different opportunities (microsystems) during development, one may infer the relative functions and statuses of those different groups.

One key point is that *microsystems are defined by their access* (Lott & Maluso, 1993). Although girls and boys are apt to share many of the same microsystems, many contexts will be gender typed. In other words, some contexts are privileged according to gender. Girls will have access to doll play while boys will have relatively more access to sports games. Access in turn provides opportunities to observe and to practice particular behaviors (as described below). Furthermore, practice enables the formation of particular outcome expectancies, preferences, and skills.

Thus, gender differences in childhood opportunities may be viewed as early forms of discrimination that perpetuate the reproduction of gender inequities in adulthood. In other words, girls' and boys' participation in different activities in childhood become the training ground for later role and status differences in adulthood (see Goodnow, 1988; Huston, 1985; Leaper, 1994; Liss, 1983). In addition to practicing different behaviors themselves, girls and boys learn gender roles by observing the other gender. Girls may observe boys being more domineering while boys may observe girls being more deferential. On many playgrounds, boys tend to occupy more space; they are also more likely to invade and disrupt girls' space than the reverse (Thorne & Luria, 1986). Additionally, inside many classrooms, boys receive more attention from teachers than girls do (American Association of University Women [AAUW], 1992).

To this point my review has focused on the impact of different macrosystems and microsystems on children's gender development. In the next section, relevant social and cognitive processes that contribute to the maintenance of gender-segregated experiences are reviewed.

Psychological Processes within the Microsystem

In front of, and defending, the political-economic structure that determines our lives and defines the context of human relationships, there is the micropolitical structure that helps maintain it. This micropolitical structure is the substance of our everyday experience.

—Nancy Henley

If one takes an interactionist position that assumes that both person attributes and situational factors have a dynamic relationship in a person's development, it becomes necessary to look at the impact of both proximal factors in the immediate setting (emphasized in the social constructionist approach) as well as the cumulative impact of historical factors (emphasized in the socialization approach). Proximal factors in the immediate setting—such as people's expectancies and situational demands—constitute the underlying processes that teach children the meaning of gender. To the extent that these kinds of experiences become regular in their lives, children can be expected to infer patterns about gender. Cognitive representations of gender, known as gender schemas, will guide children's (and adults') self-concepts, motivations, and expectations about others. To reiterate Vygotsky's general genetic law of human development (see Wertsch & Tulviste, 1992), the child internalizes culture through her or his transactions with other people.

To understand the processes underlying gender development within particular microsystems, we can integrate ideas from social learning, sociocultural, social identity, and gender schema theories. Modern social learning theory and sociocultural theory both emphasize the role of social interactions as contexts for learning cultural practices. In Bandura's (1986, 1997) model, learning a particular behavior is influenced by a combination of situational, cognitive, and motivational factors. Situational factors include the opportunities a person receives to practice particular behaviors as well as the corresponding incentives for repeating the behaviors. The importance of opportunity structures in the acquisition and maintenance of gender was addressed earlier. Although modern social learning theory addresses the importance of cognition in learning, gender schema theory and social identity theory provide a fuller account of the cognitive aspects of gender development.[3] Thus, a hybrid or eclectic model can be assembled that addresses the dynamic influences of cognition, motivation, and situations on gender learning. This model is discussed next.

Cognitive Learning

Modern social learning theory emphasizes the importance of cognition in learning. In *observational learning*, children may infer gender norms by observing family members, television characters, or peers. For example, research indicates that children learn characteristics of their own gender group by observing several members of that group (J. R. Harris, 1995; Perry & Bussey, 1979). Therefore, it is important to take into consideration the dominant gender-role models that children perceive in families, neighborhoods, television, books, and schools. One difficulty in overcoming gender biases in children's (and adults') lives is the pervasive presence of gender stereotypes in people's daily lives (Wood, 1999). For instance, children can readily infer dominant gender stereotypes in the culture from cartoon and other television programs (Calvert & Huston, 1987; Leaper, Breed, Hoffman, & Perlman, 1999; Wood, 1999). More TV shows are directed toward boys than girls. Also, male characters are overrepresented in number; they are typically portrayed as leaders; and they are more often depicted using physical aggression. In contrast, female characters are more often portrayed in supportive roles, and they are often depicted as victims of aggression. Furthermore, from TV shows and commercials girls soon learn how much the culture emphasizes their physical appearance. Although gender-stereotyped images are pervasive, children regularly exposed to nontraditional role models within the family (e.g., mother-headed households), in schools (e.g., nonsexist curricula), or on television are apt to be less gender-stereotyped in their own thinking (e.g., see Bem, 1993; Calvert & Huston, 1987; Lockheed & Klein, 1985; Stevenson & Black, 1988; Wood, 1999).

Observational learning can also occur through *direct tutelage,* which overlaps with a form of cognitive learning emphasized in sociocultural theory known as *guided participation* (Rogoff, 1990). Guided participation occurs when a more competent member of a cultural community, such as an adult or more skilled peer, demonstrates a new behavior and guides the child in her or his own participation in the activity. In guided participation, the tutor provides instruction within the child's capacity to understand. The tutor subsequently encourages the child to practice the activity. For example, guided participation could include a father teaching his son how to throw a ball or a mother guiding her daughter in the use of a sewing machine. Deliberate efforts could be made to instruct children in cross-gender-typed as well as gender-typed activities. Girls as well as boys could be taught both to sew and to throw a ball.

Another aspect of the learning process is the *motivation* children develop to enact certain behaviors. According to social learning theory, motivation results from the positive or negative consequences a child experiences for demonstrating a particular behavior. For example, a girl who approaches a doll, may receive approval from a parent or peers whereas a boy may receive disapproval. Children may also vicariously experience this lesson by observing the consequences that others receive for their behavior. For example, a boy may learn not to play with dolls by observing his peers tease another boy for demonstrating that behavior.

In addition to influencing play activity interests, peers can shape one another's preference for gender-typed styles of social interaction. For example, girls' peer groups tend to discourage directly confrontive communication. In contrast, boys' groups typically emphasize power-assertive strategies (see Leaper, 1994, for a review). In these ways, boys and girls are regularly rewarded for using different influence strategies.

Thus, through shaping, the child internalizes the incentives for particular behaviors in the form of outcome expectancies. In her review of social learning theory, P. H. Miller (1993) summarized the relationship between environmental consequences and learning as follows:

> The influence of the environment becomes cognitive as children symbolically represent the relationship among the situation, their behavior, and the outcome. The essence of reinforcement is that it provides information about what effect the behavior has in the environment. (p. 199)

Bandura (1997) views outcome expectancies as bearing directly on a person's sense of *self-efficacy*. Self-efficacy refers to people's expectations regarding their ability to influence some aspect of their lives. Having a sense of self-efficacy is positively associated with a person's motivation and achievement. However, people may have a high sense of self-efficacy in one domain but not in another (see Harter, 1996b). For example, whereas a girl may perceive herself as being highly competent in her close relationships, she may view herself as incompetent in math and science.

A person's sense of self-efficacy in a particular domain reflects prior opportunities for practice and the corresponding consequences that followed (Bandura, 1997). To the extent that a child (or adult) gets the chance to practice a skill and is rewarded for it, a sense of self-efficacy is apt to follow. In contrast, if insufficient opportunities are available or if negative consequences follow, low self-efficacy is likely to occur. Thus, subordinate groups are especially at risk for low self-efficacy in domains where prejudice and discrimination exist (Bandura, 1997). To illustrate, consider Eccles's (1989) longitudinal research on gender differences in children's math achievement. In her study, parents generally endorsed the stereotype that mathematics was more natural for boys than girls. Also, despite the absence of grade differences in math during elementary school, parents tended to underestimate girls' math ability and to overestimate boys' ability. Eccles found that over time, girls' own self-perceptions reflected the parents' stereotype. The girls increasingly lost confidence in their mathematics skills. At the same time, they lowered their evaluations of the usefulness of mathematics for their future. Thus, in high school, girls spent fewer years studying mathematics than boys did. Gender differences in math self-efficacy in high school are related to later gender differences in occupational achievement. For example, Hackett (1985) found that high school math self-efficacy was correlated with choosing a math-related major in college. Gender inequities in achievement in math-related majors translate into corresponding gender inequities in technological careers.

Bandura (1997) underscored the significance of these imbalances for society:

> Our society will have to rely increasingly on the talents of women and ethnic minorities to maintain its scientific, technological, and economic viability. Societies must come to terms with the discordance between their occupational socialization practices and the human resources needed for their success. Societies that fail to develop the capabilities of all their youth jeopardize their social and economic progress. (p. 430)

Indeed, there is evidence to support the contention that gender equality is positively related to the social and economic progress among societies around the world (Eisler, Loye, & Norgaard, 1995).

Self-efficacy is a useful construct in considering power and status asymmetries between groups. When subordinate group members are denied access to certain opportunities and experiences, they are less apt to gain the confidence and the skill to succeed in those areas from which they have been disenfranchised—as illustrated by the findings on gender inequities in math achievement. To counteract these inequities, schools can adjust their curricula to address various forms of gender discrimination (AAUW, 1992; Connell, 1996; Lockheed & Klein, 1985).

The foregoing discussion of self-efficacy calls attention to the ways in which gender discrimination can influence people's construction of self during development. Other cognitive aspects of gender development are discussed in the next section. Most notably, the impact of forming a gender concept on subsequent group identity processes is reviewed.

Social Cognition, Self-Understanding, and Group Behavior

The important point about human groups is that they are social categories. When children categorize themselves as members of a group, they take on its norms of behavior.... In dyadic relationships, children learn how to behave with [specific individuals]. In the peer group they learn how to behave in public.

—Judith Harris

Between ages one and two years, children begin to demonstrate the first clear signs of a gender concept through their use of gender labeling. Gender labeling refers to the verbal classification of other people's gender. One's *in-group gender identity*—that is, the capacity to identify one's own gender—emerges around two and three years of age. The child's gender concept becomes an organizing mental framework, known as a *gender schema,* that guides information processing.

Around the same age that children begin forming an in-group gender identity, they begin to demonstrate a preference for same-gender peer affiliations. Gender segregation leads to the establishment of different primary peer groupings for boys and girls (see Leaper, 1994; E. E. Maccoby, 1998, for reviews). As with racial segregation, gender segregation can be viewed as a problematic social process that contributes to the creation and maintenance of status and power inequities between groups. Therefore, understanding the development and impact of children's social gender identities is a key concern for feminist developmental psychology.

According to both gender schema theory (Martin, 1994; Martin & Halverson, 1981) and social identity theory (Archer, 1992; J. R. Harris, 1995; Tajfel, 1982; Turner, Hogg, Oakes, Richer, & Wetherell, 1987), the emergence of an in-group identity guides children's subsequent thinking, motivation, and behavior. Several processes are associated with group identity and group socialization: in-group favoritism, out-group hostility, between-group contrast, and within-group assimilation (see J. R. Harris, 1995, for a review). Additionally, asymmetries in these group processes can occur when one group has higher status than the other. This is the case for boys and men in patriarchal societies. The relevance of each of these group processes in relation to gender segregation is reviewed next.

In-Group Favoritism and Out-Group Hostility

Having an in-group identity increases the distinctiveness and positive evaluation of one's own gender group (i.e., *in-group favoritism*). Therefore, children are more likely to engage in activities associated with their in-group gender identity (Bussey, 1983; Fagot, 1977; Martin, 1994; Perry, White, & Perry, 1984; Powlishta, 1995). Conversely, out-group members and characteristics associated with them tend to be devalued (i.e., *out-group hostility*). Correspondingly, we see that children tend to reject cross-gender-typed objects, activities, and behaviors (Bussey, 1983; Fagot, 1977; Martin, 1994; Perry et al., 1984). Bradbard, Martin, Endsley, and Halverson (1986) tested how gender schemas might guide information processing and behavior. They presented novel, gender-neutral objects to children between four and nine years old. Objects were randomly labeled as "for girls," "for boys," or "for boys and girls." The researchers found that the children paid more attention to and remembered more about objects labeled as appropriate for their own gender than those objects labeled for the other gender. Thus, children showed a preference for learning about own-gender objects and a corresponding disinterest in other-gender objects. Children may also learn to associate certain styles of social interaction with their respective in-group. For example, physical aggression may be allied more with boys while polite behaviors may be associated more with girls.

Between-Group Contrast

In addition to in-group favoritism and out-group hostility, another related consequence of having in-group identity is that members of an in-group become invested in demarcating the differences between groups (i.e., *between-group contrast*). For one thing, group identity becomes the basis of social organization. As noted previously, gender segregation becomes prevalent around the same time as the emergence of a gender identity. Gender segregation is also associated with forms of social interaction that reaffirm the boundaries of and asymmetries between girls' and boys' groups—known as either *borderwork* (Thorne & Luria, 1986) or *gender boundary maintenance* (Sroufe, Bennett, Englund, Urban, & Shulman, 1993). Such forms of social interaction include, for example, criticizing peers who play with the other gender as well as ritualized forms of cross-gender contact such as heterosexual teasing (e.g., "Jimmy likes Beth") or oppositional games (e.g., kiss-and-chase). Children who regularly violate the rules regarding the maintenance of gender boundaries tend to be less popular with their peers (Sroufe et al., 1993). (As discussed later, girls and boys tend to differ in gender boundary maintenance.)

In the process of demarcating group identities, people tend to exaggerate and distort the extent of actual differences between groups (Messick & Mackie, 1989). For example, Martin and Halverson (1983) showed five- and six-year-old children a series of gender-stereotyped pictures (e.g., a woman sewing) and reverse-stereotyped pictures (e.g., a woman sawing wood). When children's recall for the pictures was tested one week later, they tended to recall the gender of the actors as changed in the stereotyped direction (e.g., recalling a man sawing wood). In these ways, children (and adults) can be very resistant to evidence that contradicts their gender schemas (see Cross & Markus, 1993).

Within-Group Assimilation

Part of viewing the in-group as different from the out-group is establishing certain social norms that define the in-group. Thus, conforming to the group's social norms (i.e., *within-group assimilation*) is another correlate of having a social identity. J. R. Harris (1995) argued that the peer group plays a key role in transmitting culture to individuals through this process. As discussed earlier, children effectively socialize one another to conform to gender norms. Conformity typically leads to approval and acceptance; nonconformity may lead to negative sanctions and possibly ostracism from the peer group (Leaper, 1994; Sroufe et al., 1993). As children get older, conformity pressures from the outside are no longer needed to motivate the child. Group norms are internalized as personal standards, which self-regulate behavior (Bussey & Bandura, 1992; J. R. Harris, 1995). Gender differences in group norms traditionally have included a greater emphasis on independence, competition, and dominance among boys and a greater emphasis on interpersonal sensitivity and closeness among girls (see Leaper, 1994, for a review). These differences set in motion the expectations that boys will be dominant leaders and girls will be supportive subordinates. However, one possible way to counteract these pressures during childhood is for parents and teachers to encourage collaborative cross-gender activities (see Leaper, 1994).

Boundaries and Status

Often, when different group identities occur, one group has higher status or greater power than another group. This differential is seen with gender, ethnicity (race), economic class, and sexual orientation, as stressed in various feminist analyses (Chow et al., 1996; Collins, 1986; Hurtado, 1996; Peplau et al., 1999; Reid & Comas-Diaz, 1990). In the case of gender, men have higher status than women in patriarchal societies such as the United States. Among women in Western cultures, European-American (white) women have derived higher status than ethnic-minority women (Collins, 1986; Hurtado, 1996; Trepagnier, 1994).

A pertinent corollary of social identity theory is that members of high-status groups are more invested in maintaining group boundaries than members of low-status groups (*asymmetries in borderwork*). Accordingly, two manifestations of asymmetry between girls and boys in borderwork can be noted. First, boys are more likely to initiate and maintain role and group boundaries (Bussey & Perry, 1982; Fagot, 1977; Sroufe et al., 1993; Thorne & Luria, 1986). For example, boys are generally more likely than girls to receive negative sanctions for initiating cross-gender contacts or demonstrating cross-gender-typed behavior (Bussey & Perry, 1982; Fagot, 1977; also see Leaper, 1994). Second, the characteristics associated with a high-status group are typically valued more than those of a low-status group. Thus, members of low-status groups are more likely to adopt characteristics associated with high-status groups than the reverse.[4] For example, as illustrated in Broverman, Broverman, Clarkson, Rosenkrantz, and Vogel's (1970) landmark (and since replicated) study, attributes traditionally associated with being male (independence, assertiveness) tend to be valued more than those traditionally associated with being female (nurturance, compassion). Additionally, cross-gender-typed behavior tends to be more common among girls, given the greater status afforded masculine-stereotyped characteristics in society (see Leaper, 1994). As Feinman (1981) commented, "males experience status loss and females experience status gain in cross-sex-role behavior" (p. 290). We see this distinction reflected in the different connotations for the words "sissy" (highly negative) and "tomboy" (relatively neutral).

Some authors refer to men's (and boys') avoidance and devaluing of feminine-stereotyped qualities as *masculine protest* (see Broude, 1990; Mosak & Schneider, 1977; M. O. Nelson, 1991). Masculine protest manifests as excessive masculine-stereotyped behavior, or machismo, and reflects "the belief that men are accorded preferential treatment in the culture and have rights, obligations, and privileges, and opportunities that women do not possess" (Mosak & Schneider, 1977, p. 193). Masculine protest may therefore lead to sexist discrimination against women. Researchers observe that masculine protest is further associated with men's violence against women and gay men (Ember & Ember, 1993; Herek, 1992; M. O. Nelson, 1991) as well as the sanctioning of aggression between men in violent sports (Messner, 1992).

Masculine protest may be a consequence of the group processes previously described.[5] As mentioned earlier, in-group identity tends to lead to between-group contrasts. It was also noted that people often exaggerate the extent of actual differences between groups in order to maintain their beliefs about group differences (see Cross & Markus, 1993; Messick & Mackie, 1989). Negative distortions may apply especially when processing information about low-status-group members. For example, Lockheed, Harris, and Nemceff (1983) found that school-age children viewed boys in the classroom as more competent and leader-like than girls, despite objective measures indicating no gender differences in relevant leadership behaviors. However, once girls were trained to be experts on a task, they were viewed as having leadership competence equal to boys'. The study by Lockheed et al. reveals the extent to which children's gender beliefs can bias their perceptions. At the same time, the study also shows that it is possible to counteract the stereotypes.

It is worth reiterating that the girls trained as experts were viewed as *equally* as competent (leader-like) as the boys, when the girls were actually *more* competent than the boys. As is often the experience of ethnic minorities as well, in order to be viewed as equally good in a work situation, a low-status-group member's performance may have to be superior to others' performances in order to dispel others' prejudiced expectations.

Furthermore, to counteract stereotypes, the subordinate person has to downplay whatever external pressures there might be to conform to the stereotyped expectation. In contrast, members of the high-status group will enjoy relative privilege in being the ones to whom others will turn for leadership.

Thus, asymmetries in group status have different implications for how low- and high-status-group members are viewed by outsiders. Discrepancies between how a person views the self and how others view that person are apt to be greatest for low-status-group members. When this type of discrepancy occurs, a person must decide how to present one's self. Factors related to self-presentation are addressed in the next section.

Self-Presentation

> *Social interaction is a process of identity negotiation whereby perceivers and selves... attempt to attain their negotiation goals.*
> —Kay Deaux and Brenda Major

To the extent that gender becomes an important component of a person's self-concept, gender schemas not only play a role in how information is interpreted but also influence how a person presents the self to others (Bem, 1993). Accordingly, theoretical models of the self often distinguish between the private self and the public self (see Deaux & Major, 1987, for a review). The *private self* refers to one's personal attitudes, values, and self-definitions. Maintaining a stable self-concept, or private self, is known as *self-verification.* The *public self* refers to a person's presentation to others (*self-presentation*). Generally, we tend to seek out social contexts in which our private and public selves will coincide. For example, a person who values gender equality is likely to choose friends who endorse the same attitude. However, in some situations, concerns for self-verification and self-presentation may conflict. For example, a man with gender-egalitarian ideals may find himself in a situation with other men who are making sexist jokes. Social desirability may lead to a form of self-presentation that is consistent with others' expectations (i.e., the self-fulfilling prophecy). For example, he may laugh at the sexist jokes. Alternatively, this man's wish to maintain his self-concept as nonsexist may lead to a form of self-verification. For example, he may express offense at the sexist jokes.

The distinction between private and public selves highlights the fact that people's behavior is not always consistent with their underlying attitudes and motives. As an illustration, we can consider the often cited finding that physical aggression is more likely to occur among males than among females. Both the popular press and scholarly texts generally attribute gender differences in aggression to higher levels of testosterone among males. Contrary to what people generally assume, however, the empirical evidence for a causal connection between testosterone and aggression is contradictory and inconclusive (see Sapolsky, 1997).[6] Of particular relevance to the topic of self-presentation and self-verification is recent research indicating an absence of gender differences among children when both physical and relational forms of aggression are scrutinized. Physical aggression (e.g., hitting) is more likely to occur among boys, but relational aggression (e.g., ostracism) is more likely among girls (Björkqvist, 1994; Crick & Bigbee, 1998). Moreover, rates of physical aggression among boys are comparable to rates of relational aggression among girls (see Björkqvist, 1994). Thus, to the extent that both types of aggression reflect malevolent motives, girls and boys may be viewed as equally aggressive in intent (i.e., in their private feelings), despite apparent differences in how similar underlying motives are shown (i.e., in their public presentations). Normative social pressures for girls to act "nice" and avoid direct confrontation may lead girls to express their aggressive motives indirectly by manipulating their social networks. In contrast, the relatively greater tolerance in Western societies of overt aggression among males ("Boys will be boys") may make it more acceptable (and even desirable) for boys to use physical aggression. Indeed, Huesmann, Guerra, Zelli, and Miller (1992) found that among elementary schoolchildren, "not only are boys more physically aggressive than girls…, they are also more likely to believe that aggression is an acceptable behavior across a range of circumstances" (p. 84).

Further support of the self-presentation explanation for gender differences in aggression comes from studies of cultures where physical aggression is much less frequent than in the United States. For example, Lepowsky (1994) provided an ethnographic description of the Vanatinai society of New Guinea, among whom rates of physical violence are rare. The culture is characterized by "prevailing ideologies of gender equality, no indigenous system of formal authority, and a high value on assertiveness and personal autonomy for both sexes" (p. 200). When acts of physical violence occur, they are associated with strong social disapproval. Although a causal connection is not proved, Lepowsky proposes that the gender differences in rates of physical violence may be generally related both to the tolerance of aggression among males and to the institution of male dominance in a given society.

If self-presentation concerns lead people to present a public self that is different from their private self, what kinds of factors make these pressures more or less likely? Social psychologists have found that people tend to favor self-presentation over self-verification when the audience is highly salient (see Deaux & Major, 1987). Four kinds of social situations with high audience salience can be pointed out. First, other people are more salient when they have control over desired resources. In other words, those higher in power and status are more salient than those lower in power or status. Therefore, boys and men are less apt to be concerned with self-presentation than girls and women (N. Henley, 1977). Second, a person is more sensitive to others' expectations in unfamiliar situations, when the audience may be used for a reality check or social comparison. For example, as heterosocial interactions increase during adolescence, teens are apt to rely on their peers to establish conventions about dating behavior (see Hansen, Christopher, & Nangle, 1992; Leaper & Anderson, 1997). Third, an audience is more salient when the person can expect future interactions with members of that audience. Therefore, a peer group typically has greater salience than casual acquaintances. Finally, self-presentation concerns increase when others make the person feel that her or his attitudes are deviant. In this regard, developmental psychologists additionally note that conformity is more likely in a group than in a dyad (see J. R. Harris, 1995).

To the extent that groups have a stronger socializing influence than dyads, it is pertinent to consider gender differences in peer versus dyadic experiences. Researchers find that during childhood, boys are more likely than girls to affiliate in larger groups, whereas girls are more likely than boys to play in dyads (see Benenson, 1993; Leaper, 1994). Also, boys are more apt to engage in peer-structured activities, while girls are more likely to participate in adult-structured activities (Carpenter, 1983). Thus, socialization in groups may be more persistent for boys than for girls. Accordingly, gender differences in group socialization may partly explain how and why gender typing and gender boundaries tend to be more rigid among boys than girls during childhood. By spending more time in groups, boys may be subjected to more conformity pressures than girls. Conversely, by participating in more dyadic relationships, girls may have more flexibility to engage in a wider range of behaviors because they need to negotiate social expectations with only one person at a time. The situation for girls appears to change dramatically during adolescence, however. At this time, the traditional gender role for girls tends to become more restricted (Archer, 1984; Hill & Lynch, 1983). Whereas "tomboyish" behavior may be acceptable in childhood, new pressures emerge for girls to act in ways that are viewed as attractive to boys. At the same time, girls are participating in cliques that are often composed of both boys and girls (Hansen et al., 1992). Norms for dating roles during this age period may conflict with norms for academic success or other forms of personal agency (Bush, 1987; Eccles, 1984; Marini, 1978). Perhaps partly for these reasons, some studies indicate a decline in girls' self-esteem during this age period (AAUW, 1992).

Summary

I have highlighted some of the ways in which a person's gender identity and subsequent membership in a group can contribute to the development of gender asymmetries and inequities during development. Gender identities influence how the self and others are viewed as well as how people act with and react to others. Although children experience external pressures to conform to gender norms in childhood, such conventions typically become internalized as personal standards during development. Nonetheless, concerns with self-presentation continue to exert an influence throughout life. Even when individuals are able to transcend traditional gender roles (e.g., see Eccles, 1987), there are apt to be ongoing challenges from other members of society that make it difficult to maintain a nontraditional identity. However, as gender roles in American society undergo change, children and adults with nontraditional identities are increasingly finding their own in-group.

Charting a Path for a Feminist Developmental Psychology

In this chapter, I have offered some preliminary sketches for a feminist developmental psychology. Feminists have stressed how gender (as well as ethnicity and economic class) is embedded in the social structures that define status and power in society. Social psychologists have highlighted the ways in which gender inequities are constructed in daily interactions. In a complementary manner, developmental psychologists can help explain how and why people are socialized to act in ways that perpetuate gender inequities in society. Consistent with a feminist analysis, I have argued that considering the macrosystem, or larger sociocultural context, should be the starting point. Specifically, the feminist researcher needs to consider cultural contexts at the macrosystem level that support the maintenance of gender divisions in daily interactions operating at the microsystem level. Analyses of differences between cultures or variations within societies are potentially useful research strategies. With regard to within-culture investigations, I have recommended examining variations in social-structural factors such as socioeconomic conditions as well as variations in opportunities to practice cultural tasks.

Analyses at the microsystem level help us understand how gender is constructed through the social interactions that make up children's and adults' daily lives. To paraphrase Henley (1977, p. 3), social-psychological processes operating within particular microsystems constitute the micro-political structure that maintains the patriarchal political-economic structure operating at the macrosystem level. To the extent that specific contexts are associated with particular behaviors, we better see how imbalances in opportunities may lead to later gender differences in expectations, preferences, or skills. In turn, children are apt to select activity settings that are consistent with their expectations, preferences, and skills.

Having outlined a conceptual model for a feminist developmental psychology, I close the chapter by suggesting four research directions. First, we need a better understanding of how different microsystems (and their corresponding macrosystems) influence children at different ages or developmental periods. For example, whereas family members may be especially influential in early childhood, peers appear to have more impact on gender socialization during middle childhood (J. R. Harris, 1995). Additionally, the onset of puberty and sexuality during adolescence changes the social construction and socialization of gender (D'Augelli, 1998; Leaper & Anderson, 1997). Some researchers suggest that adolescence is a period when opportunities for girls become dramatically constrained (Archer, 1984, 1992; Hill & Lynch, 1983; Leaper, 1994).

Second, when average gender differences in behavior are observed, we need to explore whether there is an underlying gender difference in (1) expectations and beliefs, (2) preferences, or (3) knowledge and skills leading to those behavioral differences (see Huston, 1985, for a similar point). In some instances girls and boys (as well as women and men) may act differently because of beliefs about how they are expected to behave, despite an absence of any underlying difference in preference or competence (Deaux & Major, 1987). Alternatively, there may be an underlying gender difference in preferences but not in competencies. For example, according to some studies men are not apt to disclose with men but will disclose with women (see Leaper, 1994, for a review). That these men can and do disclose with women partners indicates that they are not incapable of self-disclosure. Instead, perhaps they either believe it is more appropriate to disclose to women than to men (e.g., owing to a belief that their male friends will consider them less strong for being expressive) or they prefer to disclose to women (e.g., owing to having experienced more overt support from women than from men). A related proposal is to investigate if and when behavioral differences based in expectations or preferences eventually lead to differences in competence.

A third recommendation is to explore the interrelationship between children's developmental domains and aspects of their gender development. This research would include examining the development of children's gender schemas and knowledge (see Martin, 1993) as well as looking more specifically at how children come to associate gender with status (e.g., Bussey & Bandura, 1984; Hyde, 1984; Lockheed et al., 1983). Also, we can explore if and how children's understanding of power and status asymmetries is related to gender-related variations in children's social behavior.

By better knowing how sexist prejudice and discrimination develop in children, we may learn where and how to prevent or reverse their occurrence (Lutz & Ruble, 1995). Accordingly, the final suggested research direction for feminist developmental researchers is to study interventions aimed at reducing gender typing in children. Some researchers have already explored ways to reduce forms of gender bias in children's attitudes and behavior (e.g., see Connell, 1996; Katz, 1996; Leaper, 1994; Lockheed & Klein, 1985, for reviews). The effectiveness of particular intervention strategies may depend on when and how they are applied. For example, children's responsiveness to programs designed to reduce stereotypes may require the acquisition of certain cognitive strategies (Bigler & Liben, 1992). Additionally, even when interventions are effective, it is likely that they will need to be maintained in order to counteract other ongoing influences (see Leaper, 1994). For example, although a program designed to increase cross-gender cooperation worked, children reverted to prior patterns when the intervention was stopped (e.g., Serbin, Tonick, & Sternglanz, 1977). Therefore, the effectiveness of long-term intervention programs in childhood and adolescence needs to be considered.

Achieving gender equity will depend on changes occurring at both the macrosystem and microsystem levels. At the macrosystem level, continued structural changes in our economic, political, and legal institutions are necessary to foster greater gender equality. Change also must occur at the microsystem level in the context of particular relationships and settings. People can and do change their attitudes and behaviors as adults. At the same time, we can endeavor to free children from the gender stereotypes, restricted opportunities, and other biases that begin to limit their potential early in life.

Notes

The author thanks Kristin Anderson, Faye Crosby, Patricia Miller, and Ellin Scholnick for their helpful comments on earlier drafts of this chapter.

1. There are multiple forms of feminism (e.g., see Donovan, 1992; Wood, 1999, for reviews). The present paper is largely premised on the radical feminist perspective. According to radical feminists, gender differences and inequalities are rooted in structural practices—in institutions and social interactions—that favor male power and privilege.
2. Deaux and Major (1987) emphasize proximal variables in their model but also acknowledge the potential influences of distal factors such as socialization or biological predispositions.
3. To the extent that Bandura's (1986) social learning theory and Martin and Halverson's (1981) gender schema theory both reflect information-processing approaches, they may be viewed as compatible and complementary. For example, some investigators who take a social-learning approach have incorporated aspects of gender schema theory in their conceptual model (e.g., Fagot & Leinbach, 1989).
4. Attributes associated with high-status/high-power groups are not always viewed positively by members of low-status/low-power groups. Depending on the particular cultural frame of reference, members of disenfranchised groups may form an "oppositional identity" that rejects attributes associated with the dominant group. Ogbu (1993) finds that an oppositional identity is more likely to occur among involuntary than among voluntary minority groups in a culture. For example, school success is generally viewed positively by recent immigrants but may be negatively disparaged as "acting white" by inner-city African-American youth. One difference between gender and ethnic groupings is that girls and women have more access to the world of boys and men (e.g., within the family) than inner-city African-American youth have access to the suburban, European-American world. To my knowledge, the corresponding factors that might lead some girls or women to form oppositional *gender* identities

remain largely unexplored. For some women, however, the emergence of a feminist identity may reflect a form of oppositional identity (e.g., see Downing & Roush, 1985; Myaskovsky & Wittig, 1997).

5. Chodorow's (1978) object-relations theory may also be pertinent. She argued that because women typically are caregivers, boys' and girls' gender identities develop differently. For girls, having a same-gender role model who is readily available enables them to define their identities in terms of closeness and similarity to the mother. In contrast, not having a same-gender role model as readily available leads boys to define their identities in terms of separation from and difference to the mother. The masculine identity is therefore based, according to Chodorow, on being "not-female," and feminine qualities become devalued in boys' (and men's) minds.

6. The connection between testosterone and aggression is less clear than typically assumed (see Sapolsky, 1997). First, many studies find no correlation between testosterone and aggression. Second, baseline testosterone levels do not appear related to the likelihood of physical aggression. Third, when a correlation between testosterone and aggression is found, the direction of influence may not reflect the causal relationship typically assumed. Increased levels of aggression may be a *response* to enacting aggressive behavior more than a direct cause of aggressive behavior. As Sapolsky (1997) summarized, "study after study has shown that when you examine testosterone levels when males are first placed together in the social group, testosterone levels predict nothing about who is going to be aggressive. The subsequent behavioral differences drive the hormonal changes, rather than the other way around" (pp. 151–152). Thus, testosterone levels have been observed to increase or decrease according to situational demands. To the extent that boys' traditional peer groups emphasize competition and tolerate physical aggression (e.g., through contact sports and occasional fist fights), boys may be more apt to view physical aggression as an acceptable behavioral strategy for exerting their dominance. As a result, boys' greater likelihood of engaging in physical aggression may lead to higher testosterone levels.

Toward a Gender-Balanced

Approach to the Study

of Social-Emotional Development

A Look at Relational Aggression

Nicki R. Crick and Amanda J. Rose

Social developmental psychology is a rich area for the study of gender. Countless gender differences in children's and adolescents' social interaction and personality styles have been documented. These include gender differences in the size of play groups (e.g., Benenson, 1990, 1994), in the tendency to discuss emotions (e.g., Kuebli, Butler, & Fivush, 1995), in the proximity to adults sought during play (e.g., Omark, Omark, & Edelman, 1975), and in achievement motivation styles (e.g., Dweck & Bush, 1976; Stipek & Gralinski, 1991), to name just a few. However, despite the field's success in documenting gender differences, few attempts have been made to determine whether constructs and theories of social-emotional development can be applied in the same ways to both girls and boys (see Cross & Madson, 1997; Gilligan, 1982, for important exceptions).

In this chapter, we use the case of aggression to illustrate the idea that some theories of social-emotional development might look quite different were they developed from a female perspective. For decades, males have been considered to be the more aggressive gender, and this hypothesis has been supported by hundreds of studies. Most of these studies, however, excluded girls from the sample and defined aggression as physically aggressive hostile acts. Recent research indicates that gender differences in aggression disappear when the definition of aggression is broadened to include aggressive acts in which the victim's personal relationships are manipulated or damaged—that is, relational aggression. In this chapter we first describe how a gender-balanced approach to the conceptualization and assessment of aggression resulted in the study of relational aggression (which is more typical of females) in addition to physical aggression (which is more typical of males). Particular attention is paid to developmental differences in relational versus physical aggression. Next, we provide examples of other domains within social developmental psychology that might benefit from greater attention to both genders. Finally, we highlight some of the methodological limitations to conducting gender-balanced research and discuss methods that may be particularly helpful for understanding the experiences of girls and women.

Understanding Aggression from the Female Perspective: A Look at Relational Aggression

Hundreds of studies have found boys and men to be significantly more aggressive than girls and women. In their classic review of the literature, E. E. Maccoby and Jacklin (1974) cited this gender difference in aggression as one of the few reliable differences between boys and girls. Perhaps not surprisingly, this finding has been generalized to an overall lack of aggressiveness in the peer interactions of girls, a conclusion that has perpetuated the myth of the nonaggressive female (Bjorkqvist & Niemela, 1992). This conclusion was drawn, however, by viewing the types of aggressive behaviors that are typical of boys as the standard or normative forms of aggression and determining that, in comparison with boys' relationships, girls' relationships lack aggressive components. A more gender-balanced approach to the conceptualization and assessment of aggression would capture the types of aggression that are exhibited in the relationships of girls and women. If forms of aggression that are more characteristic of females as well as those that are typical of males are looked at, girls and women may prove to be as aggressive as boys and men.

In our own work, as we considered how to conceptualize aggression from a more female perspective, we first turned to a basic, general definition that describes aggression as the intent to hurt or harm (e.g., Myers, 1990; Vander Zanden, 1993). We hypothesized that during early and middle childhood, when children tend to interact primarily with same-gender peers, they would learn to harm others in ways that would most effectively damage the social goals of their same-gender agemates (Crick & Grotpeter, 1995). Past studies have demonstrated that boys are more likely than girls to focus on themes of instrumentality and physical dominance in their peer relations (for a review see Block, 1983). Therefore, it makes sense that boys are generally more physically aggressive than girls, because physically aggressive acts are likely to threaten the social goals of instrumentality and physical dominance. As an example, a boy threatening to beat up a peer unless he complies with a request has the potential to damage the victim's dominance status in the peer group. In contrast, girls are relatively more likely to focus on establishing intimate, dyadic relationships with peers (Block, 1983). Thus, we hypothesized that hostile acts that damage (or attempt to damage) close relationships and feelings of social inclusion would be highly effective, controlling, aversive acts for girls. For instance, a threat of ending a friendship unless a peer complies with a request is likely to be serious and upsetting to an individual who highly values relationships. We have labeled these behaviors relational aggression (for a review see Crick, Werner, Casas, O'Brien, Nelson, Grotpeter, & Markon, 1999). In contrast to physical aggression, in which the vehicle of harm is physical damage or intimidation, relationally aggressive acts use relationships as the instrument of harm (e.g., removing your own acceptance or friendship by giving someone the silent treatment; spreading nasty rumors about someone in an attempt to elicit rejection of the person by others).

Accumulating evidence demonstrates that a gender difference in aggression is minimized or disappears when relational aggression is assessed in addition to physical aggression. In contrast to the previously described male-weighted gender difference in physical aggression, relational aggression has been shown in numerous studies to be more prevalent among girls than boys, according to peer reports, teacher reports, self-reports, and naturalistic observations (e.g., Crick, 1997; Crick, Casas, & Mosher, 1997; Crick & Grotpeter, 1995; MacDonald & O'Laughlin, 1997; McNeilly-Choque, Hart, Robinson, Nelson, & Olsen, 1996). Additionally, when asked to describe the types of aggressive behaviors they observe among their peers, children cite physical aggression as the most frequent hostile event that occurs among boys and relational aggression as the most frequent hostile event among girls (Crick, Bigbee, & Howes, 1996). Finally, research on extreme groups of aggressive children has shown that boys and girls are identified as aggressive with almost equal frequency when relational aggression is assessed in addition to physical aggression (Crick & Grotpeter, 1995; Rys & Bear, 1997). Taken together, these studies provide relatively robust evidence to counter the view that girls and women are unaggressive.

Gender and Aggression: A Developmental Perspective

The differences between relational and physical aggression may be high-lighted when the two constructs are considered developmentally. Although research indicates that physical aggression decreases with age, we hypothesize that the incidence of relational aggression may actually increase with age. In addition, we believe that the types of relationally aggressive acts exhibited change as development progresses. In this section we discuss developmental differences in both the prevalence and the manifestations of relational versus physical aggression.

Surprisingly little is known about the frequency of occurrence of acts of relational aggression at different ages. It is likely that acts of relational aggression increase in frequency after early childhood, for two reasons: increased cognitive abilities and a more complex social world in which the child moves. In contrast to physical aggression, some acts of relational aggression require well-developed cognitive resources. Consider, for example, a young adolescent girl, Donika, who feels hurt because her best friend is spending a lot of time with a new girl in their class. Donika could try to damage her best friend's relationship with the new girl by telling her that the new girl is spreading rumors about her behind her back. Many factors, however, will influence whether this relationally aggressive act will be effective. Donika needs to tell her friend the story at a time when the friend feels vulnerable enough about her relationship with the new girl that she will believe the story, Donika needs to make sure the new girl seems credible enough as someone who would spread rumors, and she needs to tell the story to her friend in a sympathetic manner so that her true motives will not be discovered. Each of these factors requires insight into the workings of personal relationships, perspective taking, and timing. A younger girl might not have the cognitive capabilities to carry out this type of relationally aggressive act. In line with this hypothesis, the relationally aggressive acts of preschoolers typically involve relatively simplistic, directly confrontative behaviors that are enacted in the immediate moment and do not require complex cognitive abilities. For instance, relationally aggressive acts common among preschoolers include covering one's ears when a peer is talking to signal ignoring, and telling a peer that s/he will not be invited to one's birthday party unless s/he shares the toy (Crick, Casas & Ku, 1999).

Acts of relational aggression are also likely to become more common as the intensity and complexity of peer relationships increase with age during childhood and adolescence. Intimacy in friendships is found to increase in late childhood and adolescence, particularly for girls (see

Buhrmester & Prager, 1995, for a review), and intimate self-disclosure can effectively serve as ammunition for relational aggression. For instance, if a girl makes a negative comment about a popular girl to her friend, the friend could later threaten to tell the popular girl and the friends of the popular girl about the comment, which could lead to the first girl being ostracized by her more popular peers. Support for the idea that intimacy in a relationship can contribute to relational aggression in the relationship comes from a study of third through sixth graders' friendships (Grotpeter & Crick, 1996). In this study, relationally aggressive children were found to have friendships that were higher in intimacy than the friendships of other children and they also were shown to direct relationally aggressive behaviors toward their best friends. Relationally aggressive children may elicit high levels of self-disclosure from their friends in order to have power over them, and they may be particularly successful at eliciting self-disclosure during late childhood and adolescence, when the level of intimacy in girls' friendships is increasing overall.

The development of romantic relationships in late childhood and adolescence also adds to the complexity of the social world. During late childhood and adolescence, interaction with the opposite sex increases in frequency and importance (Blyth, Hill, & Thiel, 1982; Buhrmester & Furman, 1987; Montemayor & VanKomen, 1985), and by late adolescence (i.e., the college years) many individuals have formed close, long-lasting romantic relationships. The emergence of romantic relationships provides a new relationship context in which relational aggression can be exhibited and potentially contributes to an increase in the prevalence of relational aggression. In one study, for example, when undergraduate students were asked about how men and women aggress against others, relationally aggressive acts involving damaging romantic relationships, such as stealing a boyfriend or girlfriend or spreading a rumor to damage a romantic relationship, were frequently reported (Crick, Werner, & Shellin, 1998). This focus on romantic relationships is thought to emerge in late adolescence and adulthood because at this age, romantic relationships replace same-gender friendships as individuals' primary peer relationship (Crick, Werner, Casas, O'Brien, Nelson, Grotpeter, & Markon, 1999). One direction for future research is to identify whether there is a time in late childhood or adolescence when same-gender friendships are still primary but romantic relationships are developing, a time when children and adolescents would be particularly vulnerable to relationally aggressive acts.

The idea that acts of relational aggression may become more common during childhood and adolescence stands in stark contrast to research on physical aggression. Boys have been found to exhibit their highest levels of physical aggression when they are very young, and then these types of aggressive behavior decrease (see Coie & Dodge, 1998; Parke & Slaby, 1983, for reviews). A likely assumption is that physical aggression decreases because overtly aggressive acts are not tolerated in later childhood and adolescence. Because relational aggression can be subtle and is often covert, the societal pressures that lead to a decrease in physical aggression may not affect relational aggression. Contrary to the conclusion that aggression decreases with age, a finding based on research from a male-oriented perspective of aggression, additional research on relational aggression may reveal the opposite pattern of developmental differences in the prevalence of relational aggression (for research on developmental trends in the related constructs of indirect aggression, social aggression, and social alienation and ostracism during childhood and adolescence see Björkqvist, Lagerspetz, & Kaukiainen, 1992; Cairns, Cairns, Neckerman, Ferguson, & Gariepy, 1989; and Galen & Underwood, 1997).

If relational aggression does increase with age, this would also further call into question the conclusion that males are the more aggressive gender. If the prevalence of relational aggression, which is more typical of females, is increasing with age while the prevalence of physical aggression, which is more typical of males, is decreasing with age, then females might actually be the more aggressive gender in adolescence and adulthood. Even if males also become more relationally aggressive in adolescence and adulthood (this possibility is discussed below), females would likely be more skilled at relational aggression because relational aggression had been their modal form of aggression throughout their lives.

A final point to consider regarding the prevalence of relational and physical aggression over the life span is whether males might adopt a more female style of aggression in late adolescence and adulthood as a result of increased interaction with women, particularly in romantic relationships. Although some men are physically aggressive toward women, as evidenced by the prevalence of male-perpetrated partner abuse and date rape in the United States, many men may look for alternative ways to be aggressive toward their romantic partners (and other women in their lives), owing to the strong sanctions against men physically aggressing toward women. Additionally, some males may learn a lot about how relational aggression works through their relationships with females. For instance, they may learn about relational aggression because they are the targets of relational aggression, such as when their partners give them the cold shoulder. Also, when a man's partner is distressed about being a victim of relational aggression from a third party, the man may be motivated to understand what happened and why it was upsetting. Future research should address whether adult men manifest the same aggressive behaviors as those of adult females.

Where Do We Go from Here? Other Topics in Need of Gender-Balanced Research

In this section we first examine how a gender-balanced approach to the study of aggression may require expansion into other, related research areas (e.g., the precursors of aggression). Next, we give examples of how examining aggression from the female perspective could reverse some long-held beliefs in social-emotional development. Finally, we suggest areas of social-emotional development in which the male perspective has been understudied.

Where Else Might a Gender-Balanced Study Approach to Aggression Lead?

Study of relational aggression may lead to new pathways of inquiry in several ways. Specifically, adequate understanding of the development of relationally aggressive behaviors may involve identifying antecedents, correlates, and outcomes that have not been included in past studies that focused on physical aggression. For example, studies of family socialization practices indicate that the coercive, highly conflictual, and nonaffectionate family patterns that often characterize the homes of physically aggressive children (for a review see Coie & Dodge, 1998) are not particularly descriptive of the family relationships of relationally aggressive children, whose family relationships are instead more likely to be overly close and enmeshed (Grotpeter & Crick, 1998). Additionally, studies of the adjustment status of relationally aggressive children have demonstrated that, although they experience many of the same problems as physically aggressive children (such as peer rejection and externalizing difficulties), they also have other difficulties that have not been assessed in most studies of aggression, including borderline personality features and bulimic eating patterns (for a review see Crick, Werner, Casas, O'Brien, Nelson, Grotpeter, & Markon, 1999). The adjustment correlates of relational but not physical aggression include adjustment problems that are more typical of females than males.

Consideration of the interactional components of relational aggression has led to the study not only of relationally aggressive children, but also of the children who are the targets of relational aggression. Like physically victimized children, relationally victimized children are at risk for social-emotional maladjustment (e.g., depression, loneliness, peer rejection; Crick & Bigbee, 1998; Crick, Casas, & Ku, 1999; Crick & Grotpeter, 1996). More important, since girls are more relationally victimized than boys, this research has contributed to our understanding of the peer maltreatment experiences of girls by documenting the salience of this form of victimization. This is significant as, like past research on aggression, past research on peer victimization focused largely on boys.

Thus far this subsection has looked at the impact of the study of relational aggression on the identification and study of social developmental constructs related to relational aggression. However, further consideration of the perspective of girls and women may also lead to new avenues of inquiry in the study of physical aggression. Although males have convincingly been shown to be more *physically* aggressive than females overall, it is important to remember that some females are also highly physically aggressive. The antecedents and consequences may be similar in many ways for physically aggressive girls and boys, but there may also be important differences that were overlooked in earlier studies. Greater attention to the female perspective (largely lacking in past research and theory) may reveal new developmental processes that are more salient for physically aggressive girls than for physically aggressive boys. An example is the recent research on social information processing (SIP) and aggression.

Numerous SIP studies have demonstrated a significant association between biased SIP patterns and physical aggression. These studies have focused primarily on children's processing of social cues in provocation situations that involve conflicts of an instrumental nature (e.g., someone takes your spot in line; for a review see Crick & Dodge, 1994). However, recent research in which the female perspective was considered has shown that, although instrumental conflicts are highly salient for boys, girls are more likely to be provoked by conflicts of a relational nature (e.g., not getting invited to an important party or activity; Crick, 1995; Crick, Grotpeter, & Bigbee, 1998). Interestingly, physically aggressive girls have been shown to exhibit maladaptive SIP patterns in response to *both* instrumental and relational conflicts, whereas the maladaptive SIP patterns of physically aggressive boys appear to be activated by instrumental conflicts (Crick & Werner, 1998). It seems likely that aggressive girls' difficulties with rela-

tional conflicts would not have been identified through the more traditional, male-based avenues of study. Without the assessment of SIP in
response to relational conflicts, the SIP biases of physically aggressive
girls would look comparable to those of physically aggressive boys—that
is, both would exhibit biases for instrumental conflicts only. Future
research utilizing a gender-balanced approach to the study of other "similarities" between physically aggressive boys and girls seems warranted.

What Aspects of Social-Emotional Development Might Benefit from Greater Attention to the Female Perspective?

Aggression is only one of the many areas of social-emotional development
that might benefit from a gender-balanced approach that begins with the
perspective of girls and women. Another verity that needs reexamination
is that development involves becoming more individualistic, autonomous,
and separate from others with age. According to Erikson's theory of the
development of the self (1963), for instance, the developmental crises that
need to resolved from about age one to about age twenty include establishing autonomy, developing initiative, becoming industrious, and developing an identity (a view that typifies the Western European ideal). Cross
and Madson (1997) recently questioned, however, whether the view of the
self as an *independent* self is as applicable to females as it is to males (for a
similar point see Gilligan, 1982). Based on research that finds cultural
variability in individuals' self-construals (Markus & Kitayama, 1991; Triandis, 1989), Cross and Madson proposed that women's self-construals are
more *inter*dependent than *in*dependent because women frequently define
themselves in terms of their relationships with others (this perspective is
also widely held by both men and women in some cultures, such as Asian;
see Shweder, Goodnow, Hatano, LeVine, Markus, & Miller, 1998, for a
review). Cross and Madson's argument illustrates at a very basic level how
different some aspects of our understanding of social-emotional development might look were the theories developed based on the experiences of
girls and women.

The effect of studying social-emotional development from a female
perspective would also be felt in research on the relation between gender
role orientation and self-esteem, which has generally supported the masculinity model. In other words, the studies usually find masculinity to be
related to self-esteem more strongly than femininity is related to self-

esteem (for reviews see M. C. Taylor & Hall, 1982; Whitley, 1983). These findings may turn up, however, because global self-esteem measures do not tap the areas of self-esteem that are particularly important to girls and women (Cook, 1985; Rose & Montemayor, 1994; Whitley, 1983). Evidence for this view comes from a study of high school and college-age students in which femininity was found to be related more strongly than masculinity to certain areas of self-concept, including having high-quality relations with parents, perceiving oneself as honest and reliable, and feeling positively about one's religious and spiritual beliefs (Marsh & Byrne, 1991). Future research should focus on identifying additional areas of self-esteem, such as self-esteem regarding communicating, being empathetic, and caretaking, that are particularly important to girls and women and are likely to be related to femininity.

Another topic that could be reexamined from the female perspective involves understanding delinquent behavior in girls. Most research on delinquency has focused on boys; much less is known about girls' delinquent behavior (Campbell, 1980, 1990; Chesney-Lind, 1989; for an important exception see the work of Giordano and colleagues, e.g., Giordano, Cernkovich, & Pugh, 1986). In fact, theories regarding the developmental pathways to delinquent behavior that highlight the role of inconsistent, coercive parenting, academic failure, and association with deviant peers (Patterson, DeBaryshe, & Ramsey, 1989) were largely based on studies involving only boys (e.g., Patterson, 1986; Patterson, Dishion, & Bank, 1984) and may not be as applicable to girls. Empirical support for this idea comes from a recent longitudinal study in which McFayden-Ketchum, Bates, Dodge, and Pettit (1996) found that coercive parenting, assessed prior to the child's entrance into kindergarten, predicted increases in physical aggression for boys from kindergarten to third grade but predicted *decreases* in aggression for girls.

In contrast to the framework posited by Patterson and colleagues, Chesney-Lind (1989) proposed a feminist model of female delinquency that is based on the exploitation of young girls' sexuality. She argues that many young girls run away from home because they are victims of sexual abuse. Often, these girls either are convicted in juvenile court (running away from home is a status offense) and returned to their abusive homes or they are forced to survive on the streets, which frequently involves prostitution. Research on delinquent girls is needed to test this feminist model of delinquency. In addition, when trying to identify precursors of female delinquency, researchers should pay attention to problem behaviors that are more typical of girls than boys. For instance, relational aggression has been shown to significantly predict some aspects of antisocial personality features (e.g., engagement in illegal activities) for women, but not for men (Werner & Crick, in press).

What Aspects of Social-Emotional Development Might Benefit from Greater Attention to the Male Perspective?

This chapter has dealt primarily with the importance of examining social-emotional development from a female perspective. In working toward a gender-balanced view of developmental psychology, however, the importance of paying attention to both the female and the male perspective cannot be overstated. Considering both perspectives not only enriches our understanding of the phenomenon under study but may also lead to the discovery of new concomitants of social-emotional development.

For some aspects of social-emotional development, our knowledge is limited because the male perspective has not received enough attention. An example is research on children's early relationships, which until recently focused almost entirely on children's attachment relationships with their mothers. This is unfortunate, because research that has included fathers indicates that children do have attachment relationships with their fathers (e.g., Belsky & Rovine, 1987; Lamb, Hwang, Frodi, & Frodi, 1982; Main & Weston, 1981) and that fathers'sensitive interaction with their children is predictive of secure father-child attachment relationships (Cox, Owen, Henderson, & Margand, 1992). Future research should address the social-emotional outcomes for children with secure versus insecure attachment relationships with their fathers.

Another area in social-emotional development that bears more consideration from a male perspective is children's friendships. Research has consistently found girls' friendships to involve more intimate self-disclosure than boys' friendships (e.g., Bigelow, 1977; Bukowski, Hoza, & Boivin, 1994; Parker & Asher, 1993), and it is sometimes assumed, based on these findings, that girls' friendships are closer relationships than boys' friendships. This assumption should be challenged, however, insofar as boys report as much satisfaction with their friendships as girls do (Furman & Buhrmester, 1985; Parker & Asher, 1993). In fact, some researchers have moved toward a gender-balanced approach to studying friendships by proposing that boys develop close relationships through processes other than intimate self-disclosure (Buhrmester & Furman, 1987; Rose & Asher, 1999). For instance, being an available and interesting companion may be particularly important for boys' friendships.

In exploring future directions for understanding boys' social-emotional development, we have focused on studying traditionally female-oriented constructs from a male perspective (e.g., studying fathers' role as caregivers). However, given the large within-gender variation that typically exists for most social-psychological constructs, it seems likely that assessing typically male-oriented constructs from a female perspective could also enhance our understanding of boys. We have found this to be the case for relational aggression. For example, in a recent study of the association between aggression and social-psychological adjustment it was shown that, although relationally aggressive children of both genders were significantly more maladjusted than their nonaggressive peers, relationally aggressive boys were significantly more maladjusted than relationally aggressive girls (Crick, 1997). Moreover, research on the friendships of relationally aggressive children showed that relationally aggressive boys, but not girls, had significantly fewer mutual friendships than nonaggressive children (Grotpeter & Crick, 1996). These findings indicate that relational aggression, a construct assessed in these studies in an attempt to understand better the social development of aggressive girls, may also enhance our knowledge of an important subset of aggressive boys. They also point to the potentially detrimental impact of behaving in a non-gender-normative manner (Crick, 1997). Finally, these studies highlight the importance of gender balance in recruiting research participants and in assessment methodologies, issues discussed in the next section.

Methods for Gender-Balanced Research on Social-Emotional Development

In working toward a gender-balanced understanding of social-emotional development, researchers will need to carefully examine their research methods. Methodological limitations in previous research have contributed to a number of gender-biased views of social-emotional development. In this section we examine how methodological constraints can contribute to a gender-biased view of social-emotional development, and we provide suggestions for conducting gender-balanced research.

The most obvious methodological flaw that can bias the conclusions of research has been the failure to include both female and male research participants and to view constructs from both male and female perspectives. Studies of aggression that include only boys eliminate the possibility of discovering forms of aggression that are more typical of girls. It will be important in future studies to remember this limitation and to refrain from introducing a similar bias by focusing solely on the female perspective (i.e., by failing to include boys and men in research or by studying social-emotional constructs from a female perspective only).

To gain a deeper understanding of the diverse experiences of girls and women, it will also be vital to conduct research with participants from different ethnic backgrounds and socioeconomic status groups. Much of our knowledge about developmental psychology is based on research with white, middle-class samples. This is unfortunate, for the experiences of girls and women are not uniform across ethnic and social class groupings. In our own research we have made a concerted effort to obtain diverse samples whenever possible. For example, in a study of relational aggression (Crick & Grotpeter, 1995), the sample included schools from a largely working-class town and comprised approximately 40 percent African-American children. In this study and others, we found that relational aggression is not unique to white, middle-class girls (or boys). These findings are consistent with work by Goodwin (1990, 1997), who has shown that African-American girls in a working-class neighborhood engage in "he said, she said" disputes that involve acts of relational aggression. In addition, recent cross-cultural work on relational aggression has demonstrated that children in China, Italy, Russia, and Germany exhibit relational aggression in their peer interactions (for a review see Crick, Werner, Casas, O'Brien, Nelson, Grotpeter, & Markon, 1999). One limitation of these studies is that they have employed measures of relational aggression that were developed for use in the United States. Thus, research is needed to determine whether there are differences in the ways in which relational aggression is manifested in other cultures and subcultures. Research of this type is also needed with other ethnic groups in the United States, where research on minorities has been largely limited to African-Americans.

Adopting a bottom-up approach to understanding the experiences of girls and women will also be important for conducting gender-balanced research. Cultural psychologists argue that we cannot gain a true understanding of different cultures simply by applying theories and methods developed with one culture (usually European-American) to other cultures, and therefore that we should work toward a better understanding of the experiences and practices of a culture before developing theories and methods for research with that culture (Fisher, Jackson, & Villarruel, 1998; R. A. Shweder et al., 1998). This reasoning is also relevant for studying girls' experiences in areas such as aggression and delinquency, where the research has largely focused on boys. That is, it is important that we do not simply apply to female development theories and methods that were developed for research on boys. Instead, research methods should be used that will allow us to better understand the experiences of girls and women in order to develop accurate hypotheses about female development.

Ethnographic research methods could prove useful for generating hypotheses about female social-emotional development (see Fisher et al., 1998, for a discussion of how qualitative research can be used to guide quantitative research). Participant observation enables the researcher to discover subtle as well as overt processes within a group and to understand the meaning of those processes for the participants (Corsaro, 1996). In terms of better understanding girls' experiences, the rich ethnographic work on the elementary- and middle-school culture by Eder (1985), Thorne (1986), and Schofield (1981) could provide a useful grounding for future research on issues relevant to early adolescent girls, including gossip, popularity, teasing about boys, and issues involving weight and appearance.

In addition to participant observation, naturalistic observation could be useful for better understanding processes involved in female social-emotional development. However, in understanding girls' experiences, it will be vital to use observational methods that allow researchers to hear girls' conversations. Several studies have found that girls spend more time than boys in social conversation with their peers (Ladd, 1983; Moller, Hymel, & Rubin, 1992; Omark et al., 1975), but social conversation is not a unitary construct. The girls could be talking about day-to-day activities, revealing intimate secrets, or even being relationally aggressive. In fact, one reason why physical aggression probably received more attention initially than relational aggression is that physical aggression, although relatively rare, is straightforward to observe when it occurs and, for the most part, does not require audio recordings. In contrast, techniques that enable researchers to hear conversations would be vital for valid observation of relational aggression.

Another way in which researchers can be guided by the actual experiences of the girls in developing their theories and methods is by conducting interviews eliciting open-ended responses from participants. In our own research we have relied on this type of interview in the early phases of work with a new age group, a new context, or a new construct. For instance, interviews were always conducted before we developed measures of relational aggression for a particular age group (e.g., preschoolers, children, adolescents/adults; see Crick, Bigbee, & Howes, 1996; Crick, Casas, & Mosher, 1997; Morales, Crick, Werner, & Shellin, 1999, for examples and further discussion of this issue). In these interviews, we asked participants (in an age-appropriate manner) to describe the "mean" (i.e., aggressive) behaviors that are most typical of their peers. Content analyses were then used to identify categories of responses (e.g., physical aggression, verbal insults, relational aggression). It was largely through these interviews that we gained confidence in the salience of relational aggression to our research participants (because relationally aggressive behaviors were cited quite frequently), and that we captured the various manifestations of relational aggression at different developmental periods. In addition to interviews with children, we have also found that talking with adults, including parents, teachers, and day care providers, about children's experiences can be helpful, because of adults' greater cognitive abilities and their often more complex insight into interpersonal relationships.

Finally, in conducting gender-balanced research, it is important to be open to the perspectives of scholars in different fields. The interest among researchers in such fields as anthropology and women's studies in understanding the diverse experiences of individuals has resulted in many well-developed ideas about the experiences of girls and women. Developmentalists should take advantage of this research in formulating their own hypotheses about female social-emotional development. Formats need to be created for scholars from these different fields to share ideas, and scholars in each field need to look critically and nondefensively at their own assumptions and methods.

Summary

Our discussion of relational aggression demonstrates that adding a female perspective to a social-emotional construct that was previously defined according to the experiences of boys and men is a multilevel process. Following this process is likely to result in significant changes in our understanding of the definition, description, and explanation of the development of aggressive behavior patterns (and other social-emotional constructs). Understanding aggression from a female perspective involves, first, taking the experiences of girls and women as a starting point, rather than viewing the experiences of boys and men as the norm. Identifying the types of aggression that are more typical of girls, however, is not sufficient for a complete understanding of aggression from a female perspective. It is important to examine developmental differences rather than simply assume parallel developmental trajectories for girls and boys. Finally, research on relational aggression suggests the importance of identifying precursors and outcomes that are theoretically relevant for girls rather than studying just the precursors and outcomes that have been shown to be important for physical aggression. It seems clear that the collective future research agenda should include a more gender-balanced perspective, an approach that holds great promise for increasing our understanding of the social-emotional development of both genders.

Acknowledgments

Preparation of this chapter was supported by a FIRST award from the National Institute of Mental Health (No.MH53524) and a Faculty Scholars Award from the William T. Grant Foundation to the first author, and by a Doctoral Dissertation Completion Fellowship from the University of Illinois at Urbana-Champaign to the second author.

Gender Essentialism

in Cognitive Development

Susan A. Gelman and Marianne G. Taylor

In May 1998, *Newsweek* published a cover story entitled "Boys Will Be Boys" (Kantrowitz & Kalb, 1998). The writers noted that boys are different from girls in a number of respects, both obvious and subtle. They posited biological roots to these differences. They speculated that these differences are universal and difficult (if not impossible) to alter. They framed research findings in terms of broad generalizations ("Boys..."), without circumscribing the claims either by noting confounding factors (e.g., "White, middle-class boys ages ten to 12 who were raised in the Midwest...") or by noting exceptions (e.g., "56 percent of the boys in this sample..."). One of the most interesting things about this article was how the authors treated gender (in this case, differences between boys and girls) from an essentialist perspective.

Essentialism is the view that categories have an underlying reality or true nature that one cannot observe directly but that gives an object its identity (Gelman & Hirschfeld, 1999; Locke, 1894/1959; S. P. Schwartz, 1977). In other words, according to essentialism, categories are real, in several senses: they are discovered (versus invented), they are natural (versus artificial), they predict other properties, and they point to natural discontinuities in the world. Essentialism requires no specialized knowledge, and people may possess an "essence placeholder" without knowing what the essence is (Medin, 1989). For example, a child might believe that girls have some inner, nonobvious quality that distinguishes them from boys and that is responsible for the many observable differences in appearance and behavior between boys and girls, before ever learning about chromosomes or human physiology. Although numerous feminist scholars have noted and discussed the errors and perils of essentialist thinking (e.g.,

Bohan, 1993), essentialism persists throughout a number of disciplines, arguably including feminist theory itself (e.g., Belenky, Clinchy, Goldberger, & Tarule, 1986; Chodorow, 1978; Fuss, 1989; Gilligan, 1982; but see Gilligan, 1986; Goldberger, Tarule, Clinchy, & Belenky, 1996, for the argument that such theories are not essentialist).[1]

In this chapter, we focus not on the accuracy (or inaccuracy) of essentialist accounts of gender but rather on why essentialist accounts are so ubiquitous. We argue that essentialism is a powerful explanatory device in human reasoning, evident as early as preschool age, and that essentialist construals of gender also emerge early. As evidence, we review recent experimental studies of children's early concepts, suggesting that essentialism is an early reasoning bias that emerges spontaneously in young children. The persistence of essentialism in adulthood may be traced to its developmental antecedents.

The chapter is in three sections. First, we explain what an essentialist view of gender entails and why it is often argued to be problematic. Next, we review the ongoing literature on essentialist construals of gender in children. We end by discussing the implications of essentialism for gender concepts, the study of gender, and the study of development.

Essentialism and Feminist Theory

To begin, it is crucial to distinguish metaphysical from psychological claims. Metaphysical essentialism is a set of claims regarding the world. In the case of gender, these claims concern the true (objective, measurable, reality-based) nature of males and females. In contrast, psychological essentialism is a set of claims regarding human belief systems—how people represent and understand gender. When studying social concepts, it is not possible to separate altogether metaphysical from psychological claims, because with gender (as with any social category) people's representations feed back into and influence reality (e.g., the belief that girls are more nurturing might lead people to provide more opportunities for girls to nurture others, and thus for girls to become in fact more nurturing). Nonetheless, psychological essentialism and metaphysical essentialism are at least somewhat separable. Indeed, as we will argue, there are powerful psychological tendencies for children (and adults) to be essentialist regarding gender, even though many of the metaphysical claims regarding gender essentialism are overstated. Indeed, even essentialism of animal species is somewhat inaccurate (see also Dupré, 1993; Mayr, 1982, 1991; Sober, 1994), though pervasive in human thought (Gelman & Hirschfeld, 1999). This section focuses on the metaphysical claims; the following section turns to psychological claims.

Characterizing Gender Essentialism

Gender essentialism has been characterized in several distinct ways in the literature. Spelman (1988) notes "a tendency in dominant Western feminist thought to posit an essential 'womanness' that all women have and share in common despite the racial, class, religious, ethnic, and cultural differences among us" (p. ix). This essentializing focuses on a subset of women (namely, white middle-class women) as representative of all women, thus universalizing what is in fact diverse. It also fosters treating male and female as mutually exclusive (e.g., Markman, 1989)—what Tavris (1992) calls "the habit of seeing women and men as two opposite categories" (p. 55). Thus, two largely overlapping distributions (e.g., in males' versus females' math SAT scores) are erroneously conceptualized as nonoverlapping (Tavris, 1992, pp. 41–42). Likewise, Spelman (1988) notes that essentializing women leads to treating gender identity as distinct from race and class identity, and leads to "the assumption behind contrasting the situation of 'women' with (for example) the situation of 'Blacks' or 'Jews' " (p. x). Likewise, Hare-Mustin and Marecek (1988) note that gender differences are often exaggerated (which they term alpha bias).

Bem (1993) views gender essentialism as a form of *biological* essentialism in which sexual differences and inequalities are viewed "as the natural and inevitable consequences of the intrinsic biological nature of women and men" (p. 2). Thus, socially constructed differences are "naturalized." In other words, essentialism assumes that gender and gender-linked properties are *discovered* (rather than invented; Hare- Mustin & Marecek, 1988). Bem does not deny the reality of biological differences between men and women, but nonetheless argues "that these facts have no fixed meaning independent of the way that a culture interprets and uses them, nor any social implications independent of their historical and contemporary context" (pp. 2–3). Gender essentialism is, in Bem's view, dangerous in part because it is an implicit ("hidden") assumption that shapes not only "how people perceive, conceive, and discuss social reality, but because they are embedded in social institutions, they also shape the more material things—like unequal pay and inadequate day care—that constitute social reality itself" (p. 2).

Hare-Mustin and Marecek (1988) contrast essentialism with a constructivist stance: "The current interest in constructivism and deconstruction is part of a widespread skepticism about the positivist tradition in science and essentialist theories of truth and meaning (Rorty, 1979). Both constructivism and deconstruction assert that meanings are historically situated and constructed and reconstructed through the medium of language" (p. 455). Similarly, Bohan (1993) views essentialism as a model in which gender qualities are viewed as inherent (versus socially constructed). In other words, an essentialist would view gendered properties as *belonging to* or *residing in* an individual, as contrasted with a constructivist view, in which the properties are the outcome of person-context interactions.

The various definitions sketched out above, though not identical, share a family resemblance. One can consider essentialism as a range of models toward one end of a theoretical continuum (table 1). On one end, the essentialist end, gender-typed properties are inherent in an individual by virtue of biology and hence are unalterable. As a consequence, gender categories encourage many gender-based generalizations (what we will refer to as "high inductive potential"), one can readily generalize over the entire gender category and ignore differences within a category, and the two gender categories are mutually exclusive. On the other end, properties are a product of the social interaction (rather than residing "in" the individual).[2] On the nonessentialist end, gender categories are relatively weak in their inductive potential, there are important differences within a gender category, and there are important similarities across gender categories, resulting in two largely overlapping functions. One can be more or less essentialist by adhering more or less strongly to the essentialist end of one or more of these dimensions.

Table 1. Essentialist versus nonessentialist positions regarding the nature of gender differences

Essentialist	Nonessentialist
Discovered	Invented
Biological	Social
Inherent in individual	Product of social interaction
Unalterable	Easily changed
Enduring	Transient
High inductive potential	Low inductive potential
Nonobvious/underlying differences	Superficial differences
Universal	Individual
Mutually exclusive traits	Overlapping traits
Alpha bias (exaggerating male-female differences)	Beta bias (minimizing differences)

Evaluating Gender Essentialism

Although some scholars find essentialism philosophically neutral (Fuss, 1989) or even positive in giving voice and value to women's own experiences (Gilligan, 1982), others are emphatically negative about the implications of essentialism for feminism. Bohan (1993) argues that essentialism is problematic in several respects, both empirical and political. On the empirical side, essentialism is vulnerable to universalizing assumptions, in which properties of women are erroneously viewed as timeless, universal, and "natural" rather than the consequence of social, historical, and political forces. Moreover, essentialism fosters an inappropriate tendency to contrast male and female, according to which that which is female cannot be male and that which is male cannot be female (Tavris, 1992). As Bohan notes, "It is but a short step from affirming women's ways of being to disclaiming for women all other modes" (p. 11). Finally, there are methodological limitations and failures to replicate particular essentialist theories (see, e.g., Kerber, Greeno, Maccoby, Luria, Stack, & Gilligan, 1986).

Bohan also notes several political dangers of essentialism. Perhaps most obviously, essentialist accounts contribute to a "deficiency model" of women. When men and women are encouraged to occupy separate spheres of activities and role, this serves to legitimize and reinforce the model of women as possessing devalued qualities. Furthermore, by attributing women's oppression to inherent qualities, the implication is that change must rest with individual women (rather than with systems). This is a form of victim blaming.

There is continuing controversy as to how apt essentializing assumptions are. Almost all theorists would agree, however, that folk theories of gender exaggerate whatever differences there are (e.g., Caplan, MacPherson, & Tobin, 1985; Hyde, Fennema, & Lamon, 1990; Kinsbourne, 1980; Maccoby & Jacklin, 1974).[3] Moreover, doing so comes at a political cost for women. So why do people (both women and men) essentialize gender? We turn to this in the next section.

Psychological Essentialism and Gender

Children provide an important opportunity to examine the source of essentialist tendencies. Because children have little scientific knowledge and are less directly informed regarding Western philosophical traditions, they provide a measure of early reasoning biases that are relatively less influenced by complex cultural belief systems. (This is not to deny, however, the potential influence of language and culture on children's essentializing.) Furthermore, because children have a strong tendency to focus on overt, obvious, perceptual qualities, evidence for essentializing in children can be considered relatively powerful evidence for this as an early reasoning bias.

Recent research with young children is finding that essentializing tendencies—including minimizing within-group differences, exaggerating between-group differences, forming nativist theories, and discounting social constructivist theories—are early emerging. Most of the available research has focused on children's concepts of biological kinds (primarily animal species). By age two and one-half years, children hold essentialist beliefs about animal categories. They expect category members to share nonobvious similarities even in the face of salient perceptual dissimilarities. For example, on learning that an atypical exemplar is a member of a category (e.g., that a flamingo is a bird), children and adults draw novel inferences from typical instances to the atypical member (e.g., from a blackbird to a flamingo; Gelman & Markman, 1986). By age four, children judge nonvisible internal parts to be especially crucial to the identity and functioning of an item. Children also treat category membership as stable and unchanging over transformations such as costumes, growth, or metamorphosis (Gelman, Coley, & Gottfried, 1994; Keil, 1989).

Finally, children often treat species-characteristic properties as being innately determined at birth and unlikely to change with changing environmental conditions (such as adoption; Gelman & Wellman, 1991; Hirschfeld, 1996; Springer, 1996). For example, when given thought experiments in which they need to consider whether nurture or nature is more predictive of how an animal will grow, preschool children weight nature more heavily (e.g., reporting that pigs raised by goats will look and act more like pigs than like goats; in other words, they have an inborn quality that determines their appearance and behavior). In short, psychological essentialism has at least three manifestations: (1) members are viewed as alike across diverse instances of the category, (2) properties are thought to remain stable over time and over transformations, and (3) properties are considered to have innate origins.

Evidence from Gender Concepts

Analogously, several studies suggest that an essentialist bias appears to shape children's expectations about gender. We review evidence of three types: inductive potential, exaggerating group differences, and nativist theories. We then consider children's difficulty on tasks tapping their understanding of gender constancy, an apparent exception that is actually compatible with essentialism.

Inductive Potential. One essentialist implication is that entities from the same category are alike in hidden, nonobvious ways. Thus, a new property learned about one category member is often assumed to hold true for other members of the category. As noted above, children expect animal categories to have this structure very early. Two items from same category (e.g., a blackbird and a flamingo) are assumed to share novel properties (e.g., diet, bone structure), despite their dissimilar appearances (Gelman & Markman, 1986). Even when children do not initially realize that both a flamingo and a blackbird are birds, for example, language readily conveys this implication to children as young as age two and one-half years (Gelman & Coley, 1990). Thus, the category name is especially important for conveying category membership and inductive potential.

This assumption of a link between naming and inductive potential also holds true for gender categories, for both adults and children. Martin (1989) reports that adults readily make a wide range of sex-differentiated inferences (regarding physical characteristics, role behaviors, occupations, and traits) on the basis of a person's sex, even when provided with no additional information beyond that the person is male or female. Children also make stereotypic judgments about others even when all they know is their sex (Berndt & Heller, 1986). For example, they assume that an unknown girl would find feminine toys interesting even when no information is available about the girl's actual toy preferences.

Even more striking, children assume that gender categories have inductive potential even when perceptual appearances run counter to a character's gender identity. Gelman, Collman, and Maccoby (1986) conducted a study in which preschool children learned new properties for specific boys and girls and were asked to say which property a new child would have, given a gender label that conflicted with the child's appearance. For example, on one item set, children saw a typical girl, a typical boy, and a boy with long hair (who resembled the girl). They were told the gender category of each picture ("girl," "boy," "boy"), and then learned, of the typical girl and boy, that they had "estro" and "andro" in their blood, respectively. The key question was what the third child (the boy who resembled the girl) would have inside his blood. Children inferred many sex-linked properties on the basis of category membership, ignoring conflicting perceptual information (e.g., inferring that the boy with long hair would have andro in his blood). Specifically, 81 percent of children's inferences were based on gender category information, and only 19 percent of their inferences were based on perceptual similarity. Thus, four-year-old children assume that the gender categories "girl" and "boy" indicate nonobvious properties that extend beyond surface perceptual cues.

Exaggerating Group Differences. There are at least four ways that children exaggerate gender group differences. First, children often deny or misremember anomalies, such as a female firefighter. This can be seen in children's memory errors (reviewed in Liben & Signorella, 1987), in their absolute responses (e.g., claiming that only boys can do a certain activity; Berndt & Heller, 1986; Martin, 1989), and in their assumption that cross-gender roles are mutually exclusive (e.g., that one cannot be both a mother and a doctor; Deák & Maratsos, 1998; Florian, 1995; Saltz & Medow, 1971).

Second, even when children come to accept such anomalies, they view them as affectively negative, and at times even morally wrong (Levy, Taylor, & Gelman, 1995). Levy et al. assessed traditional and evaluative aspects of flexibility regarding gender-role transgressions in four-year-olds, eight-year-olds, and undergraduates. Although participants became increasingly flexible with age on traditional measures (i.e., who *can* do X, and cultural relativity), participants in *all* age groups were consistently negative in evaluating masculine gender-role transgressions (e.g., a boy who wears dresses), reporting that they would not like to be friends with such a person, that the behavior is bad, and that they would be surprised and disgusted on seeing the behavior. Some children even reported, on open-ended questions, that they would act aggressively if they encountered the transgressor (e.g., "I'd kick the dress off").

The third way that children exaggerate gender-group differences is by treating males and females as opposites. Specifically, children use knowledge of what girls will do to predict the opposite for boys (and vice versa). Martin, Eisenbud, and Rose (1995) found that four- and five-year-old children use knowledge of whether a toy is "for girls" or "for boys" to guide their toy preferences and their inferences regarding the toy preferences of other children. Specifically, children were presented with a series of novel toys and asked to rate their own liking and that of girls and boys. Martin et al. found a "gender-centric" pattern that they characterize as follows (p. 1468): "what I like, peers of my sex will like; what I like, peers of the other sex will not like." For example, in one study, the absolute difference between own liking and other-sex liking was more than double the absolute difference between own liking and same-sex liking. Likewise, correlations of liking scores across toys were higher between own and own-sex liking (.77 for the girls, .87 for the boys) than between own liking and other-sex liking (.18 for the girls, .12 for the boys). As Martin et al. conclude, "Children and adults seem to develop abstract theories about gender that go beyond the explicit gender knowledge that they have been given. Their abstract gender theories seem to be of two forms. One form is a theory of group *differences:* what one sex likes, the other does not. The other form is a theory of within-gender-group *similarity:* what a person of one sex likes, other people of the same sex also will like" (p. 1468).

In an interesting extension, Martin et al. conducted a follow-up study that manipulated the gender appropriateness of toys by means of gender labels (e.g., "this is a toy girls really like"). One researcher labeled the toys; a second researcher asked children for their liking ratings. As expected, children preferred toys that were labeled for their own sex. Moreover, even attractive toys were judged as less attractive when labeled for the other sex. As Martin et al. put it (p. 1470), "explicit gender labels ... [make] even very attractive toys lose some of their appeal when labeled as being for the other sex."

A fourth way that children exaggerate within-group similarity is by means of natural language. Specifically, even young children produce *generic noun phrases* to refer to a category as an abstract whole (Carlson & Pelletier, 1995). For example, compare the generic statement "*girls* play with dolls" with the nongeneric statement "*those girls* are playing with dolls." In the first statement, and in contrast to the second, "girls" refers to the abstract set of girls in general. Furthermore, generics typically refer to qualities that are relatively essential (nonaccidental), enduring (not transient), and timeless (not contextually bound) (Lyons, 1977). Use of a generic thus implies that a category is a coherent, stable entity. In English, generic noun phrases are expressed with bare plurals (e.g., "*Bats* live in caves"), definite singulars (e.g., "*The elephant* is found in Africa and Asia"), or indefinite articles (e.g., "*A male goose* is called a gander"), and are accompanied by present-tense verbs.

Unlike utterances containing universal quantifiers such as *all, every,* or *each,* generic statements allow for exceptions. Whereas even a single counterexample would negate the generalization "all boys play with trucks," the generic statement "boys play with trucks" can persist in the face of counterexamples. Thus, the dual nature of generics (as attributed to most members of a category but robust against counterevidence) may mean that properties expressed with generics will be particularly persistent in children's developing knowledge systems.

Furthermore, generics may foster greater category coherence, even when the properties expressed have minimal informational content. Bigler (1995) has found that for children in elementary school, reference to gender dichotomies leads to increased stereotyping, even when teachers simply note the categories without making reference to gender stereotypes or distinctive properties. Similarly, we predict that reference to a gender category in generic form (e.g., "I wonder if *girls* can do this") may highlight the coherence of the category for young children, even when no information about shared properties is conveyed.

Despite long-standing linguistic interest in the semantics of generic noun phrases (Carlson & Pelletier, 1995; Dahl, 1975; McCawley, 1981), scholars have only just begun to examine how they are used in actual speech or how they guide children's reasoning (e.g., Gelman, Coley, Rosengren, Hartman, & Pappas, 1998; Pappas & Gelman, 1998). None of the available work has focused specifically on gender categories. However, preliminary evidence suggests that this will be a promising direction to look for essentialist language in the future. Initial analyses of longitudinal data of eight children's speech (from the CHILDES database; see MacWhinney & Snow, 1990, for a description of the database) reveal that children spontaneously produce gender generics as early as two and one-half years of age (Gelman, Rodriguez, Nguyen, & Koenig, 1997). Indeed, of the generic noun phrases that three- and four-year-old children produced about people, roughly one-fourth concerned gender (Gelman et al., 1997). These included utterances such as the following:

> "That shirt's not for girls."
>
> "Girls need girl kitties and boys need boy kitties."
>
> "Because I hate brothers."
>
> "Daddies like every cheese, right?"

It is interesting to note that a good many of children's gender generics were overstated or inaccurate, thus implying that these young children are exaggerating gender differences that they encounter, and are forming general rule-like statements about differences that are only probabilistic. It will be useful in future research to explore what information about gender is conveyed in parents' and children's generics, how use of gender generics changes over development, and how children interpret gender generics that they hear from others.

Nativist Theories. Essentialism can also entail the belief that nature contributes more than nurture to the development of gender roles (see Anderson & Jayaratne, 1998, for a discussion of adults' genetic explanations of social group differences). This belief need not be a biological theory per se; it could instead reflect an assumption that certain properties are inherent in an individual and so present from birth. A number of studies now suggest that there are age-related changes in beliefs about the causes of gender differences, with younger children assuming a more nativist (i.e., essentialist) stance.

Ullian (1976) interviewed six- to eighteen-year-olds and found that causal beliefs shifted with age from a biological orientation (focus on innate physical differences) to a socialization orientation (focus on social roles and obligations), and finally to a psychological orientation (focus on requirements of individual and interpersonal functioning). J. Smith and Russell (1984) reported a similar shift from a biological to a societal orientation in their interviews with seven- to fifteen-year-olds but found little evidence for a psychological orientation. By adult age, samples of parents (Antill, 1987) and college students (Martin & Parker, 1995) mentioned both biology and socialization in their explanations of gender differences. When asked which factor they saw as more important, both groups favored socialization (although a third of the parent sample saw both as equally important). Causal beliefs varied by domain; for example, parents viewed differences in interests as more socially determined than differences in personality traits.

M. G. Taylor (1996) examined these issues with children ranging in age from preschool through late elementary school. Participants were told about infants of one sex who were raised on an island populated by members of the opposite sex (e.g., a boy raised with girls and women). For each story, subjects were asked to predict how the hypothetical children would grow, specifically, whether they would show sex-stereotyped properties (e.g., would a boy raised among females still prefer to play with trucks?). The younger children typically answered based on innate potential rather than environmental influence; older children (ten years and older) and adults gave more weight to environmental influence. Taylor found similar results in a second study that used unfamiliar properties (e.g., unfamiliar games the child would like to play) rather than familiar gender stereotypes (e.g., playing with trucks versus a tea set). Thus, children appear to hold stronger beliefs about gender category essences than do adults.

Taylor and Gelman (1999; see M. G. Taylor, 1997) further extended this finding by examining children's causal explanations for their answer choices. Children were asked, for a variety of biological and behavioral properties, not only whether nature or nurture would win out, but also *why*. For example, they were asked why a girl raised with boys would have girl blood inside (versus boy blood inside [biological property]), or why a girl raised with boys would prefer to play with a tea set (versus a toy truck [behavioral property]). In the first of two studies, five- and ten-year-old children were simply asked, in an open-ended way, to provide their own justifications. Table 2 lists a sample of the justifications children provided. As can be seen, children at both ages provided inherent and essentialist explanations for gender-stereotyped behavior, mentioning the brain, "instinct," and desires to engage in sex-stereotypical behavior. It is also interesting that a number of the children couched their explanation using generic noun phrases (e.g., "boys," "girls").

In a second study, five-, seven-, and ten-year-old children received the nature-nurture scenarios (as described above) and were asked for their explanations. However, this time they were provided with possible responses and were asked to endorse or reject each one. Possible responses included being born a certain way, being taught by others, learning, really wanting to, or others really wanting the child to. Here we report participants' justifications for their *nature* choices, that is, for those trials on which they said that a child would retain gender-characteristic properties. For biological properties, children nearly always (> 95 percent of the time) endorsed the mechanism of birth (being born a certain way), although the youngest children also sometimes endorsed wanting (51 percent) or learning (32 percent). This result validates our assumption that birth is interpreted as a biological mechanism. It also illustrates that even young children expect that different mechanisms can act in concert (e.g., innate tendencies and learning can work together; see also Marler, 1991).

We then turned to the behavioral properties (e.g., play preferences), which were our primary interest. For category responses to these items (i.e., trials on which children reported that a child raised with opposite-sex others would nonetheless show gender-stereotyped properties), the mechanisms endorsed most frequently at all ages were those that involved the child himself or herself—really wanting to be a certain way (81 percent),

Table 2.   Sample justifications

A girl raised with only boys and men:

- Wears a dress rather than a football shirt: "Because the boys have footballer clothes and the girls have those notchy things that go 'shake, shake' [pompons], and the girls have dresses—white dresses or pink." (Girl, age five)
- Grows up to be a nurse rather than a firefighter: "There's more of a chance she would want to be a nurse. Some females are firefighters, but whenever I watch *Rescue 911*, you see the males around there and the females for nurses." (Boy, age ten)
- Likes to play with a tea set rather than a toy truck: "Because usually since she has a girl brain, she'd like to play with a tea set." (Boy, age ten)
- Grows up to be a ballet dancer rather than a football player: "Because girls, a lot of girls, would more like to be a ballet dancer than a football player, and again it always depends on what she thinks." (Boy, age ten)

A boy raised with only girls and women:

- Plays with a truck rather than a tea set: "Because boys play with boy things and girls play with girl things." (Boy, age five)
- Wears army boots rather than hair ribbons: "Because he doesn't like them. Because he's a boy, and boys don't wear hair ribbons." (Boy, age five)
- Goes fishing rather than puts on makeup: "Cause that's the boy instinct." (Girl, age ten)
- Grows up to have a boy brain rather than a girl brain: "Because, you see, there's the difference in who gets boy brains and girl brains. Boy brains stay in the boy and girl brains stay in the girl." (Boy, age five)

Source: Data from M. G. Taylor and Gelman (1999).

learning to be a certain way (69 percent), or just being born a certain way (52 percent). Those that involved others (others teaching the child, or others really wanting the child to be a certain way) were deemed much less relevant (15 percent and 17 percent, respectively). These patterns were remarkably stable over the period from five to ten years of age. Thus, both essentialist mechanisms (being born a certain way) and nonessentialist mechanisms (wanting, learning) are endorsed, but what they have in common is that the mechanism is a self-guided, self-directed one. Furthermore, endorsement of nonbiological mechanisms (e.g., learning, wanting) does not entail rejecting essentialist mechanisms. Children at all ages (five, seven, and ten) viewed both sorts of mechanisms as mutually operating.

Thus, when explaining the maintenance of gender-stereotyped properties, children consistently appeal to either inherent qualities in the person or outright essentialist accounts.

Gender Constancy: An Apparent Exception. In apparent contrast to children's essentialist theories of gender, it is well known that young children tend to fail gender-constancy tasks, reporting that boys can turn into girls, that girls can turn into boys, and that superficial properties (such as hairstyle and clothing) can determine gender (Emmerich, Goldman, & Kirsch, 1977; Kohlberg, 1966). At first blush, this result would seem clear evidence that children are not gender essentialists. However, such a conclusion would be premature, for two reasons. First, gender constancy can (and does) emerge earlier, depending on how it is tested. For example, Siegal and Robinson (1987) found that merely changing the order of item presentation leads to much improved performance, due to pragmatic biases in the original order. Others (e.g., Johnson & Ames, 1994), using modified questioning techniques, have also found gender constancy at earlier ages.

The second point is that constancy itself is not a precondition for essentialism. One of the things that needs to happen for children to appreciate gender constancy fully is for them to have particular biological knowledge about sex (Bem, 1989). Until children have this, they can be mistaken about *which* properties are essential while still holding essentialist beliefs. A related point is that, although one of the suggested characteristics of essentialism is unalterability (see Rothbart & Taylor, 1992), we contend that one can be essentialist even about categories one does not view as fixed over time. For example, people are essentialist about age groupings (babies, teenagers, old people), even though these are temporary categories (i.e., one moves in and out of these groupings over time). In support of this point, Gelman et al. (1986) found that preschool children who were highly essentialist about gender on an inductive inference task (see above) nonetheless performed poorly on a standard gender-constancy task. Likewise, as noted earlier, we are finding generic statements about gender even in children as young as two and three years old—well before the standard age of achieving gender constancy.

Developmental Change. To this point we have argued that preschool children are gender essentialists, and that remnants of this way of reasoning persist through adulthood. However, this does not mean that gender concepts are static over development. In fact, over the course of childhood, conceptions of gender do become more flexible, probabilistic, and attentive to individuating information. Whereas adults have extensive probability-based stereotypes of the sexes (Martin, 1987), very young children's stereotypes appear to be less probabilistic and more absolute (Martin, 1989). For instance, younger children tend to embrace simple generalizations such as "girls play with dolls," whereas older children learn more probabilistic notions such as "many girls, but not all girls, play with dolls" (Carter & Patterson, 1982; Leahy & Shirk, 1984).

Martin (1989) suggests that the increasingly probabilistic nature of gender knowledge may allow children to perceive and notice variability within gender groups in addition to noticing similarities across gender groups. She found that young children, but not older ones, made interesting, non-adult-like judgments about others, indicating a failure to recognize within-gender group variability. For example, when told about a boy whose best friend is a girl and whose favorite activity is playing with dolls (i.e., a boy with feminine interests), five-year-olds predicted that the boy would like playing with trucks more than playing with kitchen sets. They ignored the information that distinguished this boy from others (i.e., his interests) and thus based their judgments entirely on his sex. Older children and adults were more likely to say that the boy would like other feminine toys as much as masculine toys.

In addition to becoming more probabilistic, children's beliefs about the origins of sex differences are changing with age. As noted earlier, children move from a primarily nativist theory of sex differences at preschool age to a more complex, environmental theory of sex differences by age nine or ten (M. G. Taylor, 1996). With added flexibility, children start to treat gender differences more as social conventions than as fixed physical or moral laws (Carter & Patterson, 1982; Levy et al., 1995; Stoddart & Turiel, 1985).

With age, children also become better able to differentiate biological from social properties, limiting essentializing to certain kinds of properties (Solomon, Johnson, Zaitchik, & Carey, 1996; M. G. Taylor & Gelman, 1999). We illustrate with data from a recent nature-nurture study we conducted. As described earlier, children were told brief scenarios in which an infant boy (or girl) goes to live on an island with only females (or males). Children were then asked which of a series of properties the hypothetical child would have at age ten years. At the youngest age (five years), children treated both biological properties (e.g., having boy versus girl blood inside) and behavioral properties (e.g., playing with a toy truck versus a tea set) as innately determined. In contrast, by seven and ten years of age, children largely differentiated the two sorts of properties, treating the biological properties as innately determined but the behavioral properties as at least partly the result of environmental influences.

Implications and Conclusions

Studies of implicit gender essentialism in children have implications for three sets of issues: the acquisition of gender stereotypes, the psychological study of gender, and the impact of essentialism on behavior. Furthermore, there are implicit tensions between the current approach and feminist theories of essentialism, which we explore.

Implications for Acquisition of Gender Concepts and Sex Typing

The evidence of children's essentializing suggests that it reflects a larger developmental process, and is part of how children think about categories more generally. In other words, we suggest that gender essentializing is not a historical aberration (cf. Rorty, 1979) but a consequence of how children organize their knowledge about the world (see also Hirschfeld, 1996). If anything, young children are *more* essentialist than older children or adults.

This does not mean that cultural and historical forces have no effect. After all, categories are essentialized to different degrees—we essentialize animal species but not artifacts. Cultural and historical forces may serve to heighten (or dampen) what is an essentializing tendency (see also Bem, 1981). Specifically, we suspect that gender-typed practices in the culture serve as a powerful mechanism for fostering both the presence and nature of gender essentialism in children. Children are not born knowing *which* categories to essentialize. We suggest that they look for categories with many converging, correlated cues: if a category already has a cluster of correlated properties, children will expect it to have even more correlated properties. Thus, a single dimension (e.g., color) by itself is not expected to be an essentialized kind; dimensions must cluster. Stereotyping and gender-typed practices in the culture then serve to magnify and highlight correlational cues. For example, hair length, clothing design, clothing color, and choice of accessories all magnify and highlight male/female differences, thus leading children to consider gender as an essentialized kind. In support of this view, Bigler (1995) finds that use of gender as a functional category in the classroom (i.e., making use of physical/spatial dichotomies and verbal categorizations based on gender) indeed leads to increased gender stereotyping, especially among children with less advanced categorization skills.

Implications for the Study of Gender

Although the research reviewed in this chapter focused on *beliefs about* gender (and not on the accuracy or inaccuracy of these beliefs), the fact that we are essentialist may have implications for the study of gender per se. To the extent that gender differences are in fact biological and deep-seated, an essentialist perspective is probably useful. It poses difficulties, however, when our lens, to use Bem's term, does not match the phenomenon under study. The issue of which aspects of gender roles are biologically constrained and which are linked to socialization factors continues to be debated by scientists (see Hyde, 1990, for a review of this literature). In this regard, we believe that the value of feminist approaches that are often interpreted as essentializing (e.g., Gilligan, 1982; Chodorow, 1978) will be decided on an empirical basis. Nonetheless, certainly many gender differences are stereotypes rather than deep-seated differences (Maccoby & Jacklin, 1974).

Regardless of the answers to the questions posed above, we need to be wary of studies that essentialize gender by (1) contrasting male and female without recognition of overlapping distributions (Hare-Mustin & Marecek's [1988] alpha bias), (2) looking for inherent causes rather than environmental or contextual causes of gender differences, (3) overgeneralizing to an entire gender category without recognition of contrasting (or interacting) dimensions, subgroups, or exceptions, particularly regarding social class, race, and culture, and (4) assuming that surface differences have underlying causes, even when those surface differences are often artificially imposed (e.g., hair length). As Bird (1998, p. 92) writes, "Experimental designs which examine differences between groups based on the variable of 'gender' tend to produce results which are limited to supporting or not supporting the existence of a gender difference." In other words, more interesting questions may be obscured by this narrow focus. Similarly, Z. Luria (1986) points out that studies focusing on mean differences between male and female can lose sight of complexities in the data, including range and overlap of distributions. Interactions of gender with other categories such as race, social class, and ethnicity tend to be ignored.

How to deal with these biases is not altogether clear. In her earlier work, Bem (1981) urged that we dismantle gender polarization by shrinking the relevance of gender and noting that its scope is extremely limited (e.g., to certain biological functions such as childbearing). More recently, Bem has acknowledged that the weight of culture and history may make her first suggestion impossible. In contrast, she now offers a radically different suggestion, that of "exploding or proliferating gender categories" (1995, p. 330). In other words, rather than focus on the binary opposition of male/female (with all of its associations), Bem suggests classifying people in one of many different "genders" (e.g., based on a combination of sex, gender, and desire).

The extent to which it is possible to change the course of children's gender-role development using either of these approaches has not been tested empirically. It seems that given the salience of gender differences in our culture and given young children's strong expectations concerning category structure, it would be difficult to raise "gender-aschematic" children. However, if an intervention is to work at reducing gender stereotyping it would have to provide children with not only another way to divide up the world, but also another (nonessentialist) explanatory schema or underlying causal theory about the nature of sex differences.

One common approach in intervention programs has been to expose children to counterstereotypic role models (Bigler & Liben, 1990). Reviews of these types of intervention programs have generally concluded that they have had only limited impact (e.g., Katz, 1986; Liben & Bigler, 1987). Bigler and Liben (1990) argue that the reason for their relative lack of success is that children forget or distort information that runs counter to the initial stereotype (Bigler & Liben, 1990). Consistent with this interpretation is the finding that some interventions have actually led to increased rather than decreased stereotyping (e.g., Guttentag & Bray, 1976).

Bigler and Liben (1990) designed a different kind of intervention for elementary schoolchildren (ages seven to eleven) that entailed teaching them directly about nonsexist criteria for determining who can do various activities and occupations. First, they taught children about the irrelevance of gender in making inferences about whether men or women could perform gender-typed occupations. They then provided children with two alternative criteria for making these inferences (i.e., a person's liking some job-related function, and a person's learning how to perform some job function). The intervention did lead to a significant reduction in children's beliefs about what men and women can do. This is a promising direction for future research.

Impact of Essentialism on Behavior

In future research it will be important to study how these various strands of essentialism are related in children's and adults' reasoning, and to determine what links (if any) there are between essentialist beliefs and behavior. What kind of impact does essentialist reasoning have on sex typing? The available evidence suggests at least some coherence among different beliefs, with commonsense biological construals of gender origins having particular significance. Hoffman and Hurst (1990) found that when people assume a biological basis for group differences, they tend to attribute more differences across the groups. Martin and Parker (1995, p. 45) likewise found that "[t]he more biology was believed to cause sex differences, the more the sexes were seen to differ." Similarly, Antill (1987) found that parents' beliefs about the origins of sex differences (as primarily biological versus primarily socially constructed) predicted their child-rearing patterns.

Similarly, Eccles, Jacobs, Harold-Goldsmith, Jayarathe, and Yee (1989) provide some evidence for the claim that beliefs about the nature and origin of sex differences may influence behavior. Eccles et al. found that the more parents associated gender differences in reading ability with biological factors, the less likely they were to report trying to influence their child's reading ability. Thus, individual differences in essentialist beliefs predict other beliefs and behavior.

Tensions with Feminist Theory[4]

The present approach may appear to conflict with standard feminist accounts of essentialism. We have proposed the existence of a universal essentialist bias that may be an innate template for the starting point of development, whereas many other feminists assume that the content, form, and process of conceptual development are socially constructed. Thus, the present approach departs from many feminist accounts in positing (1) that essentialist thinking is prevalent in many domains of thought, not just gender, (2) that essentialism is the result not just of social or political tendencies but also of cognitive biases, and (3) that children broadly (as an essentialized group?) can be characterized as engaging in essentialist thinking.

Although the two approaches represent genuine disagreement regarding the source of essentialism, we believe that discussion between these perspectives will lead to new insights. The cognitive developmental approach would certainly be enriched by a consideration of feminist concerns (see also Conclusions, below). Cognitive analyses tend to neglect the interplay between cognitive biases and social/political forces. Feminist analyses reveal that societies often use essentialism as a political tool to exaggerate and reinforce social differences. Thus, the child may grow up in a social environment that reinforces gender concepts through a set of practices that begin at birth. The culture also provides a folk theory of gender that may be difficult to eradicate. The ways in which cultural biases support and reinforce early essentializing is a vital topic for future research.

Second, feminist approaches would be enriched by a consideration of the individualistic psychological forces that permit essentialism to be used as a political force. Were essentialism not such a potent core notion, we argue, it could never have been used so effectively to legitimate political divisions. Moreover, some of the debate noted in the beginning of this chapter regarding the value of essentialism (regarding whether it is a positive force, a negative force, or philosophically neutral) can be understood as stemming from its initial emergence as a cognitive bias (value neutral), which can be used for either positive or negative political ends.

A final suggestion is that both cognitive developmental and feminist approaches may find insights from studying how understanding of gender essentialism changes over development. Studies of other domains provide detailed case studies of the conditions that lead to theory change, on the one hand (e.g., Carey, 1985; Gopnik & Meltzoff, 1997; Wellman, 1990), and of children's resistance to such changes, on the other hand (Wellman & Gelman, 1997). Children's essentialist theories undoubtedly change as children learn cultural explanations, grasp causal mechanisms, encounter within-category variability, and so forth. Experience has the potential to deconstruct or reconstruct essentialist theory in powerful ways, leading to new theories that can differ radically from children's first constructions. The ways in which children's essentialist theories are not fixed may provide important models for considering alternative construals of gender.

Conclusions

Essentialism has implications not only for the study of gender concepts and of sex- typed behavior, but also for the study of development, broadly construed. Feminist critiques of essentialism may be valuable to keep in mind when considering developmental studies of children, which themselves often have essentialist assumptions built in. Siegler and Ellis (1996, p. 213) provide a cogent discussion of the issue:

Oyama [1985] argued that much of psychology is aimed at identifying *essences*. Are people at their core aggressive or peaceful, selfish or altruistic, rational or irrational? Is their behavior determined by nature or nurture, genes or culture? In the context of cognitive-developmental research, the goal of such efforts is to identify the essence of thinking at each age. This goal leads to such general questions as "What is 5-year-olds' thinking like, and how does it differ from the thinking of 8-year-olds?" It also leads to more specific questions such as "Is 5-year-olds' thinking fundamentally concrete rather than abstract?"

Siegler and Ellis go on to suggest that a more fruitful approach is to examine *variability* in performance, both across contexts and within a context over time, rather than attempting to capture a single, unifying essence (see also Gelman & Diesendruck, 1999; Gelman & Medin, 1993; Jones & Smith, 1993). The solution that Siegler and Ellis propose is "to abandon the search for essences and to substitute the more limited goal of identifying characteristic tendencies in children's thinking" (p. 213), characteristic tendencies that themselves are gradually changing. Thus, as scientists, we need to overcome our own essentializing tendencies, even as we recognize and study essentialism as a powerful reasoning bias that persists throughout the life span.

Indeed, we can focus this critique even on the studies reviewed in the present chapter. It is ironic, for example, that the developmental studies of children's essentializing have focused on a rather constrained sample (data from U.S. children, primarily white and middle class). Future research should broaden the range of samples and seriously address intersections of gender, race, and social class. In this way we can address the extent to which essentializing is itself an "essential" feature of childhood.

Acknowledgments

Work was supported by a grant from the Institute for Research on Women and Gender, University of Michigan, and by NICHD grant No.HD36043, both to the first author.

Notes

1. Bem (1993, p. 131) notes that the classifying theorists as essentialist or not can be tricky business. "With respect to biological essentialism, the verdict is a lit-

tle muddier because of the diversity among the [woman-centered or difference-centered] theorists on the question of origins. This diversity notwithstanding, the woman-centered theorists concentrate so much more on the psychological differences between males and females than on their differing social contexts, they spend so little time debating the all-important question of where those psychological differences come from, and they make those psychological differences seem to be intimately connected to the essence of what it means to be either male or female that, in the end, the impact of the discourse is to make those psychological differences between males and females seem natural, not socially constructed."

2. In contrast to most theorists, Fuss (1989) argues that social constructionists are also essentialist.

3. For example, according to Deaux (1985), adults have a tendency to view male and female as bipolar opposites, even when they acknowledge that they are overlapping categories. Despite empirical evidence that masculinity and femininity are orthogonal to one another (Bem, 1974; Spence & Helmreich, 1979), adults tend to assume that what is male is "not female," and vice versa (Foushee, Helmreich, & Spence, 1979; Deaux & Kite, 1985; Deaux & Lewis, 1984).

4. We thank Ellin Scholnick for helping us to develop the ideas in this section.

Positionality and Thought

On the Gendered Foundations

of Thought, Culture,

and Development

Rachel Joffe Falmagne

My aims in this chapter are both critical and substantive. I argue that gender in intersection with other social formations configures cultures and societies, and that *epistemic* norms (norms defining what constitutes knowledge) are developed in this gendered societal matrix and must therefore be the object of critique. I then explore the substantive implications of this argument. My discussion focuses specifically on deductive reasoning and its development, but the import of these remarks extends beyond this particular domain.

Despite the increasing recognition that development is grounded in society and culture, gender as a *social formation* that includes symbolic, social, economic and institutional elements (as opposed to an individual variable) has generally not been brought into descriptions of society and culture that inform developmental research. In sections 1 and 2 I argue that it is crucial to do so because there is a complex dialectic between that social formation, the normative discourses and practices it yields, and the individual functioning of thinkers who develop within this system.

In sections 3 and 4 I focus critically on the (gendered) social construction of epistemic norms and the underlying cultural politics, drawing from (1) historical analyses that show that the norm of formal rationality was, when initially developed, gendered in its foundations and explicitly predicated on rejecting what was symbolically construed as "the feminine," and (2) related feminist critiques of logic. In section 5 I critically examine how these norms have dominated conceptions of development, and I use Piaget's theory, which posits formal logic as the end product of development, as one case study of the gendered social construction of developmental norms (Inhelder & Piaget, 1958; Piaget, 1970a). My critique includes other approaches to the study of deductive reasoning that have been under the hegemony of the rationalist worldview.

Substantively, these remarks suggest several converging directions for research, which I explore at the end of this chapter. The first is to study the gendered social processes through which knowledge is constructed at both the cultural and the individual level. The second is to study the deployment of epistemic norms in the child's developmental niche. A third is to examine the manner in which gendered thinkers appropriate, resist, or integrate rationalist norms and other discourses within each of their specific cultural and social locations. I briefly describe current research guided by these questions.

1. The Gendered Foundations of Society and Culture

Psychology as a discipline has recently begun to emerge from its individualistic history. One major current of theory and research examines human development in its social and cultural matrix and highlights the specificity of cultural norms and the social practices that implement and reproduce those norms. Although researchers who approach development from that perspective draw on diverse theoretical and methodological frameworks, there is broad agreement that thought is constituted by and develops on a cultural foundation and that modes of knowledge are produced and reproduced through cultural practices and routines.[1]

However, cultures and societies have an internal sociopolitical structure. That crucial fact is largely underrepresented in the psychological literature, where "cultures" tend to be implicitly conceptualized as apolitical. For instance, Shweder (1996) defines culture in terms of norms presumed to be uniform and in terms of cooperative social agreements: "Members of a culture are members of a moral community who work to co-construct a shared reality and who act as though they were parties to an agreement to behave rationally within the terms of the realities they share" (p. 20). Although this conceptualization is not universally shared (see Burman, 1994 and Walkerdine, 1988, among others) and although the existence of diverse subcultures is sometimes recognized qua diversity, in much of the psychological work on development in its social and cultural setting the politics of culture is underemphasized.

It is not my intention here to critique existing approaches, which have made important contributions to our understanding of the dynamics of development. However, if a fully societal approach to development is to emerge, it must include the intrasocietal operation of social, economic and symbolic power relations between social groups, relations through which cultural norms are formulated and that constitute the internal cultural politics of the society in which development proceeds. That ideologies, norms and practices are constituted by, enforced by, and reproduced through the deployment of power relations and ideological struggles is made clear by a rich body of feminist scholarship (see below) and by other critical perspectives from various disciplines (e.g., Denzin, 1996; Fairclough, 1992; Foucault, 1980, 1982). These processes must be incorporated into the societal analyses that inform developmental theory and research (Falmagne, 1998b).

The social world is a system that involves social structures (social relations between groups), economic structures (the distribution of and access to resources across groups), and ideological formations (the conceptual frameworks and notions—for instance, conceptualizations of "work"—that are taken for granted and that shape social practices, social institutions, and social subjects). These three constituents form a system: social, economic and ideological processes support and reinforce one another in a systemic, dialectical way. They are mutually constitutive. Another aspect of the system is that individuals are constituted as social subjects through these processes, and they in turn contribute to social reproduction by instantiating these processes in their behavior, their subjectivity, and their thinking. Thus, both individual development and cultural conceptions of development must be considered within an integrated, systemic theory (Falmagne, 1998a, 1998b).

In particular, gender is a key *social formation* that includes social, institutional, symbolic, and ideological elements, as feminist theorists (e.g., Barrett, 1992; Scott, 1988; D. Smith, 1990) have explained. Gender, like other social formations such as race and class and in intersection with them, configures cultures and societies in these complex ways. As a social formation, gender has both material and discursive aspects that are closely intertwined and implemented institutionally. *Materially,* gender organizes social groups, the power relations between these groups, economic functioning and access to resources, and division of labor (for instance, the construction of housework and child care as women's domain in many societies). *Discursively,* gender configures those symbolic representations and ideologies (for instance, cultural discourses of motherhood and their internalized forms) that regulate social practices and individual subjectivity. Ideologies of gender, like ideologies of race and class and in intersection with them, both reflect and support the functioning of the social order (for instance, the functioning of housework and child care as "natural" and therefore unpaid labor, not "work"). Gender ideologies are translated into legal, educational and other *institutional* texts and practices that implement and reproduce these ideologies (Hess & Marx-Ferree, 1987; Lipman-Blumen, 1984; D. Smith, 1990). The notion of *social formation* captures the fact that these ideological, symbolic, economic, social and psychological processes support one another in a systemic manner.

Although gender has received some attention in the study of thought and development, this attention has often been in the form of treating gender as a demographic, individual variable characterizing either the child or those social actors interacting with the child, or as an examination of proximal socialization practices. Gender as a macrostructural social formation with intertwined symbolic, institutional, material and ideological components has been undertheorized within psychology, and in particular within developmental psychology, again with some notable exceptions. The next section briefly examines how the social, historical, material and symbolic processes that jointly constitute the formation of gender in intersection with other social formations contribute to the formation of self and mind in the developing person. This material serves as a prelude to the subsequent discussion of the development of epistemic norms.

2. The Formation of Self and Mind in a Societal Matrix

Within her or his particular racial/ethnic, class, and cultural niche, the developing person is situated in gendered social and material arrangements and in gendered cultural discourses and practices. One's subjectivity and one's self as a *knowing agent* (the specific focus of this chapter) are constituted by these material (structural) conditions, cultural discourses and social practices. The development of subjectivity and self is not, however, a process of passive transmission. The developing person, including the child, is a social agent who appropriates, resists, rejects or modulates cultural discourses and models. People are simultaneously both products of their societal context and collective history and unique individuals with agency and creativity.

It is important to distinguish structural gender from symbolic gender and psychological gender. *Structural gender* refers to the social roles historically constructed for women and men through normative gender ideology, social practices, and institutional arrangements. *Symbolic gender* is the meaning and representation of masculinity and femininity in a society at a particular historical time, that is, those cultural discourses that define what it means to be a woman or a man. It is critical to see that symbolic gender, a cultural construct, is distinct from psychological gender. *Psychological gender* is constructed by social agents living in a structural and symbolic world, and it is constructed through a dialectic between social constructivist processes and the individual's agency in appropriating, resisting or modulating available cultural discourses. It is this dialectic that a developmental theory must capture. The notion of a dialectic is crucial in marking that individual and societal processes are co-constitutive in development (see Falmagne, 1998b, for an elaboration of these ideas).

Different theories variously stress either the structural or the symbolic aspects of the constitution of individual subjectivity, and either individual agency or social construction. N. J. Chodorow (1995), elaborating on her earlier (1974), structural account of personality development, stresses *symbolic* gender and the person's interpretation of symbolic gender through her or his experiential history; thus, gender becomes an individual as well as a social construction. Ruddick (1982) focuses on how maternal *practice* produces particular modes of thought, in this way suggesting a materialist grounding for intellectual development.[2] Black and Chicana theorists, while also generally offering a structural analysis of society, accord greater weight to self-determination in the construction of self and mind. Collins (1990) stresses the "power of self-definition" and Black women's dual consciousness and power to develop a self-articulated standpoint (contrast, for example, Baker Miller's 1986 account of predominantly white women). Hurtado (1989, 1996) similarly argues that the structural difference between the location of "women of color" and that of white women in relation to white men yields different kinds of oppression (based on rejection versus seduction) that differently affect the development of personal power.

Along with structural factors, societal discourses and ideology are key in the constitution of subjectivity. Hennessy (1993a) sees ideology as "the array of sense-making practices which constitutes what counts as 'the way things are' in any historical moment" (1993a, p. 14), and argues that ideology is systemically related to the economic and political order. D. Smith (e.g., 1990) points out how ideological discourses as they are materially manifested in institutions and texts exercise semiotic control over social practices and individual subjectivity. (See also Bordo, 1985, and Ortner, 1974, for different accounts of ideology and the symbolic order.) The ideas presented in the next section on the links between symbolic masculinity and rationality are closely related to these analyses.

3. The Positionality of Knowledge and the Gendered Social Construction of Rationalist Norms

As both feminist theory and other critical perspectives have shown, knowledge is situated. There is no neutral knowledge that transcends the particular social context and status of knowers. The knowing subject is not generic; she or he is concrete, historically specific, and socially located. For our present concerns, this means two things. First, the knower's social location provides a particular standpoint from which the knower views the world, and that standpoint makes it possible (but it does not guarantee) for the knowing subject to see certain things clearly that would be invisible from a different standpoint.[3] Hartsock (1983) and D. Smith (1987) have explained how standpoints are grounded in an individual's material conditions and activities in the process of production, and have shown that certain kinds of understandings are not possible from certain structural locations. Postcolonial critics Collins (e.g., 1990), Anzaldúa (e.g., 1990), and Mohanty (e.g., 1991), further elaborating those ideas, reject the notion of a unitary feminist standpoint. Instead, they have developed standpoint theory so as to capture the intersectional nature of social locations, and have articulated the standpoints of women of color and "third world" women.[4] The second implication of the knowing subject's specific historical-social situatedness is that his or her subjectivity and mode of thinking are constituted by the conditions and the discourses pertaining to that location. Thus, knowledge is situated in two ways: one can only apprehend the world from a certain location, and the knowing agent has been constituted by that location. These ways in which knowledge is situated are closely related, and both ways will be important in the subsequent discussion, the first for epistemology, the second for psychological analyses.

For epistemology, the situatedness of knowledge implies that there can be no transcendent epistemic norm, no "view from nowhere" that would lead to absolute standards of justification for knowledge claims. This point has been made both in relation to science (Code, 1987a; Harding, 1990, 1991; H. Longino, 1990) and in relation to other domains (Alcoff & Potter, 1993). The notion that epistemic norms are situated subverts the Enlightenment belief in transcendental knowledge obtained through universal reason. Most relevant for our concerns here, it also subverts the foundational aim of logic, as I discuss in section 4.

But it is not merely the case that knowledge and epistemic norms are socially and historically situated. Crucially, the production of knowledge is always profoundly political: the choice of topics, the choice of methods, and the assumptions defining what counts as valid knowledge are political choices. Knowledge is part of the discourse of power (Foucault, 1980, 1982; see also Falmagne, 1996). Epistemic norms, like all norms, enforce and reproduce existing relations of power and participate centrally in cultural politics, and gender is integral to these relations, in intersection with other social formations such as racial/ethnic formations, class, and institutional privilege. It is in that context that the following discussions of rationality, rationalism and logic must be considered.

Since the Enlightenment, *rationality* has been defined as a mode of thinking that privileges abstract thought rather than concrete knowledge and that separates "reason" from emotion and values. In the modern Western world, rationality, so defined, has been considered the superior mode of thinking. *Rationalism* is the epistemological doctrine according to which rationality alone, or reason so defined, can yield basic truths about the world.

Several feminist philosophers have argued that there is a relation between (traditional) rationality and masculinity. In reviewing their ideas it will be important to keep in mind the discussion in the preceding section, and to see that the relations between masculinity and rationality are at once historical, symbolic, social and psychological: processes at these different levels are mutually constitutive and form an intricate system. It is not the case that men are inherently rational; individual psychological processes cannot be disembedded from the broader system.

Lloyd (1984, 1993a) submits that, since the Enlightenment, reason has been associated with symbolic maleness: reason is part of the content of symbolic gender, what it means to be a man. Lloyd rightly observes that this content can be appropriated by both real men and real women; thus she distinguishes metaphorical, symbolic gender from individual gender and from socially constructed gender. It is these workings of sexual symbolism in relation to reason, as a "network of symbolic operations" (1993a, p. 82), that are at issue for her.

Flax (1993) argues that gender imagery drove Kant's formulation of the Enlightenment ideal. Kant's writings reveal that this ideal was grounded in his explicit desire to have the male child separate from the private and outgrow his dependency on the mother: "every man must think for himself." Of course, Kant was a socially constructed man whose desires, identity, and semiotic life were socially constructed in the complex gender system discussed previously. Flax's analysis shows that although reason was ostensibly to be a universal norm, it was explicitly formulated by Kant for (his view of) males only. Thus, historically, the very formulation of reason as a norm wove in a discursive construction of gender.

Bordo (1987) argues that Descartes formulated the ideals of detachment and objectivity of pure thought as a result of the cultural broadening in the seventeenth century with the discovery of new cultures through explorations, and as a result of Descartes's individual anxieties, particularly regarding individuation and separation. She describes Descartes's intellectual trajectory as a process with both psychological and historical dimensions, a " 'flight from the feminine' and a 're-imaging of knowledge as masculine.' " Bordo's is not an individual psychological account. Rather, she develops a cultural historical analysis: in asking "Why did the dominant intellectual culture take this turn in the seventeenth century?" she submits that this was "[o]ne intellectual 'moment' in an acute historical flight from the feminine, from the memory of union with the maternal world and a rejection of all the values associated with it" (p. 9).

In conclusion, two points deserve mention. First, it is important to reiterate the analytical distinction between symbolic gender and psychological gender. To be sure, the rationalist ideal of detachment and of reason divorced from emotion has been instrumental in constructing the subjectivities of Western privileged white men, in conjunction with processes such as child-rearing practices or institutionalized social roles. This, however, does not mean that Kant or Descartes (and others) generated these ideas merely by virtue of being, individually, men. The connection between rationality and masculinity results from a complex dialectic among societal discourses, social practices, and individual processes.

Second, not only are epistemic norms situated, they are inherently political. Rationalism, as a cultural doctrine that affirms the superiority of abstract reason over concrete knowledge has important political dimensions. As a discourse of knowledge (that is, a discourse that defines legitimate ways of knowing and agents of knowledge), it is inherently an exercise in power (Foucault, 1980), and it has developed through an explicit exaltation of symbolic masculinity in a social world whose economic, social, and cultural power relations are fundamentally gendered and unequal.

4. Logic as a Historically Gendered Cultural Construction

The preceding analysis extends to the discourse of logic as well. Logic has occupied a central place as a foundational system in the Western rationalist discourse, in several ways. It has been an *epistemic norm* for defining valid inferences across many discursive domains, including legal and scientific domains. It has been a *linguistic norm* in public and scientific discourse: appropriate public and scientific language is logical. And it has been a *norm for evaluating thinking:* formal deduction supersedes empirical knowledge, logic is an idealized description of human thought processes, and good thinking is logical. Logic has also been regarded by some as the *foundation of all knowledge.*

Various recent critiques call these assumptions into question. Outside of feminist analyses, while some moderate critiques advocate a reformulation of the ideal of rationality on broader or on different grounds (e.g., Harman, 1986; Rescher, 1988; Sperber & Wilson, 1986; see Falmagne & Gonsalves, 1995, for a review), more fundamental, cultural critiques expose in what ways ideas about the nature of reason are historically specific, socially situated, discursively constructed, and deployed in exclusionary ways as part of the ideology of knowledge (e.g., Rockmore, 1992).

Feminist cultural critiques of logic, like the more general feminist cultural critiques of rationality, expose the hegemonic features of formal logic and the gendered social formation that underpins the construction of logical norms. Nye (1990) argues that logics must be examined, not as purely technical systems but as human creations, each motivated by certain desires of the man who developed it (all were men) and each serving a function in a particular sociopolitical context, and she offers such a psychohistorical critique of selected moments in the history of Western logic.[5] Most germane to my focus are Aristotelian and Fregean logics.

For Aristotle, logic was to define the form of necessary inferences in language. Of the several innovations of the Aristotelian syllogism, two have remained central to modern logic and are crucial as objects of critique. The first is the distinction between truth (what is factually the case) and validity (roughly, what is logically necessary, what must be the case because of implications between statements). Nye suggests that in the Athenian institution of public debate and in the courts, contexts in which the syllogism was developed, the new notion of validity led to an undermining of the importance of factual truth: direct evidence came to be considered unreliable in courts as opposed to cleverness of argument. It is important to note that this particular phenomenon, the emergence of reason as a criterion superseding factual knowledge and human credibility, was a pivotal turn in the development of logic. Logic now superseded other forms of knowing in the epistemology of the times. This new epistemic status of logic directly dovetails with the modern rationalist tradition. The second innovation is the formalism of Aristotelian logic, a feature that characterizes modern logic as well. When valid arguments are formalized—expressed in the language of variables and forms rather than as full statements—the content of the argument is erased. Formalism made it possible to, in Nye's terms, "bracket empirical truth" (p. 47). Truth is of course not irrelevant to syllogisms, which are designed to be truth preserving. However, when logical form becomes the focus of concentration, the factual status of the premise is suspended as hypothetical. Concrete knowledge is secondary. But promulgating abstract reason over concrete knowledge is a major (situated) epistemic choice and one that has been questioned, in particular by some non-Western societies in which bracketing empirical truth is seen as an absurd practice, epistemically (Scribner, 1977/1997). It has also been questioned by dialectical logicians (Ilyenkov, 1960/1982; see Falmagne, 1995, for a discussion of Ilyenkov's ideas and their implications for reasoning).

As logic came to dominate legal and political debate in a culture in which this debate was central, it became an instrument of power, in several ways. First, it precluded any negotiation of ambiguities of meaning and of alternative forms of knowledge. Also, logic acquired normative status: as Nye observes, logic regulates the forms of discourse that define who can legitimately participate in political and public life. When logic was further developed by Aristotle as a substantive science (rather than only a tool of debate), it also became an instrument of epistemic domination: learned discourse is logical, leads to definitive knowledge and makes universal statements. Thus, logic as an epistemic norm within a rationalist culture has a silencing function.

Two observations are pertinent to this discussion. First, the gender hierarchy (social, economical, institutional and symbolic) in Athenian society has been well documented. Thus, Aristotle's logic can be analyzed critically as a masculinist production, in the manner developed by Bordo, Flax, and Lloyd (although Nye does not provide such an analysis). Second, the influence of classical philosophy on Western thought has been profound and enduring; hence this historical observation of the masculinist origins of logic has contemporary relevance.

A critical examination of Frege's work is equally significant because it has deeply influenced contemporary thought. While classical logic aimed to capture logical truths in terms of linguistic forms, Frege (1879/1970), in contrast, took mathematics as the paradigm of scientific thought; linguistic categories were too ambiguous and too rich. Through a formal conceptual notation for logical form, Frege sought to provide a unifying foundation for mathematics, language and all areas of human knowledge. For example, instead of analyzing the statement "All men are mortal" in terms of grammatical form, Fregean notation (not included here) expresses it in terms of its logical form as: "For all x, if x is a man then x is mortal." Frege's approach was unsuccessful for mathematics, but it became the grounding for contemporary logic and semantics, and his outlook on the status of logic influenced the schools of logical positivism and logical atomism that have been central to the Western intellectual tradition since the early twentieth century and that take logic to be the backbone of all knowledge.

There are two significant aspects to Frege's proposal. One is the formalism. Frege sought to eliminate all content (semantic or pragmatic) from the meaning of the sentence and to trace its core logical properties: the essence of its meaning was presumed to be its logical form.[6] He painstakingly carved out conceptual notions that would express absolute truth devoid of human concerns. Particularly striking is Frege's notion that the meaning of a sentence is a "thought" (Frege, 1918/1956), not the actual thought of a speaker but a disembodied thought, an epistemic entity that does not need to be thought by anyone in order to exist. Thus Frege essentially obliterates the human user of language. His was a passionate search for certainty and for rigor, where rigor was conceived as the elimination of all human elements from the reading of language so that the formal notation would preclude error and would "force consensus" (Nye, p. 142). Second, profound from a political point of view is the epistemic status of logic as the absolute foundation of knowledge, grounded in reality, a feature inherited by contemporary formal logic.

When Aristotle and Frege are read through the lenses of the critiques by Bordo (1987), Lloyd (1993a), or Flax (1993), the profoundly gendered makeup of both their social world and their subjectivity becomes clear. It is also striking that throughout the history of Western logic all the well-known logicians were men. Again, I make no essentialist claim with this statement. The connection between masculinity and Western rationality relies on a complex circular dialectic whereby social, economic, symbolic and psychological phenomena co-constitute one another. Within this system, however, it remains that logic shares men's location.

An area of current contention (Hass & Falmagne, 2000) is whether any logic is inherently hegemonic because it codifies legitimate arguments in a uniform manner and therefore is antithetical to feminist theories of knowledge, or whether feminist alternatives can be developed. Some feminist scholars argue that it is particular features of logic that are at issue, rather than the overall aim of any logical system. For instance, L. H. Nelson (1997) submits that formal logic is interdependent with broader bodies of theory and research; thus logic is inherently subject to change in response to changes in those and therefore is open to feminist reformulations. Plumwood (1993) centers her critique specifically on the dualistic thinking that underlies the binary negation of standard logic, in which one term is defined only relative to the dominant member of the pair and the positive and negated members are seen as "hyperseparated" (radically different), and she proposes alternatives that do not present that feature. Hass (2000) discusses Irigaray's (e.g., 1985; see also Whitford, 1988) radical critique of formal logic and shows how Irigaray proposes to develop a mode of discourse that honors fluidity of thought rather than emphasizing bounded, clear-cut categories and relations.

I have suggested (Falmagne, 1996) that formalism is oppressive by virtue of its epistemic status rather than being oppressive quintessentially. If formalism were taken to be merely a tool for capturing specific aspects of meaning, with the recognition that these aspects of meaning would have to be integrated with others, it could be subsumed into a broader epistemology. But within the logicist worldview, logical formalism is taken to capture the essence of meaning relevant for the determination of truth, while other aspects (concrete content, nuance, pragmatic context, rhetorical force) are considered irrelevant (as they were considered by Frege and proponents of formal logic after him). The problem is the underlying epistemology that promulgates formal reason over concrete knowledge. (It is not necessarily problematic that logic "descriptively" encodes some deductive forms.) Relatedly, the most problematic aspect of logic is that it is a system explicitly aimed toward providing complete closure, capturing unshakable truths: that goal, in and of itself, can be regarded as a hegemonic ideal.

5. Logic in Developmental and Cognitive Theories:
A Critical Appraisal

These critiques of logic are relevant to developmental psychology because of the sustained and unequaled dominance enjoyed by Piaget's theory, a theory that posits formal logic as the normative end point of cognitive development (Inhelder & Piaget, 1958; Piaget, 1970). This specific tenet of Piaget's theory is a case study of the social construction of developmental norms, and I will argue that it results from the same psycho-historico-cultural processes discussed by Flax (1993), Bordo (1987), and Lloyd (1993a). (I do not consider recent modulations of Piaget's theory to accommodate content, or Piaget's writings on other subjects; my task here is merely to expose the origins of that particular developmental norm, which until recently dominated the field.) Later in this section I also briefly consider how these critiques destabilize other (non-Piagetian) approaches to reasoning that give logic a central place.

Briefly, Piaget's program was one of "genetic epistemology": approaching the study of cognitive development from a perspective that fused insights from epistemology and biology, he sought to delineate the growth of knowledge in "the child." The child is conceptualized as an "epistemic subject": a particular child is but an instantiation of a genetic epistemological process and not a concrete, embodied being. Three major stages were defined: sensorimotor intelligence (characterized by a simple logic of action), concrete operations (characterized by a logic of classes and relations between classes, such as relations of set inclusion), and formal operations, characterized by the attainment of formal logic. Whereas concrete operations are tied to the nature of what is being manipulated mentally, formal operations are abstract and content independent. This characteristic (and other, technical features)[7] is what sets the stage of formal operations as the end point of development. Again, Piaget's theory is not merely a developmental theory: its intended scope is genetic epistemology (the course of the growth of knowledge).

The preceding critiques of rationality and logic make it clear that the Piagetian assumption that formal logical operations are the highest stage of development stems from a worldview that was developed through history as part of a gendered social formation. Piaget evidently appropriated this cultural worldview through formative symbolic and social processes of a nature similar to those described by Flax, Bordo, and Lloyd. It is significant and striking that his logicist conception of cognitive development was embraced vigorously by the psychological community, and we may ask, as

Bordo does in relation to Descartes and the ideal of objectivity, "Why did the dominant intellectual culture take this decisive turn [in that particular historical context]?" (Bordo, 1987, p. 9).

Piaget's and other theories that are presumed to apply universally have been criticized on other grounds. For instance Buck-Morss (1975) argues that Piaget's theory reflects a socioeconomic bias due to his bourgeois origins and conceptual framework, and that the development of abstract, formal cognition may reflect the demands of adapting to an industrialized society with abstract relations of production and exchange. Scribner (1997) and A. R. Luria (1976) have documented that some non-Westernized people's epistemology explicitly decries formal reasoning in favor of ordinary knowledge. Scribner submits that formal arguments and syllogistic tasks are a culture-specific "genre"; thus, agreeing to suspend ordinary knowledge and reason from arbitrary premises is less a matter of rationality than of compliance.

My critique is distinct in focus from these. My critique does not center on questioning the universalistic claims of the theory or on arguing that the course of development is culture specific (although both points are collateral to the present discussion). Rather, the critique exposes the gendered historical foundations of the norm itself and hence of the theory. Although the dominance of Piaget's early theory in the field of cognitive development has decreased in recent decades, partly due to the increased emphasis on the societal context of thought (and although this emphasis is reflected in Piaget's later writings), because of its extraordinary impact on even current conceptions of cognitive development it is important to expose it critically as a case study of the (historically) gendered construction of discourses of knowledge.

But beyond this case study, the substantive aim of this chapter is broader: it is to examine the implications of feminist critiques of logic for the study of reasoning and its development. Much of the current research on reasoning and its development stems not from a Piagetian framework but from a cluster of approaches within cognitive science that are shaped by their historical origins in rationalist philosophy. Though many rationalist assumptions have been relaxed, transformed, and woven with others in cognitive theories of deductive reasoning, that research area itself and its various contributors descend from the rationalist tradition directly or indirectly as they either posit or deny the centrality of logical processes (see Falmagne & Gonsalves, 1995, for review). Thus, the present critique bears on that tradition as well. In the last part of this chapter I explore how an approach to the study of reasoning can be informed by the feminist analyses discussed here, and how conceptual and descriptive tools might be reformulated accordingly.

6. Nonimplications from this Discussion

The conversations that surround the questions discussed here are intricate. First, in substance, these questions are complex. In addition, there exist diverse assumptions as to how these questions are to be construed and innumerable opportunities for miscommunication. Before examining the developmental and methodological ramifications from this critique, therefore, it is essential to make explicit several things that this critique does not imply and should not be taken to imply.

The preceding remarks do not imply that logic or logical thinking are invalid. Rather, formal rationality, and logic, must be made an object of critique as a cultural construction developed historically through complexly gendered processes. What this critique undermines are the foundational aspirations of logic as the ultimate grounding of knowledge, the hegemony of logic as an epistemic norm, and its dominance in descriptions of sound reasoning. (Some) logic may contribute one element of reasoning, but an epistemology broader than the rationalist program is needed. These critiques also generate new methodological directions, as discussed in the next section.

Importantly, the preceding discussion also does not presuppose either (1) that women and men have essentially different ways of reasoning or (2) that socially constructed women and men predominantly develop different ways of reasoning. Instead, there is a circular dialectic among the symbolic order, social structure, social practices and individual functioning. The dialectic is complex. The content of symbolic masculinity or femininity can be appropriated or resisted by both concrete men (and boys) and concrete women (and girls). And by virtue of being constructed by the practices and norms of a rationalist culture, many women and men are rationalist knowers. Gender cannot be treated as an untheorized (empirical) individual variable in studies of developmental, cognitive or affective phenomena. Gender is a multilevel social formation of which psychological processes are but one strand, and it must be treated as such analytically. The link between formal rationality and gender involves gender as a social formation, not individual gender.

Redundantly, perhaps, the preceding discussion does not imply or presuppose that rationality is gender linked at the individual level. This point merits emphasis, because it is too often the case that the complex questions examined here are reductively flattened into a "gender differ-ence" statement. Rather, formal rationality is a cultural construction orig-inating in a gendered societal matrix. That individual males may appropriate it in their construction of self is the result of the kind of com-plex developmental process outlined earlier. Thus, the framework devel-oped here precludes studying "gender differences" in predefined characteristics. Doing so forecloses the discovery of new patterns, the study of agency and resistance, and it inappropriately isolates individual processes from the gendered societal matrix through which thinkers are constituted.

7. Substantive and Methodological Ramifications[8]

These remarks suggest several complementary directions for research and theory. One direction is to examine critically both logic and the psychol-ogy of reasoning so as to expose the social processes through which knowl-edge is constructed at both the cultural and the individual level. We need to refocus the theoretical lens and the object of knowledge in studies of development from the individual, including the individual-in-context, to the society and culture as a social-political-institutional-semiotic system. In such an integrated approach to development, while the individual ulti-mately remains the focus of analysis, the individual is not the unit of analysis. Theory and research focus instead on those societal/cultural processes that constrain or enable particular modes of thinking. (Hen-riques, Hollway, Urwin, Venn, & Walkerdine, 1984, provide an illustrative collection of essays guided by this perspective, though not with a focus on gender.)

Logic has been historically produced through a gendered social process and is deployed as a norm in cultural institutions that are gendered, through the complex dialectic outlined in this chapter. The centrality of logic in the politics of knowledge production implies the need to investigate its impact as part of the dominant discourse of knowledge (Foucault, 1980). For developmental psychology, this implies problematizing not only the epis-temic norm itself but also (1) its institutional manifestations and (2) the practices that implement it. Thus, as a second complementary direction, a central task for developmental research is to study the deployment of epistemic norms in the child's developmental niche, and to examine how the resulting practices intersect with ideologies of gender. For instance, in a detailed Foucauldian analysis, Walkerdine (1988) examines the relations between (rationalist) pedagogical practices and linguistic and cognitive development.

The third, equally important agenda for research is to examine the manner in which thinkers negotiate rationalist discourses and other discourses within their specific cultural frameworks and (gendered) social locations: how they appropriate, resist, integrate, or transform these discourses. Stated differently, the agenda is to examine how the dominant discourse of rationality intersects with other discourses to produce modes of reasoning and conceptions of knowledge in thinkers who develop in a gendered social world.

Doing so is a reconstructive project. The preceding critiques call into question the epistemic scope of logic as an instrument of knowledge, its status of reasoning norm, and its centrality in descriptions of reasoning processes. However, consequential as they are, critiques are only the first step toward the reconstructive project of developing substantive theory and research on inference on feminist grounds. Thus, a new theoretical vocabulary must be developed that is liberated (to the extent possible) from the historical hegemony of the logicist worldview.

As a first attempt to develop such a theoretical vocabulary as well as a fully societal approach to reasoning, I have begun to examine the various resources on which different social agents draw in everyday deductive situations in which they must evaluate contradictory accounts or formulate conclusions from prior information, and to qualitatively investigate the interplay of these resources in the reasoning process. The research also examines the reasoner's epistemological views as to what constitutes sound reasoning in particular situations. The primary focus of this line of research is on gender as a social formation that structures the social world materially, institutionally and symbolically in intersection with specific ethnic/racial, cultural and socioeconomic formations. Therefore, the particularities of a reasoner's location and experience are built into the design of the interview and the interpretive method.

The exploratory research has been with young adult women, but it can be considered within the developmental framework developed in this chapter, and the methodology and research agenda extend to other populations as well. The study was designed as a methodological exploration aimed to develop interview and data analytic tools for this new line of research and to provide initial pointers for further inquiry (Falmagne, 1997). Women college students were offered hypothetical problems that involved adjudicating contradictory accounts (e.g., two contradictory medical diagnoses; the arguments from the prosecution and the defense in a hypothetical trial). They were offered these problems as models but encouraged to supply analogous situations from their life and to reason with these, a technique that proved fertile. Flexible semistructured interviews explored the woman's reasoning about the problems and her views on what constitutes sound reasoning in particular situations.

Specific foci of interest were (1) the modes of knowledge deployed at different moments, and in particular the specific kinds of contextual knowledge the woman utilized; (2) the constructive sense-making through which the woman appropriated the problem and constructed the functional context for her reasoning; (3) the manner in which the reasoner drew on general inferential principles; and (4) the specific ways in which logic and other kinds of knowledge were interwoven in her reasoning; and (5) the variations in modes of reasoning and in the woman's epistemic views on what constitutes "sound" reasoning in relation to situational aspects of the problem.

The concepts discussed in previous sections of this chapter formed the interpretive frame of the study and guided the interview and data analysis methods. An in-depth interview on the person's societal niche and history served to particularize her and to provide a contextual frame of interpretation of her reasoning. The data analysis was two-pronged, aimed at capturing both particularities and broader patterns. One analysis consisted of narrative sketches of each woman's reasoning, grounded in her life context. Interviews were analyzed for indications of formative cultural influences on the woman's thinking and of the manner in which she appropriated, resisted, transformed, or rejected various cultural discourses of knowledge, interpreted in the context of her societal location and cultural history, so as to highlight the contribution of gendered social processes (discursive, material, institutional) to the constitution of reasoning. The descriptive vocabulary for her mode of reasoning was derived from the second kind of analysis, to be described shortly.

Although the narrative profiles were suggestive of some formative cultural influences on the women's thinking (Falmagne, 1997), these preliminary interpretations cannot be summarized within the constraints of this chapter without undue simplification and without betraying the inherently interpretive, qualitative nature of the description. When abbreviated, rich contextual descriptions of this kind are vulnerable, almost unavoidably, to read as reductive causal relations between contextual "variables" and reasoning. Thus this discussion will focus on the second set of analyses instead.

This second set of analyses consisted of cross-sectional descriptive categories characterizing moments in the reasoning process. The categories were developed semi-inductively through in depth analysis of transcripts, guided jointly by suggestions from the data and by a frame of reference grounded in the feminist critiques and feminist epistemologies discussed above. Importantly, these descriptive constructs must not be seen as classification tools. Rather, they serve a *heuristic* function as *provisional pointers* (Falmagne, 1997, 2000). Their function is to provide a new descriptive vocabulary for the study of reasoning, in which one may contrast different modes of knowledge, perspectives on what constitutes sound reasoning, kinds of interplays between logic and other modes of knowledge, and other processes such as the sense-making through which reasoners appropriate the problem and construct the functional context for their reasoning. The analysis attempts to characterize moments of reasoning rather than categorizing the woman as a particular knower: a woman might deploy different modes of knowledge at different times either in her spontaneous reasoning or in response to epistemological probes, and this is indeed what the data appeared to suggest.

One mode of knowledge appeared to be an *empiricist process* guided by a search for facts, with the explicit or implicit notion that "facts speak for themselves." Often, but not always, perceptual metaphors, usually visual ("and then I would see that this is what I have") are used. It appears that, in the participant's view, facts are unmediated by selective or by inferential processes. The source of knowledge resides in facts, not thought. This approach contrasts with *rationalist knowledge,* whereby rational understanding is given primacy. The reasoner pursues paths that will generate a coherent (to her) explanation that she can rationally endorse. In sharp contrast to the previous approach, where the main burden is on empirical "proof," knowledge here is attained mentally and evaluated according to rationalist norms. For example, in reasoning about two contradictory medical diagnoses, one woman said, "...First I would like to understand the facts and then I could understand the reasoning for why I would have to take that medicine.... I mean there has to be a relationship between what is wrong with my body and their explanation for what is wrong with my body and what they will...give me to make my body better.... I have to see the relation." Thus her criterion has to do with understanding. In later segments, this woman showed complex interweavings of different modes, so this excerpt does not capture her overall epistemology but instead reflects a rationalist moment. In sharp contrast to both, some moments of reasoning seemed to reflect a *pragmatist epistemology*: the reasoning, rather than relying on factual knowledge, as in the empiricist process, or on mental understanding, as in the rationalist approach, was driven by a quest for "what works." For instance, in the medical situation, one woman would try out one treatment and then another, rather than evaluating the doctor's reasoning.

A more complex mode of knowledge could be provisionally described as *balanced rationalism:* logic and rationality are instruments of knowledge but only when they are articulated with other processes and used functionally according to broader goals. Two elements are crucial here: logic is highlighted (an emphasis not always present), and it is only one component of a system of knowledge (a construal that departs from pure rationalism). It is their conjunction that characterizes this mode of knowledge. For instance, one respondent praised rationality but defined it functionally, in terms of goals and values in particular contexts; abstract rationality oblivious to its function was inappropriate. For another woman, rationality was grounded not in values but in practical knowing and in social knowledge, thus yielding an approach to problems that integrated these three strands. Somewhat related yet distinct was an approach coined *concrete/historicized knowledge,* in which abstract knowing is called into question for misrepresenting the complexity of phenomena and therefore yielding misguided conclusions. For instance, in one situation, one woman articulately critiqued macroeconomics, arguing and illustrating that economic theories needed to be historicized and contextualized with respect to the specifics of the particular country.

The following four modes of knowledge have superficial features in common but are distinct in important ways. The first is provisionally described as *knowledge by immersion:* knowledge is acquired through "osmosis," by direct contact with the problem situation. This notion occurred infrequently but warrants singling out. One woman, describing a relative's problem, insisted that she and her family had to bring this relative to live with them, so that (crucially) merely by virtue of being with her at all times, they would be able to understand the problem. The second is a *relativistic view,* which often uses language such as "each person has their point of view" and appears to be guided by a concern for not privileging any point of view. This view does not appear to be grounded in an articulated epistemology, in contrast to the next two modes.

In sharp contrast to the above is *standpoint knowledge:* an articulated conception according to which knowledge is grounded in the standpoint of the knower. Unlike the relativistic view, standpoint knowledge includes an explicit assumption that the knower is part of the knowing process and that knowers are constituted by their social conditions, which give them a partial view on the world (an assumption present in the feminist perspectives on knowledge discussed previously). One woman, asked to discuss her thoughts on two opposing views about welfare, stated that she would have to go and live with people on welfare in order to know how they are thinking; a knowledge of their problems as they see them is not possible otherwise. Thus, for her, a person's thinking is grounded in the person's circumstances. This view differs from a relativistic view in that it explicitly articulates the relation between material conditions and mode of thought. It differs from the knowledge-by-immersion approach in that (in this example) one does not merely absorb the way in which people think by living with them; rather, living there gives one access to the standpoint of these knowers. Finally, another articulated perspective is that of *subjective knowledge:* knowledge is inherently subjective and personal. This approach is similar to what Belenky et al (1986) have described for "subjective knowers." Here, however, the description characterizes a moment of knowledge instantiated in a woman's response to a specific problem, not the woman as a knower. This mode of knowledge importantly contrasts with standpoint knowledge in that it stresses the individuality of the knower rather than the impact of one's social conditions on one's mode of thought.

One major focus of the analysis was the interplay between logic and other knowledges. The data of this exploratory study suggested that this interplay can take a variety of forms: (1) Logic is the guiding principle, while other knowledges—contextual, concrete, social, personal—are supportive only. (2) Logic is merely a default when no other knowledge is available; other knowledges are primary. (3) Logic is a common ground for communication but not the base on which knowledge is attained or evaluated. (4) Logic conflicts with, and cannot be integrated with other modes of knowledge. (5) Logic is one of several modes of knowledge that are useful for adjudicating contradictory accounts. These different forms of the interplay between logic and other forms of knowledge were examined through discourse analysis of extended segments of the interview, with a particular focus on tensions in the reasoning and on how these tensions were negotiated.

Interestingly, "making sense" surfaced as a rich, polysemous marker used by several women in describing how they would adjudicate contradictory accounts or arguments: they would try to determine which one made sense. "Making sense," however, appears to have vastly different meanings, including (1) generating a feeling of coherence with the woman's existing beliefs; (2) being well supported by the evidence adduced by the protagonist; (3) resulting from a reasoning process the woman deemed reasonable on the part of the protagonist; (4) being grounded in a mode of knowledge she found appropriate (for instance, sufficiently contextual as opposed to relying on abstract knowledge, in the case of one woman); (5) making sense substantively, in terms of what she knew about the phenomenon; and (6) making sense logically, structurally.

These preliminary analyses provide one illustration of the manner in which research questions can be reconfigured when logic is displaced off center in theoretical conceptualizations of reasoning. As exploratory research, the main aim was to begin to develop a descriptive vocabulary for a societal approach to reasoning liberated from the historical hegemony of the rationalist worldview (Falmagne, 1997). The research was done with women, in agreement with the recommendation of many feminist theorists that we start thought from women's lives (e.g., Harding, 1991; Hartsock, 1983; D. Smith, 1987). This strategy, however, is merely intended to take women, in their concrete ethnic/racial and socioeconomic locations, as a point of departure for developing theory, on the metatheoretical principle that the contradictions of a system are more visible from marginal locations. It is important to clarify again that the research did not aim to assess modes of reasoning specific to women, an approach I have argued to be problematic. Rather, the aim was to describe the course of reasoning both in its embeddedness in individuals' particular societal niche and cultural experience and in terms of potential cross-sectional patterns. Commonalities or partial commonalities that may emerge from this approach would be grounded in a full contextual understanding of each reasoner and shaped by interpretive data analysis.

This research is presented as one attempt to develop a substantive approach to reasoning informed by the critical considerations and the developmental theoretical framework discussed in this chapter. Clearly, it is the interplay of distinct lines of research directed by similar theoretical agendas that will advance the study of development on new ground. The three lines of investigation sketched in this section, focusing respectively on the role of logic in the societal politics of knowledge production, on the deployment of epistemic norms in the child's developmental niche, and on the manner in which thinkers negotiate various discourses of knowledge within their specific societal niche, are interwoven theoretically on a general level and, while proceeding with distinct foci and methodologies, may be seen as interacting components of an overall program.

Notes

1. This agreement includes in particular the approach known as "sociocultural" (e.g., Cole, 1992; Wertsch, 1991); the "cultural" approach, which views development within a semiotic-societal framework (Valsiner, 1998b); the "participation" approach, which takes as its primitive the joint activity and development of child and adult (Rogoff, 1997); cognitive approaches, which see development as grounded in social practices that are culturally shaped (K. Nelson, 1996); and various lines of research that seek to integrate the study of development and ethnographic methods (Jessor, Colby, & Shweder, 1996). The quotation marks around the term "sociocultural" mark the distinction between the particular strand of theory and research that has come to be known under that label and the more general concept of an approach to development as grounded in society and culture. In general parlance, the two are often fused. As is clear from this sketchy overview, and as I will argue in this chapter, there are different ways of construing the latter. It is important not to identify the generic perspective with the specific ways in which it has been instantiated.

2. "Practice" denotes an organized activity within a social system, a concrete activity that incorporates the goals and meanings of that system.

3. The authors make it clear that a feminist standpoint is achieved, not delivered automatically by one's structural location. My use of "standpoint" in this paragraph ignores that point in the interest of simplicity of exposition.

4. Standpoint theory is sometimes likened to some postmodern analyses, but the analogy is based on superficial features and is misguided: postmodern analyses stem from a critical, not a materialist, perspective, a fundamental difference. In a 1997 issue of *Signs*, Hekman provides a postmodern representation of standpoint theory; for critical commentaries on her representation, see articles by Hartsock, D. Smith, Collins, and Harding in the same issue.

5. Aside from the standard two-valued logic familiar to most nonspecialists, a variety of logics have been developed both historically and in contemporary work to address various epistemic and technical requirements. See Haack (1978) for a good overview of the issues, although an overview from the "mainstream," noncontextual perspective that Nye critiques.

6. In Frege's logic, true and false are the only two possibilities, although other logics do not have that constraint.

7. Piaget formalizes the mental operations that are possible at that stage through a theory-internal system, but these technicalities do not affect the fact that the logic posited as characterizing thought at that stage is the formal two-valued propositional calculus.

8. The exploratory research discussed in this section was supported by a Spencer Foundation Small Grant.

12

Naming, Naturalizing, Normalizing

"The Child" as Fact and Artifact

Lorraine Code

Epistemologies of Mastery

The principal, standard-setting epistemologies of Anglo-American professional philosophy and the theories and practices of cognitive developmental psychology echo and sustain one another across a range of methodological assumptions and substantive issues. Enactments of the central tenets of mainstream epistemology are in evidence throughout the practices of developmental psychology, which exemplify the effects of epistemology's normative claims and expose their limitations. And mainstream developmental psychologists find their established practices vindicated in the equally well established theories of knowledge that govern scientific and social scientific practice and "knowledge in general," while their practices confirm the viability and the hegemonic status of those very theories. Even if developmental psychologists rarely read epistemology, even if philosophers rarely read developmental psychology, these reciprocal effects are instructive. In this essay I engage in an exploratory investigation of this relationship, informed by a critical feminist consciousness. My analysis endeavors to show how dominant conceptions of knowledge and subjectivity, common to both domains, are complicit in sustaining patriarchal and other asymmetrical distributions of power and privilege. It points toward ways of developing revisionary, emancipatory, and socially-politically transformative successor epistemologies and developmental theories.

Postpositivist empiricist epistemology seeks to determine universal, necessary and sufficient conditions for knowledge in general, and to silence the skeptic who doubts that knowledge is possible. Guided by a formal conception of knowledge, it works to determine standards for justifying claims to know and for distinguishing bona fide knowledge from belief or conjecture: criteria ubiquitously valid across epistemic domains. Such epistemologies model their inquiries on perceptual knowledge of "medium-sized" physical objects, or on idealized conceptions of science and scientific method. Commonly, too, they presuppose a rational, individual knower who is everyone and no one, but whose identity is insignificant to the processes or products of inquiry.

In the developmental psychology informed and governed by the legacy of Jean Piaget, which is my focus here, analogous assumptions prevail. With the goal of demonstrating the presence of universal cognitive and moral structures that are alike in all children, Piagetians and their successors depict developmental stages as steps on an ascending ladder toward rational maturity. Commonly they, too, model cognition on perceptually based abilities to distinguish, arrange, and manipulate "medium-sized" physical objects. They work with a conception of "the child" who is every child and no child in particular, whose identity should make no difference to the processes or products of inquiry. Despite some attempts to produce social accounts of development, of which L. S. Vygotsky's (1962, 1978) is the classic example, an assumption that children can adequately be studied in abstraction from their family, community, and culture still governs developmental psychology. Even if the word from present-day developmentalists seems to be that Piagetian theory has "collapsed" (Gopnik & Melzoff, 1997, pp. 20, 221), the theoretical territory mapped out by the Piagetian project is a still fertile theoretical ground.[1]

The levels of abstraction that epistemologists postulate may seem at best elusive, at worst absurd, to nonphilosophers. But the goal of establishing reliable criteria for objective, disinterested knowing that transcends the particularities of values, partiality, and vested interests is a worthy one. Cognizant of the need for standards of objectivity and certainty to separate knowledge from conjecture, whimsy, propaganda, and power-driven struggles for epistemic ascendency and authority, epistemologists caution against the chaos that would ensue if "man" were indeed, idiosyncratically or collectively, "the measure of all things." Nonetheless, feminists and other postcolonial theorists engaged in transformative-emancipatory critique have demonstrated that the neutral demeanor of these theories of knowledge masks their complicity in sustaining a hierarchical social order marked by uneven distributions of power and privilege: that the ideals of knowledge, rationality, and agency that infuse these epistemologies and the practices they inform derive from the experiences of, and are most readily available to, affluent educated adult white men (e.g., Alcoff & Potter, 1993; Code, 1991; Keller, 1985; Lennon & Whitford, 1994; Lloyd, 1993b). These men's positioning as established authorities and experts may be a historical-sociological accident, but its effects are constitutive of the ideals that legitimate knowledge and morality in white Western societies. These are the authorities who uphold the standards by which knowledge claims are adjudicated, credibility conferred, and moral judgments enacted.

Analogously, the levels of abstraction and assumptions of universality in the received practices of developmental psychology may seem at best artificial, at worst absurd, to those cognizant of the diversity of children's lives. But the goal of constructing a regulative, guiding frame to capture what is common to all children, thus looking beneath surface inequalities and refusing to endorse favoritism or special interests out of respect for these demonstrated commonalities, is likewise a worthy one. Yet feminists and other postpatriarchal developmentalists, committed to eradicating the injustices that its universalistic pretensions sustain, have shown that the abstract impartiality of Piagetian developmentality, and of its successors and cognates, likewise masks the complicity of these theories in sustaining a patriarchal, capitalist social order that is insufficiently sensitive to structural differences and to the material-psychological-social specificities that shape the lives of children who fall outside "the norm." Thus, in her gender- and class-sensitive reading of Piaget, Valerie Walkerdine (1988) argues that "what is taken to be universal is itself the imposition of a particular truth" (p. 193).

It may seem a large step from my polite sketches of orthodox epistemology and developmental psychology to this claim that casts them as contributors to practices of privilege. Epistemology's self-presentation as the proponent of a view from nowhere, a god's-eye view of the world, and developmental psychology's universality claims, seem to hold them at such a distance from concrete particularities as to exonerate both from charges of sustaining structures of inequality. Yet I am proposing that the social-political effects of these epistemologies and psychologies feed into and are fed by an *instituted social imaginary* of mastery and domination that values knowledge for its power to predict, manipulate, and control the objects of its study, whether those "objects" be physical or human; that represents knowers as infinitely replicable, solitary and detached individuals face to face with inert and indifferent objects of knowledge to which their attitude, too, is and should be one of indifference; and that assumes without question that the child whom developmentalists study is the father of autonomous *man,* the man of reason, who claims the principal speaking parts in the public discourses of orthodox epistemology. Distancing themselves from particularities shields practitioners from any need to address the differences that difference makes.

Situated Knowing, Individualism, and Mastery

In this essay, I consider how this social imaginary constructs "the child" as an object of inquiry and as a (potential) knower whose cognitive development follows a path of "natural" maturation into autonomous man, the fictional character who occupies center stage in this same imaginary. Indeed, a narrowly delineated achievement of autonomy counts as the telos of "normal" development in white affluent (male) children: as its descriptively "natural" and prescriptively fostered goal. Discourses of development and maturation represent "the child" as a being who unfolds out of an infancy in which he is radically, vitally dependent on nurturant others to a place of full individual autonomy where he becomes his "own" person, renouncing dependence to emerge as a self-sufficient individual.[2] Development thus represented is a linear process that achieves completion at "the age of majority," the child having passed through well-marked way-stages or levels en route to this fully separated moment.[3] Cognitive and moral maturity, then, marks an end of dependence on infant and childhood nurturers. It manifests itself in achieved mastery: mastery over "one's own" body, which is so taken for granted that it rarely receives mention except as a precondition for all the rest; mastery over emotions, which aligns closely with bodily mastery; mastery over the becoming-adult's physical, social, cultural, and natural surroundings—a complex of "masteries" that represents a solitary coming of age in matters moral, epistemological, social, and personal. This masterful self, then, is the autonomous individual whose makings I discuss here.

Picking up a doubled thematic that runs through my work on knowledge and subjectivity (see the introduction in Code, 1995b), in this essay I examine the uneasy fit between the knowledge that empiricist-positivist epistemologies endorse and the human subjects—the children—who are the objects of study in developmental psychology. Concomitantly, I examine assumptions that tacitly inform these theories and practices: about what kind of creature "the child" must be in order to be knowable through the methods these assumptions sanction; what kinds of knowing he or she must master in order to achieve recognized maturity; what kind of knower an epistemologist-psychologist must be in order to produce developmental knowledge that qualifies as "normal science." For although neither parents nor developmentalists may be regular readers of epistemology texts, established theories of knowledge are enacted in the governing ideals of developmental theories and practices and in everyday assumptions about what claims deserve the label "knowledge" and who merits acknowledgment as a knower or knowledgeable moral agent. Feminist critics of the epistemologies and ethicopolitics of mastery have exposed the tacit agendas that underwrite these developmental disciplinary practices, inculcating children and inducting parents into this imaginary that represents mastery in its multiple modalities as the mark of a successful human life. Here I am proposing that naming, naturalizing, and normalizing are practices constitutive of these modes of inquiry—in their form, content, and social-political enactment. Reconfigured, these practices can reconstitute the inquiries, contesting their fundamental premises, refashioning the neutral, disinterested self-conceptions that permit them to hold mastery in place as a regulative ideal.

Post-Kantian philosophers tend to work with a curious, if standardized, conception of the (largely invisible) human subject who is their main protagonist. Although details of his identity rarely figure explicitly, in colonial and pre-second-wave-feminist theories, that subject is adult (but not old), white, and male. His natural epistemic maturation follows the exact same path regardless of its familial, social, cultural, or material location. For positivist-empiricists, neither the developmental processes that shape the adult masculinity enacted in the life of this "rational self-conscious agent"—this man of reason—nor the situations and circumstances in which knowledge is produced are epistemologically significant. Those who argue otherwise commit the "genetic fallacy": the fallacy of resting justification or explanation upon such nonepistemic details as the provenance—the genesis—of reason and of knowledge claims. Hence the relationship between epistemology and developmental psychology has been an uneasy one. When children figure in canonical philosophy texts—with two notable exceptions, in the *Émile* of Jean Jacques Rousseau (which is "really" about education, thus not about epistemology) and in the later work of Ludwig Wittgenstein—they appear in retrospective extrapolations in which autonomous man reconstructs his own knowledge from "primitive simples." Thus, typically, D.W. Hamlyn (1973) denies Piaget's work philosophical significance, reiterating an entrenched assumption that introspective reconstructions of childhood cognition are all that theorists of knowledge need. He writes, "the priority of the concrete to the abstract is something that all normal human beings *could discover by reflection* on what they know about the nature of human development, of human learning: it needs no further empirical investigation" (p. 42, emphasis added). Thus epistemologists are well advised to leave empirical particulars behind in their normative, a priori inquiries: everyone is an authority on childhood, for everyone has firsthand knowledge of it.

One exception to this disdain for developmental and "situational" questions is Ludwig Wittgenstein (1968). Consider the following:

> ...we are brought up, trained, to ask: "What is that called?"—upon which the name is given.... Now one can ostensively define a proper name, the name of a colour, the name of a material, a numeral, the name of a point on the compass and so on. The definition of the number two, "That is called 'two' "—pointing to two nuts—is perfectly exact. —But how can two be defined like that? The person one gives the definition to doesn't know what one wants to call "two"; he will suppose that "two" is the name given to *this* group of nuts!... That is to say: an ostensive definition can be variously interpreted in *every* case. (§27, 28)

Now, Wittgenstein is no developmental psychologist; and his remarks rely on everyday observation, thus not on experiment—but also not on "mere" reflection. Yet the passage stands as an implicit critique of Hamlyn's (not atypical) dismissal of any insights epistemologists might hope to gain from developmental studies, and of developmental psychology's focus on the generic individual child, separated from the concrete particularities that promote or thwart his or her cognitive development. Even so apparently simple a cognitive practice as teaching a child, ostensively, the name of a color, contests any claim that people "can discover by reflection" anything they need to know about child development. It emphasizes the complexity of even so simple an act as showing the child that it is the *redness* of the book, the sweater, the crayon that I am teaching her to name. How can she discern that my gestures "mean" the color, not the object itself, or its location or shape? Because acts of naming are socially-culturally embedded, all the way down to the most fundamental level, it is impossible to represent the process so simply as philosophers wedded to the Myth of the Given (Sellars, 1973), the certainty of a retrospective glance, and the idea that we all have equivalent "privileged access" to the nature of our childhood knowings, evidently think possible. Walkerdine, provocatively, asks,

> If there is no action which takes place outside the framework of social practices, and if the object world is understood only in terms of its mean-

ingful insertion within particular discursive practices, then why should we assume a unique and singular developmental path, a unique and singular subject? (1988, p. 30)

Here I am endorsing her contention that all actions, all meanings occur within social practices: a claim which marks a radical departure from the *individualism* of standard epistemology and psychology. And although it may be tempting to cite Vygotsky's work as evidence that developmental psychology has not been unrelievedly individualistic, it is worth noting that discussions framed in the language of social-cultural influences *on* the child still subtly hold to the conception of a self-contained *individual* who is subject to, but can be extricated from and purged of, those influences.

Nor does the color-naming episode unequivocally mark a standardized level of conceptual achievement, a readiness for the next stage of learning: it too can—indeed, must—be variously interpreted. In an epistemology of mastery, as in developmental psychology informed by it, such learning to *name* demonstrates a degree of success in mastering the environment: a level of control over objects. Yet such a reading is as much a product of the imaginary that normalizes mastery as it is a neutral reading of naming activities. A less individualistic, more socially embedded analysis might read learning to name as integral to a child's entry into a family, a group, a community where she establishes her place linguistically as she learns to name—both how to name and what is worth naming—within the form of life where she thus begins to claim membership. Here, again, is Wittgenstein: "When a child learns language *it learns at the same time what is to be investigated and what is not.* When it learns that there is a cupboard in the room, it isn't taught to doubt whether what it sees later on is still a cupboard or only a kind of stage set" (1971, §472, emphasis added). Wittgenstein's insistence that to learn a language is to learn a "form of life" amounts to a claim that naming and more elaborated learning-knowing processes do not speak for themselves but acquire meaning, and hence theoretical significance, out of the social-cultural locations within which they occur. It relocates childhood cognition within situations, communities, and social-political practices where naming is neither a solitary nor a simple act.

Walkerdine is one of Piaget's most cogent critics on issues of gender, class, and race. She develops an explicitly situational-political-material critique of the assumptions that underwrite his project: a sustained, provocative analysis of how Piagetian psychology reinscribes and reinforces the rhetorics of mastery as a universal leitmotiv of developmentality. In an analysis that shows clear affinities with Susan Buck-Morss's

(1975) now classic exposure of socioeconomic bias in Piagetian theory and with Cathy Urwin's (1984) and her own (1984) earlier social-material analyses, Walkerdine maps the narrowly local specificity of Piagetian theory: its situatedness within, as a product of, and as regulative for the lives of affluent white middle-class children and parents. She takes issue with Piagetian theory's universalist pretensions even within Western societies, offering a critical reevaluation of the scope, limits, and political consequences of this oft-declared neutral, politically innocent theoretical apparatus. Its tacit political intent, she convincingly shows, is to promote "the triumph of reason over emotion through stressing the naturally adaptive processes of organisms... [so that] animal passions would be left behind to found a better world in reason" (1988, p. 5).

Now, such a project might seem to advocate an uncontestably commendable goal, nor does Walkerdine deny its appeal. Her quarrel is with its implicitly naturalizing/normalizing agenda, and with the suppressions and silencings that result from its promotion of a formal reason that is assumed, without question, to be alike in all men (see Lloyd, 1993b). Consequent on such celebrations of the power of reason over emotion is a failure to take adequately into account the sociality—the radically diverse "practices of everyday life"—that make rational development *variously* possible. Co-opted into "bourgeois and patriarchal rule by science," Walkerdine contends, "the 'reasonable person,' in Piaget's terms, is 'in love with ideas' and not bodies" (1988, p. 186). This suppression of affectivity, and therefore of affective engagement with the differences that the diversity of human embodiment entails, is a significant cost that ideal mastery over the self and the physical-social world enacts. It at once informs the naturalizing-normalizing that I discuss below, and renders epistemologies and psychologies of mastery inimical to feminist and other postcolonial emancipatory projects.

Naming, Naturalizing, Normalizing

My intention is not to enlist Wittgenstein as a protofeminist or protodevelopmentalist but to read passages in his later work (which can also be variously interpreted) as marks of a refusal, partially congruent with the critique Walkerdine advances, of certain constraints of epistemological orthodoxy. Wittgenstein examines social practices as sites where truths about childhood cognition are produced and which create (to borrow Walkerdine's words) "a normalizing vision of the 'natural child' " (1988, p. 5). Thus I am reading Walkerdine and Wittgenstein through one another, as contributors to a *natural history* of the knowledge-and-subjectivity issues in child-adult-world cognitive relations. I intend this analysis to count as one piece in my in-progress articulation of an *ethologically* and *ecologically* sensitive naturalized epistemology. My aims are to discern what epistemologists, especially naturalistic epistemologists, can learn from developmentalists, and to show why a critical stance toward Piagetian orthodoxy and its successors and analogues matters to feminists and to participants in other successor epistemology projects, who are likewise working to undo the damage consequent on an excessive veneration of mastery.

Naturalists relinquish mainstream epistemology's search for a priori, necessary and sufficient conditions for knowledge in general, to examine how people go about knowing, variously, within the scope and limits of their (experimentally revealed) cognitive capacities. Naturalism's title, and its guiding principle, have their source in W. V. O. Quine's (1969/1994) landmark claim, "Epistemology, or something like it, simply falls into place as a chapter of psychology and hence of natural science. It studies a natural phenomenon, viz., a physical human subject" (p. 25). Thus, according to Hilary Kornblith (1990), the agenda-setting questions are: "What is the world that we may know it? And what are we that we may know the world?" (p. 3).[4] Answers will be found at places where the best theories of physical reality and the best psychological theories dovetail: in studies of "how we are adapted to the structure of the world around us" (p. 15) so that we can rely on perceptual information and the conclusions of inductive inferences.

Yet I have argued (Code, 1996) that its scientism—that is, its adherence to a strictly power-affect- and value-neutral conception of scientific inquiry as the only inquiry that yields knowledge worthy of the name—limits Quinean naturalism's promise for feminist and other postcolonial projects. Sabina Lovibond (1989) characterizes the promise that Quinean naturalists bypass, in her contention (which I endorse) that feminist theory could establish theoretical allegiances with projects of naturalizing epistemology, which

> represent the activity we call 'enquiry' as part of the natural history of human beings.... Naturalist or materialist analyses of the institutions of knowledge-production have made it possible to expose the unequal part played by different social groups in determining standards of judgement.... *They have revealed the ideological character of value-systems which have passed as objective or universally valid.* (pp. 12–13, emphasis added)

Because Quinean naturalists limit their observations to the knowing that takes place in the scientific laboratory, where values, ideology, diversity, power, and privilege are left behind at the door, they are unable to realize the full promise Lovibond envisages. The effects of this limitation are starkly apparent in Alison Gopnik's and Andrew Melzoff's (1997) commitment to (Quinean) scientistic literalness, in their "theory theory" that casts developing children as miniature rationalistic scientists, their cognitive activity as theory-constructive from earliest infancy, and old-style mastery as their ultimate developmental achievement.

Wittgenstein, I am suggesting, is a more secular naturalist whose contributions to a natural history of everyday epistemic life generate neither a full-blown theory nor a scientistic reductivism. Both Wittgenstein's work and Walkerdine's succeed, although quite differently, in "making strange" certain sedimented epistemological assumptions, in revealing their incongruity within everyday (diverse) epistemic lives, while Walkerdine's book also exposes the ideological complicity of the value system implicit in the work of Piaget and his successors. Walkerdine (1988) astutely observes that "experimental studies, while they are an important source of data...reveal relatively little about how non-experimental contexts operate" (p. 11). Feminists' commitment to eradicating real-world injustices precludes their reliance on an overblown conception of the reach of experimentally derived analyses; the gap between theory and practice is too wide. Thus I am casting scientism as inimical to feminist naturalistic projects because of its contention that natural science is in order as it stands. Implicit in that contention are the beliefs that there is no need to contest the universal-applicability assumptions of scientific orthodoxy that mask the power- and privilege-sustaining agendas behind its claims to account for everything that is knowledge-worthy. Nor is there any need to question the abstract individualism it takes for granted, in which knowers figure only incidentally, and inconveniently, as producers of the knowledge that matters: they need not be identified because every one is substitutable for every other. Within such a frame there is no place to ask "Whose knowledge are we talking about?"—a question pivotal to feminist and other postcolonial epistemologies and the disciplinary projects they inform.

Wittgenstein does not address equality or ideology, but his observations of how children know within "forms of life" count as contributions to a "natural history of human beings" that could radicalize the potential of a science-derived naturalism that looks only occasionally to developmental psychology—and often to a mode of developmental practice, of which Gopnik and Meltzoff's (1997) work is a representative state-of-the-art example, that characterizes itself as a "specific version of the naturalistic-epistemology story" (p. 18). Their project is almost as narrowly scientistic as the sources to which Quine-line naturalists appeal, for they enter these debates fully equipped with before-the-fact assumptions about the child as a little scientist and about the "naturalness" both of laboratory life and of solitary, self-reliant information processors as paradigmatic knowers. This is the scientism Jeanne Marecek (1995) attributes to mainstream psychology, historically

> committed to the discovery of presumed universals in human experience—"laws of human behavior" that transcend history, culture, class, caste, and material circumstances. Thus, the valued means of producing knowledge has been the experiment, in which behavior is extracted from its usual social context. (p. 110)

Yet experimentation need not be confined to the laboratory: Walkerdine relocates it in the schoolroom. Even there, she cautions, universalistic assumptions could function reductively, as a prefabricated grid, if an experiment is treated simply as a means for producing quantifiable analysis, and the classroom is represented as a site for straightforwardly scientific "naturalistic observation." In such circumstances, she suggests, the process "evades and elides" issues of how the truth of specifically located practices is produced, fails to address how that "truth" is registered in the institutionalized aptness of certain kinds of response (1988, p. 51). Yet Walkerdine shows how such assumptions can be problematized in observings that depart from empiricist orthodoxy to participate in what I think is best characterized as a critical, *negotiated* empiricism where perceptual "data" have always to be debated, interrogated, interpreted, and analyzed, not merely "read off" the surface of events and practices.

With these thoughts in mind, in the following sections I give content to the terms of my title, "naming," "normalizing," and "naturalizing." My intention is to show how they figure as emblematic practices within mainstream developmental psychology and to suggest why and how they might be reconfigured in feminist developmental projects.

Naming

Naming, in my title and in Wittgenstein's reminders about the ambiguity of ostensive definition, is a trope for the "primitive simples" that classical and some later empiricists represent as the basics of human knowledge: for the assumed immediacy, simplicity, and atomicity of childhood knowing, where the simple, prepropositional naming of discrete physical objects counts as an originary cognitive moment. Rhetorically, it functions as the moment where it all began, the moment that is recuperable in analyses rigorous enough to reconstruct the discrete building blocks from which knowledge can be rebuilt "from the bottom up" to reveal the conditions of its possibility. Classical empiricists, as I have noted, arrive at these simples by introspecting retrospectively to what a child "must have known for certain"; the thought experiments of such sense-data theorists as Bertrand Russell (1912) and H. H. Price (1933) strip observations of simple objects down to their barest presentational moments; logical positivists (see Ayer, 1936) contrive sanitized observations where simple propositional knowledge claims map perceptual "givens" to yield straightforwardly verifiable protocol statements. Analogously, laboratory psychology favors experiments that yield simple verbal responses, naming sensory input so clearly as to admit of minimal interpretive variation, believing that in honoring such requirements, social science displays its true scientificity. Rarely, in these traditions, is the possibility taken seriously that "naming" practices could vary, even dramatically, perhaps incommensurably, according to race, gender, class, culture, ethnicity, or any of the other specificities that radically shape and inflect cognitive processes in the everyday world.

The pivotal place that epistemologists and developmental psychologists accord to naming as a paradigmatic act of knowing, indicative of an achieved moment of mastery, naturalizes and normalizes the picture of the abstract, interchangeable knower—the *individualism*—which, in a complex feedback loop, gives content to and acquires content from a conceptual apparatus whose central pillar is a form of objectivity possible only through the exercise of pure reason. Developmentalists' chartings of rational progress attest amply to this point. Thus, representing quantifiable input-output experiments as exemplary of "ordinary" human knowing attests to the residual power of a positivistic "unity of science" credo, even after "the naturalistic turn." And when developmentalists rely on uninterpreted, uninterrogated "namings" as demonstrations of a child's readiness to pick out objects in her surroundings or to make comparative "bigger/smaller," "more/less" judgments, they perpetuate these same assumptions, oblivious to what Wittgenstein notices about the radical interpretability of the simplest naming practices.

Walkerdine, in instructive contrast, details experiments with children's responses to the story of Goldilocks and the Three Bears, in studies designed to reveal their readiness to proceed to complex object comparisons once they have demonstrated an ability to distinguish "small/bigger/biggest." The unquestioned background assumption is that all children will recognize that baby bear is smaller than mommy and daddy bear, mommy bear is smaller than daddy bear, and daddy bear is biggest. Walkerdine notes how deeply observers had to challenge their own fundamental, governing assumptions in order to be able to *hear* answers that spoke against their sedimented assumptions; to understand that physically, affectively, and conceptually-psychologically, children who kept insisting that mommy bear was bigger than daddy bear were often *right,* even if "objective" measurement showed that mommy bear was (physically) smaller. These children's answers reveal variations, emotional and empirical, on "normal" patriarchal family structure: variations in which either daddy was not present at all; daddy's was an insignificant, minimal presence; mommy was physically or affectively/psychically bigger, and so on. Here even size is neither a simple physical attribute nor a "natural," namable trait. (Recall comparable claims in Carolyn Steedman's *Landscape for a Good Woman.*) Walkerdine notes, "These children can clearly make size comparisons, but these comparisons are relations within particular and specific practices" (1988, p. 72). The experiment exposes the minimally informative potential of the disembedded question; it reveals the complex interplay among observer, observed, and the politics of the larger social-cultural situation that enter into the negotiative interpretation of empirical results. Yet it is not adequately explicable in the vocabulary of "context" and "contextualization," where the assumption is that text and context are separable, that text explains itself more easily when it is inserted into, or returned to, context; but the two are distinct.[5] In the practices Walkerdine details, "kinds," namings, practices are mutually constitutive in ongoing interpretive negotiations. Thus consider bell hooks (1996):

> We are so confused by this thing called Race.
> We learn about color with crayons. We learn to tell the difference between white and pink and a color they call Flesh. The flesh-colored crayon amuses us.... Flesh we know has no relationship to our skin, for we are brown and brown and brown like all good things. (pp. 7–8)

What better example of the cultural saturation of simple names, of the cooptation of everyday naming practices into the language of the dominant, of the power-infused nature of the simplest of knowings and notknowings? The issue is not just about naive naming but about how cultural beliefs are entrenched in the smallest perceptual-naming practices. Nor could simple translation bridge the divide, for it leaves the power-knowledge relations that structure this "difference" completely *hors de question,* preserving a dominant wisdom of materially replete societies about disinterested relations to objects that generate uniform, straightforwardly translatable naming practices that never need examine their underlying assumptions of mastery, even as they take for granted a dislocated interchangeability of experiences and perceptions.

"Naming," then, is emblematic of the dislocated one-liner responses in input/output experiments and simple everyday paradigm-generating knowings. Disengaged from the social-cultural-material practices that make them meaningful, these responses appear in the epistemologies of mastery as neutral, apolitical, and thence universal markers of developmental progress. Yet these practices are embedded in and constituted (though not determined) by epistemic and linguistic community: nor could they be otherwise, the cleansing and disentangling steps that present them as ostensibly free of cultural taint notwithstanding. Whereas Gopnik and Melzoff comment that "even extremely young children appear to organize their categorization in terms of "natural kinds," underlying essences with causal efficacy" (1997, p. 31), Walkerdine contests the very idea of a natural kind, observing the "multiple signification of many signs within particular practices [which] demonstrate...the way in which the participants are positioned and regulated, and how emotionality and desire are carried within these relations themselves" (1988, p. 92). I am suggesting that Walkerdine's critical stance—her experiments in "naturalizing" to working-class lives rather than standard "bourgeois" lives—at once refuses to allow hegemonic practices to supply the contents of "the natural" and keeps her investigations "truer" to the subjects they study than unnegotiated empirical studies that "read results" neat, from a smooth, seamless surface, can be.

Naturalizing

Naturalizing is a term I invoke in two senses in this inquiry. First, in its critical dimension, I use it to contest the implicit, subterranean "naturalizings" both of human knowers and of exemplary kinds or moments of knowing, within the very scientific psychology from which naturalists draw their evidence about who/what "we" are. Second, in a different and more positive register, this analysis catches the promise for feminists and other postcolonial theorists in naturalism's turning away from speculation to relocate theoretical analyses within the epistemic practices of real, specifically situated, "natural" knowers.

With reference to critiques of implicit "naturalizing," a classic point of feminist reference is Naomi Weisstein's (1971) "Psychology Constructs the Female," in which she shows that natural (female) human "kinds" are as artifactual as they are factual: constructs of the very experiments and studies that claim to know them (see also Crawford & Maracek, 1989). Similarly, Walkerdine observes that "The liberal order of choice and free will had to be created by inventing a natural childhood which could be produced and regulated in the most invisible of ways... it is mothers who are held responsible for the emergence of the 'natural' " (1988, pp. 212–13).[6] For both Weisstein and Walkerdine, it would strain credulity to suggest that names could simply be read off the surface of events and practices: they have to be interpreted, negotiated, in every case. Indeed, interpretations, negotiations, and the ensuing politics of knowledge vary radically across differences of class, race, gender, ethnicity—across the myriad differences that the epistemologies of the mainstream mask in their demeanor of dislocated ubiquity.

By contrast, although Wittgenstein is no psychologist, the naturalistic face of his thought reveals itself in specific appeals to what children *do*. He writes, for example, that "[c]hildren do not learn that books exist, that armchairs exist, etc. etc.—they learn to fetch books, sit on armchairs, etc. etc." (1971, §476). He observes, "The child, I should like to say, learns to react in such-and-such a way; and in so reacting it doesn't so far know anything. Knowing only begins at a later level" (1971, §538). Wittgenstein's repeated reminders that the norms of epistemic practice are fundamentally social again have the effect of "making strange" some of the more standard abstract philosophical puzzles about knowledge and language use. The connections he draws between learning a language and learning a form of life contest the usefulness of dislocated naming practices. Wittgenstein looks—perhaps at how his pupils go about knowing (see Monk, 1990, pp. 193–209), he tests his thinking against his observations of practices. Thus he naturalizes his inquiry, interrogating by example the canonical individualistic assumptions of mainstream epistemology, exposing the oddity of the questions philosophers regard as epistemically primitive. Thus too he becomes a distant ally for feminist naturalizing projects, while showing that epistemology cannot just fall into place as a chapter in psychology. For neither epistemology nor psychology can be assumed to be in order as it stands.

In its more positive register, then, naturalism reclaims a place for *everyday*—as opposed to standardized, sanitized—empirical evidence within the hitherto a priori confines of epistemology. Equally significantly, it contests the orthodox theory-practice relation, where conflicts between practice and theory tend to come out in favor of established theory, discounting practical occurrences that appear to challenge the theory, labeling them mere exceptions, aberrations. It is in part because of its refusal to perpetuate this theory-over-practice ascendency that Carol Gilligan's work claims landmark status for feminist philosophers and psychologists. Gilligan shows that the experimentally demonstrated "fact" of women's moral immaturity is an artifact of the insensitivities of Kohlbergian theory: of its incapacity to connect gender-related developmental differences with the social production of male/female-gendered children, rather than reading them as signs of "natural" (in)abilities. At issue for feminists, Gilligan shows, is the adequacy of the theoretical apparatus, not the "failure" of female subjects to measure up to its demands.

Whereas Quinean naturalists assume homogeneity within the "natural kind" *human,* feminist naturalistic studies of cognitive and moral practices in the 1990s are simultaneously gender sensitive and multiply aware of the diverse axes along which gender is enacted. Feminists, for example, cannot operate effectively with a model of vision as a passive mirroring of empirical reality; they cannot assume that, simply by looking, people will see things as they are. Rather, in Donna Haraway's (1991) words, feminists are caught up in "the problem of responsibility for the generativity of all visual practices... answerable for what [they] learn how to see" (p. 190). Thus feminist research has to be methodologically vigilant; sufficiently perceptive to notice and contest theory-constitutive assumptions that permeate everyday life and professional psychological discourse, about the naturalness of traits, behaviors, dispositions; prepared to submit the researchers' activities to scrutiny that is just as meticulous as the observational practices required to study the subjects of its research (see Code, 1995a).

Even Gilligan's work does not wholly escape the naturalizing assumptions that sustain patriarchy. The developmental narrative that runs from Jean Piaget to reemerge in Lawrence Kohlberg's stage theory, and to inform popular child development manuals, is complicit in legitimating the ongoing hegemony of the status quo of the middle-class Western world: the values of the patriarchal nuclear family in cold-war (Norman Rockwell) America are inscribed in Kohlberg's developmental stages, as are the disciplinary practices of the (masterful) father and the acquiescence, albeit often silently coerced, of the mother.[7] Gilligan (following Nancy Chodorow, 1978) reclaims a place for maternal agency in this relatively uncontested family arrangement even as she pays unprecedented heed to the voices of female children.

Yet her analysis, radical in its time, concentrates more on the internal dynamics of nuclear family structure than on the social mileux, and the power-infused relations that permeate and sustain it. Gilligan exposes the gendered texts and subtexts in developmental practices that enable girls to bring to their moral and cognitive lives a "caring" that is stereotyped as "natural" within the dominant social imaginary and that is missing and/or devalued in the rights-and-justice-based, autonomy-promoting lives that are the template for male development in those same segments of society. In so doing she prepares the ground for renewed debates about nature and nurture, gender essentialism, difference, and power that are as crucial for feminist developmentalists as for feminist epistemologists.

But Gilligan's are as markedly *white* texts as they are middle-class and heterosexual, two-parent-family centered. Their racial specificity contrasts sharply with developmental stories from other racial and cultural locations, of which a striking example again comes from bell hooks's (1996) *Bone Black:*

> [I]n traditional southern-based black life, it was and is expected of girls to be articulate, to hold ourselves with dignity.... These are the variables that white researchers often do not consider when they measure the self-esteem of black females with a yardstick that was designed based on values emerging from white experience. (p. xiii)

Naturalizing female development as it is fostered in affluent segments of white societies can only render such expectations "unfeminine" and hence "unnatural." Standard developmental theory thus legitimates deep social divisions. The white Western individualistic "I" remains intact throughout this story, living out scripted patterns of gender-, class-, and race-specific development: this individual who is also represented as so transparent to her-/himself as readily to see the conditions of her-his oppression and to evade them. Structural, systemic oppression recedes from view.

Cynthia Willett (1995) offers a subtle analysis of mother-infant relations that indicates just how different studies of cognitive development would be if they were prepared to see the infant, from the beginning, as a social, erotic, desiring and creative being, learning to live in an affect- and meaning-saturated world. The contrast with the mastery-oriented Piagetian-

Kohlbergian story is stark, as is the contrast with appeals to the retrospective reflection of disengaged, disinterested adults and with the restriction of Quinean attention to visual observations of "a *physical* human subject." These more orthodox framings, although variously, reduce the child to mere appetite that has to be disciplined, mastered, even as the developmental significance of the social eroticism that, from the beginning, binds together mother and children, caregiving fathers, nannies, day care workers, teachers and children falls below the threshhold of theoretical notice, along with the extent to which the child's agency shapes developmental processes from the very beginning. "Nurturing" the child reduces to abstract, mechanical activity in theories that accord cognitive developmental significance neither to touch nor to the kind of communication and listening that are also "wrap-around" processes: the early expressive relationships from which infants and children develop, or are thwarted in developing, faith in their environment and a sense of trust in other people and in themselves. As Willett observes,

> By "naturalizing" the work of the nurturer, patriarchal institutions of motherhood subject the nurturer to the same subjectless asociality as her infant. Together parent and infant are rendered mute before the forces of a masculinized reason and an oppressive social system. (p. 32)

Yet only a full acknowledgment of these affective-erotic processes can foster the mature affectivity that makes properly *communal* lives and practices possible. Cathy Urwin (1984) makes a related point:

> [T]he separation between affect and cognition in Piaget's theory bypasses the question of what actually motivates children's communications; and the universalist paradigm...renders the study of systematic differences in development inaccessible within the account. (p. 269)

The alienated and estranged autonomous individual who is the exemplary mature adult for Piaget and Kohlberg emerges as a solitary creature on an indifferent landscape peopled by rational Others with whom his interactions are primarily competitive.

Normalizing

Normalizing consequences follow from naturalizing practices, as naturalistic inquiry normalizes certain experiences, certain ways of being, thus endorsing standards according to which behaviors, among them putative knowings, can be cast as acceptable, "normal," or aberrant. Developmental analyses normalize the trajectory fostered in a "normal" affluent heterosexual two-parent patriarchal family, reading past the power relations that patriarchy enacts and the abuses of women and children it frequently condones within the confines of a protected, "private" domain. The ubiquity of patriarchal power relations makes of the idea of a "normal," situationally neutral developmental line more a fiction (a fabrication) than a "natural" fact. (The variations exposed in Walkerdine's Three Bears study exemplify this point.) Feminist developmentalists have to look at power in a new way within child-raising situations, to show (again citing Urwin, 1984) how "desert-islanded" views of mother-child relations "pre-empt[ ] any examination of material conditions, ideology and questions of power" (p. 270).

In short, "normal" rarely functions just descriptively in philosophy, psychology, or everyday discourse; deviations from or failures to achieve the normal—whether a cognitive-developmental stage, an IQ score, or a social skill—invite disapproval and evoke strategies for "improvement." The very idea of "the normal child" performs a powerfully normative, regulative function, generating acute anxieties and compensatory measures when a child appears not to fit within it (see Wong, 1996). Thus, while some critics worry that naturalistic epistemology is merely descriptive, that it falls short of the normative, criteria-establishing demands that a "real" theory of knowledge should meet (see, e.g., Kim, 1994), my interest is in the normative force of its tacit normalizing of mothers, infants, and social arrangements. My intention is to clear space for feminist interrogations of developmental psychology that ask what kind of engagement with childhood—childhoods—an appropriately gender-sensitive developmental epistemology must promote in order to avoid gross reductivism, at one end of a spectrum, and anecdotal randomness at the other.

Given the complicity of mainstream epistemology and psychology in sustaining a patriarchal social order, given the extent to which that social order underwrites white supremacist and ecologically exploitative practices, *feminist* epistemology, even if it is naturalized, cannot simply "fall...into place as a chapter of psychology and hence of natural science." Here I have looked at practices out of which "the natural child" emerges more as construct than a discovery, but neither in order to essentialize developmental psychology by representing "it" as a unified project, nor to assume that its practices are uniform or univocal. I have been critical of epistemologies that dismiss appeals to psychology as "psychologism" and of psychological practices that normalize and naturalize the abstract individuals who are the subjects of their inquiry so as to preserve conceptions of human development that erase the differences and the affectivity and sociality that characterize human cognitive, moral, and emotional experiences.

The Child as Fact and Artifact

Who, then, or what is this child whom I represent as both fact and artifact, both found and made? Just as, for Quinean naturalists, the human knower is a *fact*ual physical entity, a natural kind whose cognitive processes are available to objective inspection, so for Piagetians and their successors "the child" is the natural, *fact*ual given in genetic inquiry. Neither Piagetians nor Quineans consider the possibility that this very "natural" kind—this human knower, this child—could be as much an artifact of experimental situations as a natural given. Indeed, such intimations of "social constructivism" do not sit easily with cognitive science–based developmentalists, who tend to caricature it as antithetical to realism and hence as symptomatic of a postmodern slide into chaos. Gopnik and Melzoff (1997) are typical on this issue. They deflate "constructivism" into "socialization" and chide would-be constructivists as follows:

> Assimilating *all* cognitive development to the model of socialization is, however, a dreadful mistake, allied to the dreadful mistake of postmodernism in general.... Purely social-constructivist views discount this fundamental link between mind and the world. (p. 72, their emphasis)

Were this view not so common a misrepresentation of social constructivism it would merit no further discussion. Nothing in the contra-Piagetian views I have discussed implies that *all* cognitive development is attributable to socialization or that "the child" as an embodied, feeling, needy being is not materially, really *there,* part of the social and physical world in which it learns to *be* and that makes its knowing possible. Nowhere do Gopnik and Melzoff offer a characterization of this "postmodernism in general" that they cast as a dreadful mistake; hence it is impossible to agree or disagree with them. But the successes of postmodern theories in opening out and exposing the oppressions, exclusions, and colonizing practices—and the narcissism—consequent on humanistic assumptions of universal sameness caution against so peremptory a dismissal. The range of positions that characterize themselves as postmodern—of which feminism itself, on many readings, counts as one—render references to "postmodernism in general" quite unilluminating.

The positions I draw on from Walkerdine's, Urwin's, and Willett's work entail that the child is at once thrown into and made by the world of which it is a part: made but not determined, yet not "influenced" so superficially as "socialization" implies, with its sense that the effects of socialization are mere accretions on a core being who remains somehow "discoverable" beneath them, so that the accretions could be stripped away and the "real" child—or adult—would emerge. Children—real, embodied, feeling and feeding children—are born into complexes of familial-social-cultural-affective meanings and expectations, and studied within disciplinary expectations, that shape, *even if they do not determine*, who the child can be, what she can know, how she can respond and negotiate with and within the material and affective, circumstances in which she participates in constructing her becoming-adult subjectivity. The simple contrast between the interlocking grid of semantic, affective, and material expectations in which white American girl children enact their subjectivity, in Gilligan's account, and those within which black American girl children enact their subjectivity, in hooks's example, counts as telling evidence for the implausibility of any idea that "the child" could be extracted from the conditions that make her particularly realized maturation possible; could be transplanted to mature, interchangeably, in a frame so different that she could not *be* the same person within it. The normalizing assumption that she should, nonetheless, want to conform to the "standard" group attests further to the colonializing effects of dominant norms.

Disenchanted with post-Kantian "philosophical psychology's" speculative, introspective approach, its belief in "a power peculiar to philosophical thought, which, in determining the preliminary methods necessary for science, places itself above it" (1971, p. 57), Jean Piaget argued for the superiority of "scientific psychology." Yet Piagetians and post-Quinean naturalists assume a human sameness that blocks adequate engagement with the constitutive differences that are the focus of feminist and other postcolonial inquiry. They claim a formalistic advantage that allows them to stand outside the fray of knowledge-making, as spectators "from nowhere." Thus dislocated, their specificities as inquirers count for naught; and the specificities of objects of inquiry also count for naught, be they physical objects or human subjects. Scientific inquiry is about uniformity, lawlike behaviors, deductively achieved conclusions, none of which need to address idiosyncratic, local variation. Yet once inquiry locates itself "down on the ground," in the midst of and answerable to the integrity of real people's cognitive practices, it faces imperatives that extend as far beyond the walls of the laboratory as beyond the walls of the philosopher's study. These imperatives are about responsible inquiry, about being "true to" the experiential situatedness of everyday knowings. No longer can inquiry assume before-the-fact (= a priori) sameness of human subjects either as inquirers or inquired into or before-the-fact (= a priori) objective rational sameness on the part of inquirers themselves, whose inevitable situatedness cannot remain, epistemologically, *hors de question.* Nor can inquiry mask its artifactual side, casting its object of inquiry—"the child"—in a predetermined (a priori after all) image of a situationally indifferent, naturally developing biological organism.

Most strange is the support these assumptions have provided for the belief that people—subjects who are the objects of inquiry—can adequately be known in this way, a belief that requires social scientists to restrict their observations to separate, discrete behaviors and overt utterances of people extracted from the circumstances that generate those behaviors and make them possible, appropriate, and meaningful. They separate their subjects-objects of study out from their affective, cultural, racial, and economic circumstances; their bodily specificities as variously gendered, aged, abled beings; and the narratives that carry their psychosocial histories, constructing and constantly reconstructing the meanings that shape their lives.

Developmentally, what is most curious about these assumptions is that recognizing nurturant others, learning what she or he can expect of them, comprises the very earliest infant learning (see Code, 1991, chap. 2). An infant learns to respond affectively-cognitively to carers who touch, hold, and feed her long before she can name the simplest physical object: her access to the objects she comes to know is embedded in and mediated by affective-cognitive relations with carers, and not just "intersubjectively" but in and in relation to culturally and historically specific social practices. Studies of the effects of sensory-emotional deprivation in the development of subjectivity, sociality, and agency (of which the example of the wild child of Aveyron is only the best known) amply show how closely a child's growing capacity to make trusting sense of and within the world, both physical and personal, is bound up with her caregivers' nurturance, which is in its turn shaped, and enabled or thwarted, by the social-educational-material-value-saturated milieu in which the caregiving occurs (a classic study is Goldfarb, 1945). There is no neutral originary place, no untouched "individual," no pure moment that can be separated out for study.

Yet there are practices, myriad practices, communal, collective practices, which are the sites where knowledge is produced and within which,

I am suggesting, knowledge has to be studied, developmentally or otherwise. Nor does the idea that knowledge necessarily grows out of collective practices amount to a simple amendment to or expansion of established epistemological wisdom. It poses a radical challenge to the individualistic tradition, resituates and reconfigures it, rewrites its agenda. Taking seriously Wittgenstein's demonstration that the norms of cognitive practice are fundamentally social, Walkerdine's that they have to be studied in their material-cultural situatedness, and Willett's that they are as affective as they are rational, I have proposed some directions in which feminist developmental psychology and feminist epistemology can work toward a radical future.

Notes

1. Gopnik and Melzoff comment, "Nonetheless, ... we and other theory theorists are staking out the same conceptual territory as Piaget ... many of those working in this area come out of a broadly Piagetian tradition and see themselves as Piaget's inheritors" (1997, p. 221).
2. The masculine pronoun signals the masculine character of autonomy in Western post-Enlightenment discourse. See also in this connection Code (1991, chap. 2; 1999). For an analysis of the bounded masculine separateness that autonomy ideals foster, see Schmitt (1995).
3. Both classic popular child-raising manuals such as Spock and Gesell and the theories of Rousseau, Durkheim, Kohlberg, and Piaget represent it thus. Nancy Chodorow (1978) contrasts female connectedness with this autonomous disconnectedness fostered in male children.
4. For an introduction to the central debates in epistemological naturalism, see Kornblith (1994).
5. Cathy Urwin makes a similar point. She writes, "The appeal to context not only fails to explain; it also conceals.... [It] puts the context outside the child, who is viewed as a point of origin which interacts with or is affected by external factors.... [T]he relation between the situation and the process of production is left out of the account. So, too, is the child's motivation or power to speak" (1984, p. 273).
6. Naturalistic assumptions also pervade Phillipe Rushton's studies of "natural" links between brain size and genital size, and the bell curve controversy.
7. In formulating these thoughts I am grateful to a paper Cynthia Willett presented at a conference of the American Philosophical Society in Los Angeles, March 1998.

THE OTHER HALF

OF THE PARTNERSHIP

DEVELOPMENTAL PSYCHOLOGY

CAN INFORM FEMINISM

Engendering

Development—Developing

Feminism

Defining the Partnership

Ellin Kofsky Scholnick and Patricia H. Miller

Why would feminist scholars want to read this book? At first glance the chapters seem unidirectional. The authors attempt to persuade other psychologists that the language by which we describe developmental processes and products and the methods by which we study development are gendered. Their chapters illustrate how traditional conceptions of memory, reasoning, social interactions, and understanding of mental life reflect a male perspective and how each topic can be enriched by incorporating feminist thought. Ultimately, however, the interchanges between feminist scholars and developmental psychologists need to be bidirectional. As psychological processes are rethought and a feminist developmental psychology emerges, this view then changes the individual described by feminists in other venues. A combined, compatible, richer perspective on humans emerges. But feminist scholars need not wait for developmental psychologists familiar with feminist work to transform developmental psychology. This chapter explains why even now, feminists can profit from reading developmental psychology.

Developmental psychologists who read feminist scholarship find it puzzling that feminists seldom draw on theories and data from modern developmental science that are compatible with feminist perspectives. Feminist scholars rarely mention major developmental theories other than older psychoanalytic ones, and seem aware of the work of few developmentalists other than Gilligan (1982). This limited attention to developmental work may reflect, in part, feminist scholars' focus on, and critique of, theories that have permeated the popular and literary culture. Feminist scholars focus their analysis on the discursive practices of a culture and the social structures that produce and are produced by those practices. But developmentalists would add that these androcentric theories also fail to predict and explain human behavior. The perspectives of theories such as psychoanalysis are straw men that developmentalists have already dismembered, discarded, or reconfigured, and this book reflects their search for more female-friendly and empirically valid approaches. As feminism turns from deconstructing the past and present to reconstructing the future, feminist developmental psychology may offer some starting points.

Feminists also seem to adopt models of engenderment and social construction that neglect both the developing child and the complicated intertwining of biology, psychology, and sociology that development entails. Biological essentialist thinking has led to the negative stereotyping of women, and there is ample justification for calling attention to social influences while downplaying biological determinism. But an almost total focus on social construction is as limiting as a focus on biological essentialism. Children grow, and they learn. Developmentalists' description of the interplay between these processes over the life span may be of use to feminist scholars.

Thus far, feminists have convincingly critiqued a variety of disciplines by deconstructing the hidden masculine values, models, and methods of those disciplines. In the place of these biased edifices they have begun to construct models that are more inclusive and flow from the experiences of women, rather than men only. Here, too, developmental psychology can contribute by providing empirical support and theoretical models for many of the tenets of feminist thought. Developmental psychology can contribute a real-world, situated account of how the experiences of women and girls, and perhaps other nondominant groups in the margins, matter. Abstract notions in feminist scholarship such as discourse, epistemology, and dominance can be grounded in a rich database regarding specific situated speakers, knowers, and bullies. Developmental data on and models of cognition, gender, social interactions, language, awareness of others' psychological states, and appreciation of standpoints can provide support and detail for feminist blueprints. This final chapter outlines several potential contributions of current developmental psychology to a feminist vision of people, society, and change.

Changing the Feminist Toolbox

We illustrate current developmental psychology's potential contributions to feminist scholarship with four examples: categories, reasoning, parent-child relations, and appreciation of standpoints. We locate each topic in feminist theorizing, provide alternative frameworks derived from developmental psychology, and then suggest implications for feminist study.

Categories

Feminists (e.g., Code, 1991; Lloyd, 1993b) often criticize how the categories of male and female have been constructed. One facet of construction is semantic: how a category, like female, is imbued with meaning. The second aspect is syntactic. A syntactic analysis examines the nature of the rules by which members are included in a category. Feminist epistemologists and many cognitive psychologists (e.g., Gelman & Taylor, this volume) share the assumption that syntactic rules, not just semantic content, reflect a cognitive construal of the world. They also begin at the same point, dissatisfaction with classical models of categorization. Feminists lay the blame on hegemonic discourse, whereas cognitive psychologists blame inaccurate models of mental processing. Critiques must be followed by alternative models, and contemporary cognitive scientists have generated and tested new models of categorization that might provide conceptual tools for feminists.

The Classical View. A first step in rethinking gender categories is to rethink the general nature of category structure so that it is based on strategies of mental representation actually used by human problem solvers[1] rather than the putative theoretical entities postulated by epistemologists and logicians. Philosophers work within a formal abstract system of logical classes and logical relations that provides the norms for human thought (Code, 1991). In this "classical" framework categories are constructed by an "all and only" rule (Scholnick, 1999). Each class is defined by a set of criterial properties that all members possess to the same degree. Only the category members possess these features. Thus, categories are mutually exclusive and often dichotomous. Children are either boys or girls, but not both (the law of the excluded middle). Girls are children who are not male. All girls are alike. Feminists argue that these dichotomies are insidious when one pole is marked as inferior and the other pole is unmarked because it is assumed to be the standard from which the marked pole deviates (Code, 1991; Tavris, 1992).

Graded Categories. Consistent with feminist thought, few modern cognitive psychologists characterize conceptual life in an "all and only" way. Formal logic is not an apt model of how the mind works, because the logic is content free and the structure of the classical categories of formal logic is not the same as the structure humans use to group objects (Medin, 1989; Scholnick, 1999). One of the most influential alternative accounts of categorization was provided by Rosch (e.g., Rosch, 1978),[2] who demonstrated that people's mental representations of categories did not conform to the "all and only" rule. For example, the category of birds encompasses both the small flying songbird sparrow and the ostrich, which lacks flight and song and is large, but is still a bird. However, membership in a cognitive category is graded: not all instances are deemed equivalent (equally representative of the class) by humans. A set of properties characterizes the class, and some members, such as sparrows, have more of them, while others, like the ostrich, have fewer and may even possess properties seen in a contrasting class. Do people think of bats as birds or mammals? Is a whale a mammal or a fish? No property is present in all members of a class and only in class members. However, some properties, like wings in birds, are more prevalent than others. Some members of the category have many of the most frequent features associated with the category. These instances serve as prototypes or best examples. The resemblance to the best example of a category like vehicle declines as we move from cars to wagons, elevators, and skis.

Research by Armstrong, Gleitman, and Gleitman (1983) underscores how people represent categories. Like Rosch, they found that adults took longer to verify that an ostrich was a bird than that a sparrow was a bird, and rated the ostrich as a worse example of a bird than a sparrow. The same pattern occurred even for categories such as numbers or females. When asked to verify whether a "widow" is a female, or to rate whether "widow" is a good example of a female, adults took longer to answer and gave lower ratings than when the exemplar was "aunt."

This approach to categorization provides a different understanding of gender. For most people gender is not a homogeneous category. Males and females possess many overlapping behavioral traits, abilities, and anatomical characteristics. The excessive attention to gender differences in abilities ignores the research that demonstrates that our concepts, and perhaps the world the concepts represent, do not consist of sharp dichotomies (Tavris, 1992).

If all categories overlap, why do we propose dichotomies? Rosch (Mervis & Rosch, 1981) suggests that the best exemplar is the conceptual glue for a category and that other instances are organized around it. When children learn to name the instances of a category, they begin with the label for the best and most distinctive exemplar. Parents also label for children the best examples of a category before they name other instances. Children learn to call shirts "clothing" before they identify belts as clothing. They may also associate "girl" with the most stereotypic female. Young children are likely to be sexist because their attention is drawn to the features that are most diagnostic and differentiating for gender. Even when children build a richer concept of gender, the best example—the stereotype—is the most accessible. People reason better about typical instances than less typical ones, presumably because it requires more cognitive processing to detect and associate less typical instances with the category. Thus, Rosch's work lends itself to a key distinction between people's categorical construals and the heuristics they use to simplify demanding tasks.

In cognitive analyses, descriptions of the structure of categories are tied to accounts of the content, origin, and use of the categories, whereas logicians assume that the features of a category are inherent in its definition and universally understood and used. Rosch suggested that people learn categories by detecting a set of loosely bundled features that are correlated with the category. The connections among features reflect the structure of the environment and the naming practices of the culture (Mervis & Rosch, 1981). Rosch underestimated just how powerful culture and expertise are in determining the content of categories, but many cognitive scientists accept her account of the syntax of categories as a graded, overlapping structure. Three other accounts of concepts have gained currency among psychologists. They postulate a different conceptual structures or different story of its acquisition.

Essentialist Concepts. In this volume Gelman and Taylor introduce another approach that builds on Rosch's insights into the structure of psychological categories but add semantic analyses. Gelman (Gelman, Coley, & Gottfried, 1994) claims that the attributes associated with a category like "bird" are integrated by a story line or an intuitive, folk theory. The child initially assumes that the appearances and behaviors of all organic life forms are expressions of some biological essence or design for survival. Thus, birds are often small and have hollow bones because these enable flight. Although feminists may not be attracted to an essentialist theory, Gelman suggests that essentialism is a default assumption that enables children to simplify the diversity they encounter and to provide meaning to the information they receive. Their intuitive theory explains why categories of creatures are the way they are. This early theory may account for the prevalence of biological essentialism in many theories of gender. In his chapter, Leaper suggests that essentialist categories also help social groups solidify and clarify group membership.

Feminists can use Gelman's concepts-as-theories approach to understand why biological essentialist notions are hard to eradicate, and can characterize cognitive development as a shedding of essentialism in order to build concepts on another causal core. Perhaps experience arising from membership in a marginalized group, which attunes members to the diverse ways categories are defined, enables the individual to abandon early essentialism as a cognitive strategy (Harding, 1991).

Schema Theory. Rosch and Gelman work within mainstream cognitive analyses. Social psychologists (e.g. Bem, 1993; Ruble & Martin, 1998) have also offered an alternative view of categorization. Schema theory retains the mutually exclusive dichotomies of classical categories but offers a different explanation of the acquisition and use of concepts. Each concept is organized around a node (often represented by a label), such as "boy" or "girl." Because categories do not overlap, Bem needed to introduce "androgyny" to account for individuals who may have both masculine and feminine traits. The categories gain their meaning and definition as the child learns which behaviors, traits, and aspects of appearance are associated with the gender labels. Once these stereotypes are learned, individuals are biased to seek out information consistent with the schema and distort inconsistent information to match the schema. From a different perspective, Vygotsky (1978) described how cultures point out salient attributes of objects and group these objects together under one rubric. Cultural practices provide the basis for the child's understanding of words and things.

Interconnected Knowing. Patricia H. Miller (this volume) describes a different categorical structure and point of origin than the preceding theories, one that is more consistent with feminist epistemology and with work on situated knowing (Barsalou, 1983). She notes that categories are often embedded in overlapping and connected networks of concepts (see also G. Lakoff, 1987). Developing knowers, embedded in an epistemological community of other knowers, construct categories of gender. Because circumstances and relationships change, categories, such as gender, are not fixed entities. Simultaneously children develop, peers and parents develop, and sociohistorical contexts change. The usually hidden influences on the construction of gender categories in this dynamic, connected system are the power, status, and centrality (versus marginality) of the gender, race, and social class of the child and significant others in the particular social system. Thus, Miller's analysis links categorization to the societal system that constructs and employs social categories.

In summary, these models of thinking provide new ways for feminists to reframe gender and other social categories. Although the variety of alternative conceptual accounts may seem confusing, our conceptual systems are often heterogeneous, hybrid structures. Moreover, categories change during development. For example, gender concepts become more flexible and interconnected, and the intuitive theory that undergirds associations between gender labels and particular properties shifts with accumulating knowledge of biology, society, and the self (Keil & Lockhart, 1999; Ruble & Martin, 1998).

Reasoning

The preceding section introduced a variety of ways that humans think about categories and identified implications for analyses of gender. Discussions of human reasoning raise the same issues. Lloyd (1993b) has attacked Western notions of the "man of reason" whose thought is a realization of the masculine virtues of self-containment, objectivity, and abstraction. But the man of reason, who is the model of logic, is not the human reasoner. Traditional epistemologists use abstract norms, divorced from human mentation. If feminists wish to attack these norms, why not use the findings of psychologists?

Many social psychologists characterize the human reasoner as anything but rational, because reasoning and memory concerning the likelihood of certain occurrences are biased (Nisbett, 1993). Cognitive psychologists (Cheng & Holyoak, 1985; Johnson-Laird & Byrne, 1991) doubt that human reasoning can be modeled on scientific thinking or Aristotelian logic. They dispute that logic is based on a set of inherent rules for drawing valid conclusions. Instead, they suggest that reasoning is based on meaning and on pragmatic rule structures for interpretations of social interactions. Use of conditional (if-then) reasoning illustrates their point. In conditional logic, whenever the condition in the if-clause occurs, it must be accompanied by the condition in the main (then-) clause. Consequently, when the condition in the main clause does not occur, neither does the condition in the if-clause. Table 1 presents three different tests of the ability to make this deduction. The first example in the table is the hardest

Table 1. Three modus tollens problems

1	2	3
If p, then q	If it rains, the ground is wet.	If you vote, you must be 18.
Not q	The ground is dry.	Joan is 5.
p?	Is it raining?	Did she vote?

because the symbols, p and q, are not meaningful. The material is the most difficult kind to encode, and reasoners lack an experiential structure that could be used to check for counterexamples to their conclusion (Johnson-Laird & Byrne, 1991). The second example is easier because adults know that roads will not be dry in pouring rain. Moreover, in some cases, such as the permissions exemplified by the third problem, the social structure underlying the sentence is obvious even to young children (Girotto, Light, & Colbourn, 1988). Permissions bar people from performing the action in the if-clause unless they have met the condition in the main clause. Preschoolers cannot vote.

The introduction of meaning and awareness of social practices into logical performance changes our characterization of thinking. The issue is not simply that classical epistemology uses a normative model of logic and knowing that is grounded in masculine stereotypes but that the model is not psychologically valid. The pragmatic and semantic models that psychologists use are compatible with and lend credence to feminist theorizing. It might be better to examine how people reason in their daily lives, which would likely show that their logic is dependent on social roles and situations. Falmagne's chapter provides a guide.

Parent-Child Relations

Many feminist theories locate the acquisition of gender in the early parent-child relationship and draw their accounts of mothering from Freudian theory or its derivatives (Chodorow, 1989; Keller, 1985). These theories characterize the child as a need-driven, egocentric creature, the mother as the granter or withholder of gratification, and the relationship as sexualized. Gender is constructed in the course of the child's struggles to develop ego and superego controls over irrational and insistent instinctual demands. Current developmental approaches, buttressed by sensitive observations of parent-child interactions, do not start from the same base. Two current developmental analyses of parent-child relations illustrate alternative frameworks.

Russian Theory. Russian theorists (e.g., Vygotsky, 1978) assume that the child is social from the onset, not egocentric. Caretakers attune themselves to the child and teach the child about culture and cultural roles in ways the child can incorporate. To be effective, the parents must sense the child's receptive limitations and provide a scaffold that will extend the child's capabilities. The child uses the scaffold both as a support and as a model for building social and intellectual skills. Children learn to think by assimilating parents' ways of observing and describing others. The child uses the extrapsychic environment, as exemplified in the parents' embodiment of historical-cultural traditions, to build internal representations. Parenting is a social practice that is based on the parents' social position and cultural traditions. Feminist developmentalists would includes markers such as gender, race, and social class in their definition of social position. The child who is constructed by social interactions, regardless of gender, develops an individuated self, but one that is always framed by the cultural traditions and cultural tools that aided self-construction.

This approach motivates close examination of the ways in which parental practices and communicative exchanges transmit messages to the baby about his or her social role. The end point of development is never abstraction and independence from relationships. Affective and cognitive development are closely linked. The paradigm also separates acquisition of gender from a sexualized parental relationship.

Attachment Theory. Even Bowlby (1969), an object relations theorist who claims a biological basis for maternal behavior, provides a different cast on mother-child relations. In N. J. Chodorow's (1989) version of psychoanalytic theory, the mother provides an ambivalent choice to the child; she satisfies the child's instinctual needs at the cost of the child's self-determination. Boys break from the mother to win independence at the cost of dampening relational needs, while girls are encouraged to sacrifice autonomy to stay in relation. In contrast, Bowlby asserts that autonomy and relatedness are dual outcomes of a healthy mother-child relationship, and that the outcome of maternal-child interactions is not necessarily gendered.

Bowlby proposes that the child's basic need is for security and protection. A caretaker who sensitively attunes herself to the child's needs helps to create a secure relationship in which the child has a base of support to use in exploring the external world and a sense of the self as a well-loved and competent agent. Parental responsivity to the child's need for security enables the child to become an active shaper of his or her environment and also a competent partner. Parent-child interchanges teach children how to maintain and repair relationships. Thus, affect, social competence, and cognitive competence are linked rather than separated or opposed. These relational interchanges support agentive manipulation of the environment. Like the Russian approach, research grounded in Bowlby's theory carefully examines parental practices and is beginning to demonstrate how particular cultures vary in parenting practices and outcomes (Thompson, 1998, pp. 43–47). Feminists could easily adapt aspects of attachment theory to an analysis of the ways that particularities of gender and social position (including ethnicity and social class) modify the child's representation of the self, the external world, and social relations.

Perspective Taking

Feminists (e.g., Harding, 1991) argue that the discursive practices of a culture often are so dominated by the view of a particular class (Western European, white, middle-class males), that it is difficult to understand that other views exist, and therefore that the pervasiveness of one viewpoint reflects a social arrangement, not a natural condition. The antidote is the cultivation of views from marginalized groups whose pronouncement of their perspectives leads to the realization that each view is a perspective, not a direct reading of reality. Feminists focus on the articulation of standpoints. What does it mean to be a female in a particular social location? How does one become aware of a standpoint and the factors that determine it?

Developmentalists address the same issue from a different angle, one that might enrich feminist analyses. They study perspective taking, role taking, and theory of mind (Flavell, 1992; Flavell & Miller, 1998). The ability to identify a standpoint rests on assumptions that representations of the world differ from reality, that one's "position" or "perspective" determines particular aspects of one's view, and that occupying a different position has specific implications for one's view. Awareness of these assumptions is a developmental achievement. Children know that people differ in perspective before they understand how differences in position affect the content of different points of view, and they appreciate how certain factors influence points of view before they understand the impact of other conditions. These fundamental lessons are acquired in the preschool and early school years, but their implications in particular content areas are worked out throughout life. Two-year-olds know that someone who stands in front of an object sees a different view than one who stands behind the object, but not every adult recognizes that a dominant group has a different attitude toward specific social practices than a marginalized group.

Feminists and developmentalists can join forces to work out how appreciation of social standpoints develops. In that joint venture, feminists may continually remind developmentalists of the impact of social practices on the appreciation of different standpoints, but developmentalists may also demonstrate the ways that the developing brain and developing conceptual content and organization of knowledge influence acquisition and appreciation of standpoints. Appreciating different perspectives places strains on immature cognitive systems because it requires the ability to hold in mind two perspectives while calculating how different informational conditions might lead to different views. External conditions stimulate cognitive development, so frequent experiences in comparing shared experience (see the chapters by Fivush and Welch-Ross, this volume) may foster the child's capacity to appreciate diverse perspectives on events.

Rethinking Development

The greatest resource that developmental psychology can offer feminists is the appreciation of development itself, and its complexities. Development is a polysemous term. Because it refers to changes over time within the individual and within societies, it is tempting to assume similar causes for change, for example, shifting social and economic conditions. Consequently, feminists and developmental psychologists confront the same problem: Are their categories—male and female, child and adult—socially constructed?

Currently, the analytic categories of male and female are threatened because multiple situational and social variables produce variations that question the reality of the distinctions. The danger, and perhaps the promise, of postmodern feminism is that it will deconstruct the concepts of male and female to the point that those concepts will vanish. Similarly, developmental psychologists faced with variations across individuals of the same age in different settings and different groups might envision discarding age categories (Siegler, 1996). These challenges have caused developmental psychologists to reassess the meaning of development. Their discussions may be useful for feminists who look at gender and may even lead to a careful differentiation of psychological from societal development.

Nature-Nurture

One frequently debated issue is the limits of human plasticity, or the role of nature and nurture in developmental change. Rather than suppressing one influence, recent analyses describe the interplay or co-action between biology and the environment (Baltes, Lindenberger, & Staudinger, 1998; Gottlieb, 1997; Lerner, 1998; Overton, 1998). Experience shapes the brain by contributing to the pruning and forging of particular connections. The brain also shapes experience. We are receptive to only certain colors in the spectrum. The immaturity of the forebrain limits the child's capacity to integrate and anticipate environmental structure. Constraints in development originate not just in the environment to which the child is exposed, but also in the cortical or representational capacities of the child to make sense of experience. The influences are not just additive but interactive. For example, the age of menarche has declined as nutritional practices have improved. Consequently, girls' physical maturity has outpaced their emotional and cognitive abilities. Early-maturing girls are more likely to engage in risky social and sexual interactions (Lerner, 1998).

Baltes (Baltes et al., 1998) has proposed that development reflects a shifting balance between expansions of biological capacity and environmental influences. Biological development is an inverted U. Many different biological/neurological processes grow to some peak and then decline, whereas cultural factors can be inhibitory or suppressive at every age. Because our biological plasticity varies over the life course, so does the influence of the culture. Older individuals need more cultural support, but environmental influences may be more ineffectual due to decreasing receptive capacity. Thus, the influence and interaction of biology and environment vary across the life span and across specific domains. The application of this model to gender presents interesting possibilities for feminists.

Social Construction

Lesser receptivity to environmental influences in the very elderly is but one illustration of the limitations of a strict social constructivism. Individuals are both the product and the producer of their own development, simultaneously objects and agents. People in the same environments are not identical. They bring to situations different qualities (e.g., coping skills) and characteristics (e.g., physical appearance) that elicit different responses from their surrounds (Bronfenbrenner & Morris, 1998). During socialization, due to their own interests, abilities, and so on, they extract different meanings and interpretations.

Even receptivity to an environment is a developmental skill based on strategies, proclivities, and capacities. Children are not just novices in a gendered world who are molded by the practices associated with their social position in a society. Their subjectivity, interpretive frames, and awareness of their interpretive stance change due to their own efforts to make sense of the world and to an expanded capacity to manage their cognitive and emotional resources. Transformations in their conceptual and emotional life affect their understanding of gender and other social categories.

Feminist standpoint theory argues that one can reveal hidden social norms by taking the perspective of someone, particularly from a non-dominant group, who does not share the norms. Developmentalists argue for the importance of examining gender from the perspective of the child acquiring gender roles. Study of the processes that influence children's understanding of gender and other social roles can illuminate our theoretical analyses of the interplay of society and the individual in development.

Conclusion: The Lenses of Reciprocity

What does developmental psychology have to offer feminism? Developmentalists do more than test for sex differences and track the transformation of girls into women. They can enrich analyses of concepts, reasoning, social interactions, and perspective taking by providing new models that feminists may "engender." Psychologists offer a model of development that takes into account the developing individual who is responsive to the environment but also selective. The constraints on the process come not only from the opportunities to which the individual is exposed but also from a developing brain and cognitive and behavioral repertoire. Each approach offers a different context of understanding. Feminists situate gender in a social-historical context. Developmentalists situate the understanding and practice of gender in the context of a growing and changing organism. Each is a single lens on a two-dimensional landscape. Combining the lenses adds depth to re-vision our analyses.

Notes

1. Psychological discussions of categorization focus on the format of *representation* or *knowledge structures*. Theories provide varying accounts of the origin of knowledge, such as in the perception of the natural world, in universal properties of mental processing, or in social constructions.

2. The terminology of psychology may be confusing to biologists because it calls to mind a Linnaean taxonomic system in which terms like family, class, and prototype have specific meanings different from the ones psychologists use. Rosch's analysis applies to a larger realm of categories, including artifacts like furniture and toys, as well as to biological categories. We have tried, where possible, to use neutral terms. Another source of confusion is the definition of categories. Rosch claimed that ordinary people base their categories on perceptual appearances rather than on the criteria biologists use, such as method of reproduction or evolutionary heritage. Even Gelman, who claims that categories are based on a biological theory, asserts that this theory is a naive one (Gelman & Taylor, this volume). The psychological theory of knowing describes everyday understanding, not scientific understanding, and mental representation, not the empirical world. But if feminists claim all knowledge is situated, psychologists provide the cognitive situation.

Bibliography

Adam, A. (1997). *Artificial knowing: Gender and the thinking machine*. London: Routledge.

Adams, S., Kuebli, J., Boyle, P., & Fivush, R. (1995). Gender differences in parent-child conversations about past emotions: A longitudinal investigation. *Sex Roles, 33*, 309–323.

Albert, A. A., & Porter, J. R. (1988). Children's gender-role stereotypes: A sociological investigation of psychological models. *Sociological Forum, 3*, 184–210.

Alcoff, L., & Potter, E. (Eds.). (1993*). Feminist epistemologies*. New York: Routledge.

Allende, I. (1989). *Eva Luna*. New York: Bantam.

Alpert-Gillis, L. J., & Connell, J. P. (1989). Gender and sex-role influences on children's self-esteem. *Journal of Personality, 57*, 97–114.

American Association of University Women. (1992). *How schools shortchange girls: The AAUW report: A study of major findings on girls and education*. Washington, DC: American Association of University Women Educational Foundation.

Amsterdam, B. K. (1972). Mirror self-image reactions before age two. *Developmental Psychobiology, 5*, 297–305.

Anderson, E., & Jayaratne, T. (1998). *Genetic explanations of group differences: Old or new racism, sexism, and classism?* Unpublished manuscript, University of Michigan.

Antill, J. K. (1987). Parents' beliefs and values about sex roles, sex differences, and sexuality: Their sources and implications. In P. Shaver & C. Hendrick (Eds.), *Review of personality and social psychology: Vol. 7. Sex and gender* (pp. 294–328). Newbury Park, CA: Sage.

Anzaldúa, G. (1990). Introduction. In G. Anzaldúa (Ed.), *Making face, making soul: Creative and critical perspectives by feminists of color* (pp. xv–xxviii). San Francisco: Aunt Lute Books.

Archer, J. (1984). Gender roles as developmental pathways. *British Journal of Social Psychology, 23*, 245–256.

Archer, J. (1992). Childhood gender roles: Social context and organisation. In H. McGurk (Ed.), *Childhood social development: Contemporary perspectives* (pp. 31–61). Hove, England: Erlbaum.

Armstrong, S. L., Gleitman, L. R., & Gleitman, H. (1983). What some concepts might not be. *Cognition, 13*, 263–308.

Astington, J. W. (1996). What is theoretical about the child's theory of mind? A Vygotskyan view of its development. In P. Carruthers & P. K. Smith (Eds.),

Theories of theories of mind (pp. 184–199). Cambridge, England: Cambridge University Press.

Astington, J. W., & Gopnik, A. (1991). Theoretical explanations of children's understanding of the mind. *British Journal of Developmental Psychology, 9,* 7–32.

Ayer, A. J. (1936). *Language, truth and logic.* London: Gollancz.

Bahktin, M. M. (1981). *The dialogic imagination: Four essays by M. M. Bahktin* (M. Holquist, Ed., C. Emerson & M. Holquist, Trans.). Austin: University of Texas Press. (Original work published 1975)

Baier, A. (1985). Cartesian persons. In A. Baier (Ed.), *Postures of the mind: Essays on mind and morals* (pp. 74–92). Minneapolis: University of Minnesota Press.

Baker Miller, J. (1986). *Toward a new psychology of women* (2nd ed.). Boston: Beacon Press.

Baker-Ward, L., Ornstein, P. A., & Holden, P. J. (1984). The expression of memorization in early childhood. *Journal of Experimental Child Psychology, 37,* 555–575.

Baltes, P. B., Lindenberger, V., & Staudinger, U. M. (1998). Life-span theory in developmental psychology. In W. Damon (Series Ed.) & R. M. Lerner (Vol. Ed.), *Handbook of child psychology: Vol. 1. Theoretical models of human development* (5th ed., pp.1029–1143). New York: Wiley.

Bandura, A. (1986). *Social foundations of thought and action: A social cognitive theory.* Englewood Cliffs, NJ: Prentice-Hall.

Bandura, A. (1997). *Self-efficacy: The exercise of control.* New York: Freeman.

Bar On, B.-A. (1993). Marginality and epistemic privilege. In L. Alcoff & E. Potter (Eds.), *Feminist epistemologies* (pp. 83–100). New York: Routledge.

Bardwell, J. R., Cochran, S. W., & Walker, S. (1986). Relationship of parental education, race, and gender to sex role stereotyping in five-year-old kindergartners. *Sex Roles, 15,* 275–281.

Baron-Cohen, S. (1995). *Mindblindness: An essay on autism and theory of mind.* Cambridge, MA: MIT Press.

Barrett, M. (1992). Words and things: Materialism and method in contemporary feminist analysis. In M. Barrett & A. Phillips (Eds.), *Destabilizing theory: Contemporary feminist debates* (pp. 201–219). Stanford, CA: Stanford University Press.

Barsalou, L. W. (1983). Ad hoc categories. *Memory and Cognition, 11,* 211–227.

Bartlett, F. C. (1932). *Remembering: A study in experimental and social psychology.* New York: Cambridge University Press.

Bartsch, K., & Wellman, H. M. (1995). *Children talk about the mind.* New York: Oxford University Press.

Beal, C. R. (1995, April). Feminist views of cognitive development: Lessons from other fields. In E. K. Scholnick (Chair), *Cognitive development through the lenses of feminist epistemology.* Symposium conducted at the biennial meeting of the Society for Research in Child Development, Indianapolis.

Belenky, M. F., Clinchy, B. M., Goldberger, N. R., & Tarule, J. M. (1986). *Women's ways of knowing: The development of self, voice, and mind.* New York: Basic Books.

Belsky, J., & Rovine, M. (1987). Temperament and attachment security in the Strange Situation: An empirical rapprochement. *Child Development, 58,* 787–795.

Bem, S. L. (1974). The measurement of psychological androgeny. *Journal of Consulting & Clinical Psychology, 42,* 155–162.

Bem, S. L. (1981). Gender schema theory: A cognitive account of sex typing. *Psychological Review, 88,* 354–364.

Bem, S. L. (1989). Genital knowledge and gender constancy in preschool children. *Child Development, 60,* 649–662.

Bem, S. L. (1993). *The lenses of gender: Transforming the debate on sexual inequality.* New Haven, CT: Yale University Press.

Bem, S. L. (1995). Dismantling gender polarization and compulsory heterosexuality: Should we turn the volume down or up? *The Journal of Sex Research, 32,* 329–334.

Benenson, J. F. (1990). Gender differences in social networks. *Journal of Early Adolescence, 10,* 472–495.

Benenson, J. F. (1993). Greater preference among females than males for dyadic interaction in early childhood. *Child Development, 64,* 544–555.

Benenson, J. F. (1994). Ages four to six years: Changes in the structures of play networks of girls and boys. *Merrill-Palmer Quarterly, 40,* 478–487.

Berndt, T. J., & Heller, K. A. (1986). Gender stereotypes and social inferences: A developmental study. *Journal of Personality and Social Psychology, 50,* 889–898.

Bigelow, B. J. (1977). Children's friendship expectations: A cognitive-developmental study. *Child Development, 48,* 246–253.

Bigler, R. S. (1995). The role of classification skill in moderating environmental influences on children's gender stereotypes: A study of the functional use of gender in the classroom. *Child Development, 66,* 1072–1087.

Bigler, R. S., & Liben, L. S. (1990). The role of attitudes and interventions in gender-schematic processing. *Child Development, 61,* 1440–1452.

Bigler, R. S., & Liben, L. S. (1992). Cognitive mechanisms in children's gender stereotyping: Theoretical and educational implications of a cognitive-based intervention. *Child Development, 63,* 1351–1363.

Binion, V. J. (1990). Psychological androgyny: A black female perspective. *Sex Roles, 22,* 487–507.

Biology and Gender Study Group. (1989). The importance of feminist critique for contemporary cell biology. In N. Tuana (Ed.), *Feminism and science* (pp. 172–187). Bloomington: Indiana University Press.

Bird, L. (1998). Dances with feminism: Sidestepping and sandbagging. In E. Burman (Ed.), *Deconstructing feminist psychology* (pp. 90–114). Thousand Oaks, CA: Sage.

Birke, L. (1986). *Women, feminism, and biology: The feminist challenge.* New York: Methuen.

Bjorklund, D., & Green, B. L. (1992). The adaptive nature of cognitive immaturity. *American Psychologist, 47,* 46–54.

Björkqvist, K. (1994). Sex differences in physical, verbal, and indirect aggression: A review of recent research. *Sex Roles, 30,* 177–188.

Björkqvist, K., & Niemela, P. (1992). New trends in the study of female aggression. In K. Björkvist & P. Niemela (Eds.), *Of mice and women: Aspects of female aggression.* San Diego, CA: Academic Press.

Björkqvist, K., Lagerspetz, K. M. J., & Kaukianen, A. (1992). Do girls manipulate and boys fight? Developmental trends in regard to direct indirect aggression. *Aggressive Behavior, 18,* 117–127.

Blackwell, A. (1976). *The sexes throughout nature.* Westport, CT: Hyperion Press. (Original work published 1875)

Bleier, R. (1979). Social and political bias in science: An examination of animal studies and their generalizations to human behavior and evolution. In R. Hubbard & M. Lowe (Eds.), *Genes and gender: 2. Pitfalls in research on sex and gender* (pp. 49–70). New York: Gordian Press.

Bleier, R. (1984). *Science and gender: A critique of biology and its theories on women.* Elmsford, NY: Pergamon Press.

Bleier, R. (Ed.). (1986a). *Feminist approaches to science.* New York: Pergamon Press.

Bleier, R. (1986b). Sex differences research: Science or belief? In R. Bleier (Ed.), *Feminist approaches to science* (pp. 147–164). Elmsford, NY: Pergamon Press.

Block, J. H. (1983). Differential premises arising from differential socialization of the sexes: Some conjectures. *Child Development, 54,* 1335–1354.

Blyth, D. A., Hill, J. P., & Thiel, K. S. (1982). Early adolescents' significant others: Grade and gender differences in perceived relationships with familial and nonfamilial adults and young people. *Journal of Youth and Adolescence, 11,* 425–450.

Bohan, J. S. (1993). Regarding gender: Essentialism, constructionism, and feminist psychology. *Psychology of Women Quarterly, 17,* 5–21.

Boldizar, J. P. (1991). Assessing sex typing and androgyny in children: The children's sex role inventory. *Developmental Psychology, 27,* 505–515.

Bordo, S. (1985). The body and the reproduction of femininity. In A. Jaggar & S. Bordo (Eds.), *Gender/body/knowledge: Feminist reconstructions of being and knowing* (pp. 13–33). Rutgers, NJ: Rutgers University Press.

Bordo, S. (1987). *The flight to objectivity: Essays on Cartesianism and culture.* Albany: State University of New York Press.

Bordo, S. (1990). Feminism, postmodernism and gender-skepticism. In L. Nicholson (Ed.), *Feminism/postmodernism* (pp. 133–156). New York: Routledge.

Bowlby, J. (1969). *Attachment and loss: Vol. 1. Attachment.* New York: Basic Books.

Bradbard, M. R., Martin, C. L., Endsley, R. C., & Halverson, C. F. (1986). Influence of sex stereotypes on children's exploration and memory: A competence versus performance distinction. *Developmental Psychology, 22,* 481–486.

Bradley, B. S. (1989). *Visions of infancy.* Oxford: Polity/Blackwell.

Braham, J. (1995). *Crucial conversations: Interpreting contemporary American literary autobiography by women.* New York: Teachers College Press.

Bransford, J. D., Barclay, J. R., & Franks, J. J. (1972). Sentence memory: A constructive versus interpretive approach. *Cognitive Psychology, 3,* 193–209.

Bretherton, I. (1992). Attachment and bonding. In V. B. Van Hasselt & M. Hersen (Eds.), *Handbook of social development: A lifespan perspective*. New York: Plenum Press.

Bretherton, I., & Beeghly, M. (1982). Talking about internal states: The acquisition of an explicit theory of mind. *Developmental Psychology, 18*, 906–921.

Brewer, W. (1988). Memory for randomly sampled autobiographical events. In U. Neisser & E. Winograd (Eds.), *Remembering reconsidered: Ecological and traditional approaches to the study of memory* (pp. 21–90). New York: Cambridge University Press.

Brody, L. R., & Hall, J. A. (1993). Gender and emotion. In M. Lewis & J. M. Haviland (Eds.), *Handbook of emotions* (pp. 447–460). New York: Guilford Press.

Bronfenbrenner, U. (1977). Toward an experimental ecology of human development. *American Psychologist, 32*, 513–531.

Bronfenbrenner, U. (1979). *The ecology of human development*. Cambridge, MA: Harvard University Press.

Bronfenbrenner, U., & Morris, P. A. (1998). The ecology of developmental processes. In W. Damon (Series Ed.) & R. M. Lerner (Vol. Ed.), *Handbook of child psychology: Vol. 1. Theoretical models of human development* (5th ed., pp. 993–1028). New York: Wiley.

Brookins, G. K. (1985). Black children's sex-role ideologies and occupational choices in families of employed mothers. In M. B. Spencer, G. K. Brookins, & W. R. Allen (Eds.), *Beginnings: The social and affective development of black children* (pp. 257–271). Hillsdale, NJ: Erlbaum.

Broude, G. J. (1990). Protest masculinity: A further look at the causes and the concept. *Ethos, 18*, 103–122.

Broughton, J. M. (1987). Piaget's concept of the self. In P. Young-Eisendrath & J. A. Hall (Eds.), *The book of the self: Person, pretext, and process* (pp. 277–295). New York: New York University Press.

Broverman, I. K., Broverman, D. M., Clarkson, F. E., Rosenkrantz, P. S., & Vogel, S. R. (1970). Sex-role stereotypes and clinical judgments of mental health. *Journal of Consulting & Clinical Psychology, 34*, 1–7.

Brown, L. M., & Gilligan, C. (1992). *Meeting at the crossroads: Women's psychology and girls' development*. Cambridge, MA: Harvard University Press.

Brown, R., & Kulik, J. (1977). Flashbulb memories. *Cognition, 5*, 73–99.

Bruner, J. S. (1990). *Acts of meaning*. Cambridge, MA: Harvard University Press.

Bruner, J. S. (1992). Narrative as the construction of reality. In H. Beilin & P. B. Pufall (Eds.), *Piaget's theory: Prospects and possibilities* (pp. 229–250). Hillsdale, NJ: Erlbaum.

Buck-Morss, S. (1975). Socio-economic bias in Piaget's theory and its implications for cross-culture studies. *Human Development, 18*, 35–49.

Buffery, W., & Gray, J. (1972). Sex differences in the development of spatial and linguistic skills. In C. Ounsted & D. C. Taylor (Eds.), *Gender differences: Their ontogeny and significance* (pp. 5–19). Edinburgh: Churchill Livingstone.

Buhrmester, D., & Furman, F. (1987). The development of companionship and intimacy. *Child Development, 58*, 1101–1113.

Buhrmester, D., & Prager, K. (1995). Patterns and functions of self-disclosure during childhood and adolescence. In K. J. Rotenberg (Ed.), *Disclosure processes in children and adolescents* (pp. 10–56). Cambridge, England: Cambridge University Press.

Bukowski, W. M., Hoza, B., & Boivin, M. (1994). Measuring friendship quality during pre- and early adolescence: The development and psychometric properties of the Friendship Qualities Scale. *Journal of Social and Personal Relationships, 11,* 471–484.

Burman, E. (1994). *Deconstructing developmental psychology.* London: Routledge.

Burman, E. (Ed.). (1998). *Deconstructing feminist psychology.* London: Sage.

Bush, D. M. (1987). The impact of family and school on adolescent girls' aspirations and expectations: The public-private split and the reproduction of gender inequality. In J. Figueira-McDonough & R. Sarri (Eds.), *The trapped woman: Catch-22 in deviance and control* (pp. 258–295). Beverly Hills, CA: Sage.

Buss, D. M. (1995). Psychological sex differences: Origins through sexual selection. *American Psychologist, 50,* 164–168.

Bussey, K. (1983). A social-cognitive appraisal of sex-role development. *Australian Journal of Psychology, 35,* 135–143.

Bussey, K., & Bandura, A. (1984). Influence of gender constancy and social power on sex-linked modeling. *Journal of Personality & Social Psychology, 47,* 1292–1302.

Bussey, K., & Bandura, A. (1992). Self-regulatory mechanisms governing gender development. *Child Development, 63,* 1236–1250.

Bussey, K., & Perry, D. G. (1982). Same-sex imitation: The avoidance of cross-sex models or the acceptance of same-sex models? *Sex Roles, 8,* 773–784.

Byrne, R., & Whiten, A. (Eds.). (1988). *Machiavellian intelligence.* Oxford, England: Oxford University Press.

Cairns, R. B., Cairns, B. D., Neckerman, H. J., Ferguson, L. L., & Gariepy, J. L. (1989). Growth and aggression: 1. Childhood to early adolescence. *Developmental Psychology, 52,* 320–330.

Calvert, S. L., & Huston, A. C. (1987). Television and children's gender schemata. In L. S. Liben & M. L. Signorella (Eds.), *Children's gender schemata* (New Directions for Child Development, No. 38, pp. 75–88). San Francisco: Jossey-Bass.

Campbell, A. C. (1980). Friendship as a factor in male and female delinquency. In H. C. Foot, A. J. Chapman, & J. R. Smith (Eds.), *Friendship and social relations in children* (pp. 365–389). New York: Wiley.

Campbell, A. C. (1990). Female participation in gangs. In C. R. Huff (Ed.), *Gangs in America* (pp. 163–182). Newbury Park, CA: Sage.

Caplan, P. J., MacPherson, G. M., & Tobin, P. (1985). Do sex-related differences in spatial abilities exist? *American Psychologist, 40,* 786–799.

Carey, S. (1985). *Conceptual change in childhood.* Cambridge, MA: MIT Press.

Carey, S. (1999). Sources of conceptual change. In E. K. Scholnick, K. Nelson, S. A. Gelman, & P. H. Miller (Eds.), *Conceptual development: Piaget's legacy* (pp. 293–326). Mahwah, NJ: Erlbaum.

Carlson, G. N., & Pelletier, F. J. (Eds.). (1995). *The generic book*. Chicago: University of Chicago Press.

Carpenter, C. J. (1983). Activity structure and play: Implications for socialization. In M. B. Liss (Ed.), *Social and cognitive skills: Sex roles and children's play* (pp. 117–145). New York: Academic Press.

Carpenter, C. J., Huston, A. C., & Holt, W. (1986). Modification of preschool sex-typed behaviors by participation in adult-structured activities. *Sex Roles, 14*, 603–615.

Carruthers, P., & Smith, P. K. (Eds.) (1996). *Theories of theory of mind*. Cambridge, England: Cambridge University Press.

Carter, D. B., & Patterson, C. J. (1982). Sex roles as social conventions: The development of children's conceptions of sex-role stereotypes. *Developmental Psychology, 18*, 812–824.

Case, R. (1992). *The mind's staircase: Exploring the conceptual underpinnings of children's thought and knowledge*. Hillsdale, NJ: Erlbaum.

Cauce, A. M., Hiraga, Y., Graves, D., & Gonzales, N. (1996). African American mothers and their adolescent daughters: Closeness, conflict, and control. In B. J. Ross Leadbeater & N. Way (Eds.), *Urban girls: Resisting stereotypes, creating identities* (pp. 100–116). New York: New York University Press.

Chandler, M. J., & Boutilier, R. G. (1992). The development of dynamic system reasoning. *Human Development, 35*, 121–135.

Cheng, W., & Holyoak, K. J. (1985). Pragmatic reasoning schemas. *Cognitive Psychology, 17*, 391–416.

Chesney-Lind, M. (1989). Girls' crime and woman's place: Toward a feminist model of female delinquency. *Crime and Delinquency, 35*, 5–29.

Chodorow, N. J. (1974). Family structure and feminine personality. In M. Rosaldo & L. Lamphere (Eds.), *Woman, culture and society* (pp. 43–66). Stanford, CA: Stanford University Press.

Chodorow, N. J. (1978). *The reproduction of mothering: Psychoanalysis and the socialization of gender*. Berkeley: University of California Press.

Chodorow, N. J. (1989). *Feminism and psychoanalytic theory*. New Haven: Yale University Press.

Chodorow, N. J. (1995). Gender as a personal and cultural construction. *Signs, 20*(3), 516–542.

Chow, E., Wilkinson, D. Y., & Baca Zinn, M. (Eds.). (1996). *Race, class, & gender: Common bonds, different voices*. Thousand Oaks, CA: Sage.

Cixous, H., & Clement, C. (1986). *The newly born woman*. Minneapolis: University of Minnesota Press.

Clayton, S. D., & Crosby, F. J. (1992). *Justice, gender, and affirmative action*. Ann Arbor: University of Michigan Press.

Clewell, B. C., & Ginorio, A. B. (1996). Examining women's progress in the sciences from the perspective of diversity. In C.-S. Davis, A. B. Ginorio, C. S. Hollenshead, B. B. Lazarus, P. M. Rayman, & Associates (Eds.), *The equity equation* (pp. 163–231). San Francisco: Jossey-Bass.

Code, L. (1987a). *Epistemic responsibility*. Hanover, NH: University Press of New England.

Code, L. (1987b). Second persons. In M. Hanen & K. Nielsen (Eds.), *Science, morality, and feminist theory* (pp. 357–382). Calgary, Canada: University of Calgary Press.

Code, L. (1991). *What can she know? Feminist theory and the construction of knowledge*. Ithaca, NY: Cornell University Press.

Code, L. (1993). Taking subjectivity into account. In L. Alcoff & E. Potter (Eds.), *Feminist epistemologies* (pp. 15–48). New York: Routledge.

Code, L. (1995a). How do we know? Questions of method in feminist practice. In S. Burt & L. Code (Eds.), *Changing methods: Feminists transforming practice*. Peterborough, ON: Broadview Press.

Code, L. (1995b). *Rhetorical spaces: Essays on gendered locations*. New York: Routledge.

Code, L. (1996). What is natural about epistemology naturalized? *American Philosophical Quarterly, 33*, 1–22.

Code, L. (1998). Epistemology. In. A. M. Jaggar & I. M. Young (Eds.), *A companion to feminist philosophy* (pp. 173–184). Oxford, England: Blackwell.

Code, L. (1999). The perversion of autonomy and the subjection of women: Discourses of social advocacy at century's end. In C. Mackenzie & N. Stoljar (Eds.), *Relational autonomy: Feminist perspectives on autonomy and agency*. New York: Oxford University Press.

Code, L., Mullett, S., & Overall, C. (1988). Editors' introduction. In L. Code, S. Mullett, & C. Overall (Eds.), *Feminist perspectives: Philosophical essays on methods and morals* (pp. 3–10). Toronto: University of Toronto Press.

Coie, J. D., & Dodge, K. A. (1998). Aggression and antisocial behavior. In W. Damon (Series Ed.) & N. Eisenberg (Vol. Ed.), *Handbook of child psychology: Vol. 3. Social, emotional, and personality development* (5th ed., pp. 933–1016). New York: Wiley.

Cole, M. (1992). Culture in development. In M. H. Bornstein & M. E. Lamb (Eds.), *Developmental psychology: An advanced textbook* (pp. 731–790). Mahwah, NJ: Erlbaum.

Collins, P. H. (1986). Learning from the outsider within. *Social Problems, 33*, 514–532.

Collins, P. H. (1990). *Black feminist thought: Knowledge, consciousness and the politics of empowerment*. New York: Routledge.

Collins, P. H. (1997). Comment on Hekman's "Truth and method: Feminist standpoint revisited": Where's the power? *Signs, 22*(2), 375–381.

Condry, J., & Condry, S. (1976). Sex differences: A study of the eye of the beholder. *Child Development, 47*, 812–819.

Connell, R. W. (1996). Teaching the boys: New research on masculinity, and gender strategies for schools. *Teachers College Record, 98*, 206–235.

Conway, J. K. (1998). *When memory speaks: Reflections on autobiography*. New York: Knopf.

Conway, M. A. (1990). *Autobiographical memory: An introduction*. Buckingham, England: Open University Press.

Conway, M. A. (1995). *Flashbulb memories*. Hillsdale, NJ: Erlbaum.

Cook, E. P. (1985). *Psychological androgyny*. Eimsford, NY: Pergamon Press.

Cooley, C. H. (1902). *Human nature and the social order*. New York: Scribner.

Corea, G. (1985). *The mother machine: Reproductive technologies from artificial insemination to artifical wombs*. New York: Harper & Row.

Corsaro, W. A. (1996). Transitions in early childhood: The promise of comparative, longitudinal ethnography. In R. Jessor, A. Colby, & R. A. Shweder (Eds.), *Ethnography and human development* (pp. 419–457). Chicago: University of Chicago Press.

Cox, M. J., Owen, M. T., Henderson, V. K., & Margand, N. A. (1992). Prediction of infant-father and infant-mother attachment. *Developmental Psychology, 28*, 474–483.

Coyle, T. R., & Bjorklund, D. F. (1997). Age differences in, and consequences of, multiple- and variable-strategy use on a multitrial sort-recall task. *Developmental Psychology, 33*, 372–380.

Crawford, M., & Marecek, J. (1989). Psychology reconstructs the female: 1968–1988. *Psychology of Women Quarterly, 13*, 147–165.

Crick, N. R. (1995). Relational aggression: The role of intent attributions, feelings of distress, and provocation type. *Development and Psychopathology, 7*, 313–322.

Crick, N. R. (1997). Engagement in gender normative versus gender nonnormative forms of aggression: Links to social-psychological adjustment. *Developmental Psychology, 67*, 2317–2327.

Crick, N. R., & Bigbee, M. A. (1998). Relational and overt forms of peer victimization: A multi-informant approach. *Journal of Consulting and Clinical Psychology, 66*, 337–347.

Crick, N. R., Bigbee, M. A., & Howes, C. (1996). Gender differences in children's normative beliefs about aggression: How do I hurt thee? Let me count the ways. *Child Development, 67*, 1003–1014.

Crick, N. R., Casas, J. F., & Ku, H. (1999). Physical and relational peer victimization in preschool. *Developmental Psychology, 35*, 376–385.

Crick, N. R., Casas, J. F., & Mosher, M. (1997). Relational and overt aggression in preschool. *Developmental Psychology, 33*, 579–588.

Crick, N. R., & Dodge, K. A. (1994). A review and reformulation of social information-processing mechanisms in children's social adjustment. *Psychological Bulletin, 115*, 612–620.

Crick, N. R., & Grotpeter, J. K. (1995). Relational aggression, gender, and social-psychological adjustment. *Child Development, 66*, 710–722.

Crick, N. R., & Grotpeter, J. K. (1996). Children's treatment by peers: Victims of relational and overt aggression. *Development and Psychopathology, 8,* 367–380.

Crick, N. R., Grotpeter, J. K., & Bigbee, M. A. (1998). *Because they're being mean? Intent attributions of relationally and physically aggressive children.* Manuscript submitted for publication.

Crick, N. R., & Werner, N. E. (1998). Response decision processes in relational and overt aggression. *Child Development, 69,* 1630–1639.

Crick, N. R., Werner, N. E., Casas, J. F., O'Brien, K. M., Nelson, D. A., Grotpeter, J. K., & Markon, K. (1999). Childhood aggression and gender: A new look at an old problem. In D. Bernstein (Ed.), *Nebraska Symposium on Motivation* (vol. 45, pp. 75–141). Lincoln: University of Nebraska Press.

Crick, N. R., Werner, N. E., & Shellin, H. (1998). *Young adults' normative beliefs about aggression.* Unpublished manuscript, University of Minnesota, Twin Cities.

Cross, S. E., & Madson, L. (1997). Models of the self: Self-construals and gender. *Psychological Bulletin, 122,* 5–37.

Cross, S. E., & Markus, H. R. (1993). Gender in thought, belief, and action: A cognitive approach. In A. E. Beall & R. J. Sternberg (Eds.), *The psychology of gender* (pp. 55–98). New York: Guilford Press.

Dahl, O. (1975). On generics. In E. L. Keenan (Ed.), *Formal semantics of natural language* (pp. 99–111). New York: Cambridge University Press.

Damon W., & Hart, D. (1982). The development of self-understanding from infancy through adolescence. *Child Development, 53,* 841–864.

Damon, W., & Hart, D. (1988). *Self-understanding in childhood and adolescence.* New York: Cambridge University Press.

D'Augelli, A. R. (1998). Developmental implications of victimization of lesbian, gay, and bisexual youths. In G. M. Herek (Ed.), *Stigma and sexual orientation: Understanding prejudice against lesbians, gay men, and bisexuals* (pp. 187–210). Thousand Oaks, CA: Sage.

Dawkins, R. (1976). *The selfish gene.* New York: Oxford University Press.

de Beauvoir, S. (1974). *The second sex* (H. M. Parshley, Trans. & Ed.). New York: Vintage Books.

Deak, G. O., & Maratsos, M. (1998). On having complex representations of things: Preschoolers use multiple words for objects and people. *Developmental Psychology, 34,* 224–240.

Deaux, K. (1985). Sex and gender. *Annual Review of Psychology, 36,* 49–81.

Deaux, K., & Kite, M. E. (1985). Gender stereotypes: Some thoughts on the cognitive organization of gender-related information. *Academic Psychology Bulletin, 7,* 123–144.

Deaux, K., & Lewis, L. L. (1984). Structure of gender stereotypes: Interrelationships among components and gender label. *Journal of Personality and Social Psychology, 46,* 991–1004.

Deaux, K., & Major, B. (1987). Putting gender into context: An interactive model of gender-related behavior. *Psychological Review, 94*, 369–389.

Denzin, N. (1996). The epistemological crisis in the human disciplines: Letting the old do the work of the new. In R. Jessor, A. Colby, & R. A. Shweder (Eds.), *Ethnography and human development: Context and meaning in social inquiry* (pp. 127–151). Chicago: University of Chicago Press.

Dinnerstein, D. (1977). *The mermaid and the minotaur: Sexual arrangements and human malaise.* New York: Harper.

Donovan, J. (1992). *Feminist theory: The intellectual traditions of American feminism* (2nd ed.). New York: Continuum Press.

Downing, N. E., & Roush, K. L. (1985). From passive acceptance to active commitment: A model of feminist identity development for women. *Counseling Psychologist, 13*, 695–709. [Special issue: *Cross-cultural counseling.*]

Dubois, E., Kelly, G. P., Kennedy, E., Korsmeyer, C., & Robinson, L. S. (1985). *Feminist scholarship: Kindling in the groves of academe.* Urbana: University of Illinois Press.

Dudychea, G. J., & Dudychea, M. M. (1941). Childhood memories: A review of the literature. *Psychological Bulletin, 38*, 668–682.

Dugger, K. (1988). Social location and gender-role attitudes: A comparison of black and white women. *Gender & Society, 2*, 425–448.

Dunn, J. (1988). *The beginnings of social understanding.* Cambridge, MA: Harvard University Press.

Dunn, J. (1994). Changing minds and changing relationships. In C. Lewis & P. Mitchell (Eds.), *Children's early understanding of mind: Origins and development* (pp. 297–310). Hillsdale, NJ: Erlbaum.

Dupré, J. (1993). *The disorder of things: Metaphysical foundations of the disunity of science.* Cambridge, MA: Harvard University Press.

Duran, J. (1991). *Toward a feminist epistemology.* Savage, MD: Rowman & Littlefield.

Dweck, C. S., & Bush, E. S. (1976). Sex differences in learned helplessness: I. Differential debilitation with peer and adult evaluators. *Developmental Psychology, 12*, 147–156.

Dworkin, A. (1983). *Right-wing women.* New York: Coward-McCann.

Eccles, J. S. (1984). Sex differences in achievement patterns. *Nebraska Symposium on Motivation: Vol. 32* (pp. 97–132). Lincoln: University of Nebraska Press.

Eccles, J. S. (1987). Adolescence: Gateway to gender-role transcendence. In D. B. Carter (Ed.), *Current conceptions of sex roles and sex typing: Theory and research* (pp. 225–241). New York: Praeger.

Eccles, J. S. (1989). Bringing young women to math and science. In M. Crawford & M. Gentry (Eds.), *Gender and thought: Psychological perspectives* (pp. 36–58). New York: Springer.

Eccles, J. S., Jacobs, J., Harold-Goldsmith, J., Jayarathe, T., & Yee, D. (1989, April). *The relations between parents' category-based and target-based beliefs:*

Gender roles and biological influences. Paper presented at the biennial meeting of the Society for Research in Child Development, Kansas City, MO.

Eder, D. (1985). The cycle of popularity: Interpersonal relations among female adolescents. *Sociology of Education, 58*, 154–165.

Eder, R. A. (1990). Uncovering young children's psychological selves: Individual and developmental differences. *Child Development, 61*, 849–863.

Eisler, R., Loye, D., & Norgaard, K. (1995). *Women, men, and the global quality of life.* Pacific Grove, CA: Center for Partnership Studies.

Ellis, S. (1995, April). *Social influences on strategy choice.* Paper presented at the biennial meeting of the Society for Research in Child Development, Indianapolis.

Elman, J. L., Bates, E. A., Johnson, M. H., Karmiloff-Smith, A., Parisi, D., & Plunkett, K. (1996). *Rethinking innateness: A connectionist perspective on development.* Cambridge, MA: MIT Press.

Ember, C. R. (1973). Feminine task assignment and the social behavior of boys. *Ethos, 1*, 424–439.

Ember, C. R., & Ember, M. (1993). Issues in cross-cultural studies of interpersonal violence. *Violence & Victims, 8*, 217–233.

Emmerich, W., Goldman, K. S., & Kirsh, B. (1977). Evidence for a transitional phase in the development of gender constancy. *Child Development, 48*, 930–936.

Engel, S. (1986). *Learning to reminisce: A developmental study of how young children talk about the past.* Unpublished doctoral dissertation, City University of New York.

Erikson, E. H. (1963). *Childhood and society* (2nd ed.). New York: Norton.

Etaugh, C. (1993). Maternal employment: Effects on children. In J. Frankel (Ed.), *The employed mother and the family context* (pp. 68–88). New York: Springer.

Fagot, B. I. (1977). Consequences of moderate cross-gender behavior in preschool children. *Child Development, 48*, 902–907.

Fagot, B. I., & Leinbach, M. D. (1989). The young child's gender schema: Environmental input, internal organization. *Child Development, 60*, 663–672.

Fairclough, N. (1992). *Language and social change.* Cambridge, England: Polity Press.

Falmagne, R. J. (1995). The abstract and the concrete. In L. Martin, K. Nelson, & E. Tobach (Eds.), *Sociocultural psychology: On the theory and practice of knowing and doing* (pp. 205–228). New York: Cambridge University Press.

Falmagne, R. J. (1996). *Logic, reasoning and the politics of knowledge production.* Address, Suffolk University, School of Sciences Annual Banquet. Manuscript, Clark University.

Falmagne, R. J. (1997). *Toward a feminist theory of inference: Exploration of a cross-disciplinary methodology.* Paper presented at the enGendering Rationalities Conference, University of Oregon, Eugene, OR.

Falmagne, R. J. (1998a). A time of epistemic transformation and responsibility. [Review of the book *Ethnography and human development*]. *Human Development, 41*, 134–144.

Falmagne, R. J. (1998b). *On the constitution of self and mind in societal and cultural matrix*. Unpublished manuscript, Clark University.

Falmagne, R. J. (2000). Toward the feminist study of deductive inference: Exploration of a cross-disciplinary methodology. In M. Hass & R. J. Falmagne (Eds.), *Feminist perspectives on logic*. New York: Rowman & Littlefield.

Falmagne, R. J., & Gonsalves, J. (1995). Deductive inference. *Annual Review of Psychology, 46*, 525–559.

Fausto-Sterling, A. (1992). *Myths of gender*. New York: Basic Books.

Fee, E. (1982). A feminist critique of scientific objectivity. *Science for the People, 14*(4), 8.

Feinman, S. (1981). Why is cross-sex-role behavior more approved for girls than for boys? A status characteristic approach. *Sex Roles, 7*, 289–300.

Firestone, S. (1970). *The dialectic of sex*. New York: Bantam Books.

Fischer, K. W., & Bidell, T. R. (1998). Dynamic development of psychological structures in action and thought. In W. Damon (Series Ed.) & R. M. Lerner (Vol. Ed.), *Handbook of child psychology: Vol. 1. Theoretical models of human development* (5th ed., pp. 467–561). New York: Wiley.

Fischer, K. W., Knight, C. C., & Van Parys, M. (1993). Analyzing diversity in developmental pathways: Methods and concepts. In R. Case & W. Edelstein (Eds.), *The new structuralism in cognitive development* (pp. 33–56). Basel: Karger.

Fisher, C. B., Jackson, J. F., & Villarruel, F. A. (1998). The study of African American and Latin American children and youth. In W. Damon (Series Ed.) & I. E. Sigel & K. A. Renninger (Vol. Eds.), *Handbook of child psychology: Vol. 4. Child psychology in practice* (5th ed., pp. 1145–1207). New York: Wiley.

Fiske, S. T., & Taylor, S. E. (1991). *Social cognition* (2nd ed.). New York: McGraw-Hill.

Fivush, R. (1994a). Constructing narrative, emotion, and self in parent-child conversations about the past. In U. Neisser & R. Fivush (Eds.), *The remembering self: Construction and accuracy in the life narrative* (pp. 136–157). New York: Cambridge University Press.

Fivush, R. (1994b). Young children's event recall: Are memories constructed through discourse? *Consciousness and Cognition, 3*, 356–373.

Fivush, R., & Fromhoff, F. (1988). Style and structure in mother-child conversations about the past. *Discourse Processes, 11*, 337–355.

Fivush, R., Haden, C., & Reese, E. (1996). Remembering, recounting and reminiscing: The development of autobiographical memory in social context. In D. Rubin (Ed.), *Reconstructing our past: An overview of autobiographical memory* (pp. 341–359). New York: Cambridge University Press.

Fivush, R., Hamond, N. R., Harsch, N., Singer, N., & Wolf, A. (1991). Content and consistency of young children's autobiographical recall. *Discourse Processes, 14*, 373–388.

Fivush, R., & Shukat, J. (1995). Content, consistency and coherency of early autobiographical recall. In M. S. Zaragoza, J. R. Graham, G. C. N. Hall, R. Hirschman, & Y. S. Ben-Porath (Eds.), *Memory and testimony in the child witness*. Thousand Oaks, CA: Sage.

Flavell, J. H. (1992). Perspectives on perspective taking. In H. Beilin & P. B. Pufall (Eds.), *Piaget's theory: Prospects and possibilities* (pp. 107–139). Hillsdale, NJ: Erlbaum.

Flavell, J. H., & Miller, P. H. (1998). Social cognition. In W. Damon (Series Ed.) & D. Kuhn & R. S. Siegler (Vol. Eds.), *Handbook of child psychology: Vol. 2. Cognition, perception, and language* (5th ed., pp. 851–898). New York: Wiley.

Flavell, J. H., Miller, P. H., & Miller, S. A. (1993). *Cognitive development* (3rd ed.). Hillsdale, NJ: Prentice Hall.

Flax, J. (1990). Postmodernism and gender relations in feminist theory. In L. J. Nicholson (Ed.), *Feminism / postmodernism* (pp. 39–62). New York: Routledge.

Flax, J. (1993). *Disputed subjects: Essays on psychoanalysis, subjects, politics and philosophy*. New York: Routledge.

Florian, J. E. (1995). *Preschoolers' understanding of social role combinations*. Unpublished doctoral dissertation, University of Michigan.

Foushee, H. C., Helmreich, R. L., & Spence, J. T. (1979). Implicit theories of masculinity and femininity: Dualistic or bipolar? *Psychology of Women Quarterly, 3,* 259–269.

Fossey, D. (1983). *Gorillas in the mist*. Boston: Houghton Mifflin.

Foucault, M. (1980). *Power/knowledge*. New York: Pantheon.

Foucault, M. (1982). The order of discourse. In M. Shapiro (Ed.), *Language and politics*. Cambridge, MA: Basil Blackwell.

Franks, B. (1992). Developmental psychology and feminism: Points of communication. *Women's Studies Quarterly, 1–2,* 28–40.

Frege, G. (1970). Begriffsschrift. In P. Geach & M. Black (Eds.), *Translations from the philosophical works of Gottlob Frege*. Oxford, England: Basil Blackwell. (Original work published 1879)

Frege, G. (1956). The thought: A logical inquiry. *Mind, 65,* 289–311. (Original work published 1918)

Freud, S. (1953). Three essays on the theory of sexuality. In J. Strachey (Ed. & Trans.), *The standard edition of the complete psychological works of Sigmund Freud* (Vol. 7, pp. 135–243). London: Hogarth Press. (Original work published 1905)

Friedan, B. (1974). *The feminine mystique*. New York: Dell.

Furman, W., & Buhrmester, D. (1985). Children's perceptions of the personal relationships within their social networks. *Developmental Psychology, 21,* 1016–1024.

Fuss, D. (1989). *Essentially speaking: Feminism, nature, and difference*. New York: Routledge.

Galen, B. R., & Underwood, M. K. (1997). A developmental investigation of social aggression among children. *Developmental Psychology, 33,* 589–600.

Gallup, G. G., Jr. (1970). Chimpanzees: Self-recognition. *Science, 167,* 86–87.

Garcia, R. (1999). A systemic interpretation of Piaget's theory of knowledge. In E. K. Scholnick, K. Nelson, S. A. Gelman, & P. H. Miller (Eds.), *Conceptual representation: Piaget's legacy* (pp. 165–183). Mahwah, NJ: Erlbaum.

Gardner, H. (1983). *Frames of mind: The theory of multiple intelligences.* New York: Basic Books.

Gatens, M. (1998). Modern rationalism. In. A. M. Jaggar & I. M. Young (Eds.), *A companion to feminist philosophy* (pp. 21–29). Oxford, England: Blackwell.

Gelman, S. A., & Coley, J. D. (1990). The importance of knowing a dodo is a bird: Categories and inferences in 2-year-old children. *Developmental Psychology, 26,* 796–804.

Gelman, S. A., Coley, J. D., & Gottfried, G. M. (1994). Essential beliefs in children: The acquisition of concepts and theories. In L. A. Hirschfeld & S. A. Gelman (Eds.), *Mapping the mind: Domain specificity in cognition and culture* (pp. 346–365). New York: Cambridge University Press.

Gelman, S. A., Coley, J. D., Rosengren, K., Hartman, E., & Pappas, T. (1998). Beyond labeling: The role of maternal input in the acquisition of richly-structured categories. *Monographs of the Society for Research in Child Development, 63* (1, Serial No. 253).

Gelman, S. A., Collman, P., & Maccoby, E. E. (1986). Inferring properties from categories versus inferring categories from properties: The case of gender. *Child Development, 57,* 396–404.

Gelman, S. A., & Diesendruck, G. (1999). What's in a concept? Context, variability, and psychological essentialism. In I. E. Sigel (Ed.), *Theoretical perspectives in the concept of representation* (pp. 87–111). Hillsdale, NJ: Erlbaum.

Gelman, S. A., & Hirschfeld, L. A. (1999). How biological is essentialism? In S. Atran & D. Medin (Eds.), *Folk biology.* Cambridge, MA: MIT Press.

Gelman, S. A., & Markman, E. M. (1986). Categories and induction in young children. *Cognition, 23,* 183–209.

Gelman, S. A., & Medin, D. L. (1993). What's so essential about essentialism? A different perspective on the interaction of perception, language, and conceptual knowledge. *Cognitive Development, 8,* 157–167.

Gelman, S. A., Rodriguez, T., Nguyen, S., & Koenig, M. (1997, April). *Children's spontaneous talk about kinds: Domain-specificity in use of generics.* Paper presented at the biennial meeting of the Society for Research in Child Development, Washington, DC.

Gelman, S. A., & Wellman, H. M. (1991). Insides and essences: Early understandings of the nonobvious. *Cognition, 38,* 213–244.

Gergen, K. J. (1993). *Realities and relationships: Soundings in social construction.* Cambridge, MA: Harvard University Press.

Gergen, K. J. (1994a). Mind, text, and society: Self-memory in social context. In U. Neisser & R. Fivush (Eds.), *The remembering self: Construction and accuracy in the life narrative* (pp. 78–104). New York: Cambridge University Press.

Gergen, K. J. (1994b). *Toward transformation in social knowledge.* Thousand Oaks, CA: Sage.

Gergen, M. M. (1988). Toward a feminist metatheory and methodology in the social sciences. In M. M. Gergen (Ed.), *Feminist thought and the structure of knowledge* (pp. 29–49). New York: New York University Press.

Giddings, P. (1984). *When and where we enter: The impact of black women on race and sex in America.* New York: Morrow.

Gilligan, C. (1982). *In a different voice: Psychological theory and women's development.* Cambridge, MA: Harvard University Press.

Gilligan, C. (1986). On *In a different voice:* An interdisciplinary forum. Reply. *Signs, 11,* 324–333.

Ginorio, A. B., Gutiérrez, L., Cauce, A. M., & Acosta, M. (1995). Psychological issues for Latinas. In H. Landrine (Ed.), *Bringing cultural diversity to feminist psychology* (pp. 241–263). Washington, DC: American Psychological Association Press.

Ginorio, A. B., & Martinez, L. J. (1998). Where are the Latinos? Ethno-race and gender in psychology courses. *Psychology of Women Quarterly, 22,* 53–68.

Giordano, P. C., Cernkovich, S. A., & Pugh, M. D. (1986). Friendships and delinquency. *American Journal of Sociology, 91,* 1170–1202.

Girotto, V., Light, P., & Colbourn, C. J., (1988). Pragmatic schemas and conditional reasoning in children. *Quarterly Journal of Experimental Psychology: Human Experimental Psychology, 40,* 469–482.

Goldberger, N. R., Tarule, J. M., Clinchy, B. M., & Belenky, M. F. (Eds.). (1996). *Knowledge, difference, and power.* New York: Basic Books.

Goldfarb, W. (1945). Effects of psychological deprivation in infancy and subsequent stimulation. *American Journal of Psychiatry, 103,* 113–117.

Golombok, S., & Fivush, R. (1994). *Gender development.* New York: Cambridge University Press.

Goodall, J. (1971). *In the shadow of man.* Boston: Houghton Mifflin.

Goodfield, J. (1982). *An imagined world.* New York: Penguin.

Goodnow, J. J. (1988). Children's household work: Its nature and functions. *Psychological Bulletin, 103,* 5–26.

Goodwin, M. H. (1985). The serious side of jump rope: Conversational practices and social organization in the frame of play. *Journal of American Folklore, 98,* 315–330.

Goodwin, M. H. (1990). *He said, she said: Talk as social organization among black children.* Bloomington: Indiana University Press.

Goodwin, M. H. (1997). Crafting activities: Building social organization through language in girls' and boys' groups. In C. T. Snowden & M. Hausberger (Eds.), *Social influences on vocal development* (pp. 328–341). Cambridge, England: Cambridge University Press.

Gopnik, A. (1993). How we know our minds: The illusion of first-person knowledge of intentionality, *Behavioral and Brain Sciences, 16,* 1–14.

Gopnik, A., & Astington, J. W. (1988). Children's understanding of representational change in its relation to the understanding of false belief and the appearance-reality distinction. *Child Development, 59,* 26–37.

Gopnik, A., & Meltzoff, A. (1997). *Words, thoughts and theories.* Cambridge, MA: MIT Press.

Gopnik, A., & Wellman, H. (1994). The theory theory. In L. A. Hirschfeld & S. A. Gelman (Eds.), *Mapping the mind* (pp. 257–293). New York: Cambridge University Press.

Gottlieb, G. (1997). *Synthesizing nature-nurture: Prenatal roots of instinctive behavior.* Mahwah, NJ: Erlbaum.

Gould, S. J. (1991). Exaptation: A crucial tool for an evolutionary psychology. *Journal of Social Issues, 47,* 43–65.

Goy, R., & Phoenix, C. H. (1971). The effects of testosterone propionate administered before birth on the development of behavior in genetic female rhesus monkeys. In C. H. Sawyer & R. A. Gorski (Eds.), *Steroid hormones and brain function* (pp. 193–201). Berkeley: University of California Press.

Griffin, S. (1978). *The death of nature.* New York: Harper & Row.

Grotpeter, J. K., & Crick, N. R. (1996). Relational aggression, overt aggression, and friendship. *Child Development, 67,* 2328–2338.

Grotpeter, J. K., & Crick, N. R. (1998*). Relational aggression, physical aggression, and family relationships.* Unpublished manuscript, University of Minnesota, Twin Cities.

Grusec, J. E., Goodnow, J. J., & Cohen, L. (1996). Household work and the development of concern for others. *Developmental Psychology, 32,* 999–1007.

Guttentag, M., & Bray, H. (1976). *Undoing sex stereotypes.* New York: McGraw-Hill.

Haack, S. (1978). *Philosophy of logics.* New York: Cambridge University Press.

Hackett, G. (1985). Role of mathematics self-efficacy in the choice of math-related majors of college women and men: A path analysis. *Journal of Counseling Psychology, 32,* 47–56.

Haden, C. A., Didow, S. M., Ornstein, P. A., & Eckerman C. O. (1997, April). Mother-child talk about the here-and-now: Linkages to subsequent remembering. In E. Reese (Chair), *Adult-child reminiscing: Theory and practice.* Symposium conducted at a meeting of the Society for Research in Child Development, Washington, DC.

Halpern, D. (1992). *Sex differences in cognitive abilities* (2nd ed.). Hillsdale, NJ: Erlbaum.

Hamlyn, D. W. (1973). Logical and psychological aspects of learning. In R. S. Peters (Ed.), *The concept of education.* London: Routledge & Kegan Paul.

Haney, C., & Zimbardo, P. (1998). The past and future of U.S. prison policy: Twenty-five years after the Stanford Prison Experiment. *American Psychologist, 53,* 709–727.

Hansen, D. J., Christopher, J., & Nangle, D. W. (1992). Adolescent heterosocial interactions and dating. In V. B. Van Hasselt & Michel Hersen (Eds.), *Handbook of social development: A lifespan perspective* (pp. 371–394). New York: Plenum Press.

Haraway, D. (1988). Situated knowledges: The science question in feminism and the privilege of partial perspective. *Feminist Studies, 14,* 575–599.

Haraway, D. (1989). *Primate visions: Gender, race, and nature in the world of modern science*. New York: Routledge.

Haraway, D. (1991). Situated knowledges: The science question in feminism and the privilege of partial perspective. In D. Haraway (Ed.), *Simians, cyborgs, and women: The reinvention of nature* (pp. 183–201). New York: Routledge.

Harding, S. (1986). *The science question in feminism*. Ithaca, NY: Cornell University Press.

Harding, S. (1990). Feminism, science and the anti-enlightenment critiques. In L. J. Nicholson (Ed.), *Feminism/postmodernism* (pp. 83–106). New York: Routledge.

Harding, S. (1991). *Whose science? Whose knowledge? Thinking from women's lives*. Ithaca, NY: Cornell University Press.

Harding, S. (1993). Rethinking standpoint epistemology: What is "strong" objectivity? In L. Alcoff & E. Potter (Eds.), *Feminist epistemologies* (pp. 49–82). New York: Routledge.

Harding, S. (1997). Comment on Hekman's "Truth and method: Feminist standpoint revisited": Whose standpoint needs the regimes of truth and reality? *Signs, 22*(2), 382–391.

Harding, S. (1998). *Is science multicultural? Post-colonialisms, feminisms, and epistemologies*. Bloomington: Indiana University Press.

Harding, S., & Hintikka, M. B. (Eds.). (1983). *Discovering reality: Feminist perspectives on epistemology, metaphysics, methodology, and philosophy of science*. Dordrecht, Holland: Reidel.

Hare-Mustin, R. T., & Marecek, J. (1988). The meaning of difference: Gender theory, postmodernism, and psychology. *American Psychologist, 43*, 455–464.

Harman, G. (1986). *Change in view: Principles of reasoning*. Cambridge, MA: MIT Press.

Harris, J. R. (1995). Where is the child's environment? A group socialization theory of development. *Psychological Review, 102*, 458–489.

Harris, P. L. (1992). From simulation to folk psychology: The case for development. *Mind and Language, 7*, 120–144.

Hart, D., & Fegley, S. (1997). Children's self-awareness in cultural context. In U. Neisser & D. A. Jopling (Eds.), *The conceptual self in context: Culture, experience, and self-understanding. The Emory symposia in cognition* (pp. 128–153). New York: Cambridge University Press.

Harter, S. (1986). Processes underlying the construction, maintenance, and enhancement of the self-concept in children. In S. Suhls & A. Greenwald (Eds.), *Psychological perspectives of the self* (Vol. 3, pp. 136–182). Hillsdale, NJ: Erlbaum.

Harter, S. (1990). Issues in the assessment of the self-concept of children and adolescents. In A. LaGreca (Ed.), *Through the eyes of a child* (pp. 292–325). Boston: Allyn & Bacon.

Harter, S. (1996a). Developmental changes in self-understanding across the 5 to 7 shift. In A. J. Sameroff & M. H. Haith (Eds.), *The five to seven year shift: The age of reason and responsibility* (pp. 207–236). Chicago: University of Chicago Press.

Harter, S. (1996b). Historical roots of contemporary issues involving self-concept. In B. A. Bracken (Ed.), *Handbook of self-concept: Developmental, social, and clinical considerations* (pp. 1–37). New York: Wiley.

Hartman, M., & Banner, L. (Eds.). (1974). *Clio's consciousness raised.* New York: Bantam Books.

Hartsock, N. (1983). The feminist standpoint: Developing the grounds for a specifically feminist historical materialism. In S. Harding & M. Hintikka (Eds.), *Discovering reality: Feminist perspectives on epistemology, metaphysics, methodology, and philosophy of science* (pp. 283–310). Dordrecht, Holland: Reidel.

Hartsock, N. (1997). Comment on Hekman's "Truth and method: Feminist standpoint revisited": Truth or justice? *Signs, 22*(2), 367–374.

Hass, M. (2000). Thinking fluids/fluid thinking: Irigaray's critique of formal logic. In M. Hass & R. J. Falmagne (Eds.), *Feminist perspectives on logic.* New York: Rowman & Littlefield.

Hass, M., & Falmagne, R. J. (Eds.). (2000). *Feminist perspectives on logic.* New York: Rowman & Littlefield.

Hawkesworth, M. (1998). Social sciences. In. A. M. Jaggar & I. M. Young (Eds.), *A companion to feminist philosophy* (pp. 204–212). Oxford, England: Blackwell.

Heidbreder, E. (1933). *Seven psychologies.* Engelwood Cliffs, NJ: Prentice-Hall.

Hekman, S. (1997). Truth and method: Feminist standpoint theory revisited. *Signs, 22*(2), 341–365.

Henley, N. M. (1977). *Body politics: Power, sex, and nonverbal communication.* Englewood Cliffs, NJ: Prentice-Hall.

Henley, N. M. (1995). Ethnicity and gender issues in language. In H. Landrine (Ed.), *Bringing cultural diversity to feminist psychology: Theory, research, and practice* (pp. 361–395). Washington, DC: American Psychological Association.

Hennessy, R. (1993a). *Materialist feminism and the politics of discourse.* New York: Routledge.

Hennessy, R. (1993b). Women's lives/feminist knowledge: Feminist standpoint as ideology critique. *Hypatia,8*(1), 14–34.

Henriques, J., Hollway, W., Urwin, C., Venn, C., & Walkerdine, V. (1984). *Changing the subject: Psychology, social regulation and subjectivity.* New York: Methuen.

Henseler, S., Plesa, D., Goldman, S., Presler, N. & Walkenfeld, F. F. (1997, April). *Language and the dual representation problem in early development.* Poster presented at the biennial meeting of the Society for Research in Child Development, Washington, DC.

Herek, G. M. (1992). Psychological heterosexism and anti-gay violence: The social psychology of bigotry and bashing. In G. M. Herek & K. T. Berrill (Eds.), *Hate crimes: Confronting violence against lesbians and gay men* (pp. 149–169). Newbury Park, CA: Sage.

Hess, B., & Marx-Ferree, M. (Eds.). (1987). *Analyzing gender: A handbook of social science research.* Thousand Oaks, CA: Sage.

Hewlett, B. S. (1991). *Intimate fathers: The nature and context of Aka Pygmy paternal infant care.* Ann Arbor: University of Michigan Press.

Hill, J. P., & Lynch, M. E. (1983). The intensification of gender-related role expectations during early adolescence. In J. Brooks-Gunn & A. C. Petersen (Eds.), *Girls at puberty: Biological and psychological perspectives* (pp. 201–229). New York: Plenum Press.

Hirschfeld, L. (1996). *Race in the making: Cognition, culture, and the child's construction of human kinds.* Cambridge, MA: MIT Press.

Hobson, R. P. (1993). *Autism and the development of mind.* Hillsdale, NJ: Erlbaum.

Hoffman, C., & Hurst, N. (1990). Gender stereotypes: Perception or rationalization? *Journal of Personality and Social Psychology, 58,* 197–208.

Hollingsworth, L. S. (1914). Variability as related to sex differences in achievement. *American Journal of Sociology, 19*(4), 510–530.

hooks, b. (1983). *Feminist theory from margin to center.* Boston: South End Press.

hooks, b. (1990). *Yearning: Race, gender, and cultural politics.* Boston: South End Press.

hooks, b. (1996). *Bone black: Memories of girlhood.* New York: Holt.

Horgan, T., & Woodward, J. (1993). Folk psychology is here to stay. In S. M. Christensen & D. R. Turner (Eds.), *Folk psychology and the philosophy of mind.* Hillsdale, NJ: Erlbaum.

Howe, M. L., & Courage, M. L. (1993). On resolving the enigma of infantile amnesia. *Psychological Bulletin, 113,* 305–326.

Howe, M. L., & Courage, M. L. (1997). The emergence and early development of autobiographical memory. *Psychological Review, 104,* 499–523.

Hrdy, S. B. (1981). *The woman that never evolved.* Cambridge, MA: Harvard University Press.

Hrdy, S. B. (1984). Introduction: Female reproductive strategies. In M. Small (Ed.), *Female primates: Studies by women primatologists* (pp. 13–16). New York: Liss.

Hrdy, S. B. (1986). Empathy, polyandry, and the myth of the coy female. In R. Bleier (Ed.), *Feminist approaches to science* (pp. 119–146). Elmsford, NY: Pergamon Press.

Hrdy, S. B., & Williams, G. C. (1983). Behavioral biology and the double standard. In S. K. Wasser (Ed.), *Social behavior of female vertebrates* (pp. 3–17). New York: Academic Press.

Hubbard, R. (1979). Introduction. In R. Hubbard & M. Lowe (Eds.), *Genes and gender: 2. Pitfalls in research on sex and gender* (pp. 9–34). New York: Gordian Press.

Hubbard, R. (1990). *The politics of women's biology.* New Brunswick, NJ: Rutgers University Press.

Hudson, J. A. (1990). The emergence of autobiographical memory in mother-child conversation. In R. Fivush & J.A. Hudson (Eds.), *Knowing and remembering in young children* (pp. 197–222). New York: Cambridge University Press.

Huesmann, L. R., Guerra, N. G., Zelli, A., & Miller, L. (1992). Differing normative beliefs about aggression for boys and girls. In K. Björkqvist & P. Niemela (Eds.), *Of mice and women: Aspects of female aggression* (pp. 77–87). San Diego, CA: Academic Press.

Humphrey, N. K. (1976). The social function of intellect. In P. P. G. Bateson & R. A. Hinde (Eds.), *Growing points in ethology*. Cambridge, England: Cambridge University Press.

Hurtado, A. (1989). Relating to privilege: Seduction and rejection in the subordination of white women and of women of color. *Signs, 14*(4), 833–855.

Hurtado, A. (1996). *The color of privilege: Three blasphemies on race and feminism.* Ann Arbor: University of Michigan Press.

Huston, A. C. (1983). Sex typing. In P. H. Mussen (Series Ed.) & E. M. Hethrington (Vol. Ed.), *Handbook of child psychology: Vol. 4. Socialization, personality, and social development* (4th ed., pp. 387–467). New York: Wiley.

Huston, A. C. (1985). The development of sex-typing: Themes from recent research. *Developmental Review, 5*, 1–17.

Hyde, J. S. (1984). Children's understanding of sexist language. *Developmental Psychology, 20*, 697–706.

Hyde, J. S. (1990). Meta-analysis and the psychology of gender differences. *Signs, 16*, 55–73.

Hyde, J. S., Fennema, E., & Lamon, S. J. (1990). Gender differences in mathematics performance: A meta-analysis. *Psychological Bulletin, 107*, 139–155.

Hyman, I. (1994). Conversational remembering: Story recall with a peer versus for an experimenter. *Applied Cognitive Psychology, 8*, 49–66.

Ilyenkov, E. V. (1982). *The dialectics of the abstract and the concrete in Marx's Capital.* Moscow: Progress Publishers. (Original work published 1960)

Inhelder, B., & Piaget, J. (1958). *The growth of logical thinking from childhood to adolescence.* New York: Basic Books.

Irigaray, L. (1985). Le langage de l'homme. In *Parler n'est jamais neutre* (pp. 281–292). Paris: Editions de Minuit.

Irigaray, L. (1989). Is the subject of science sexed? In N.Tuana (Ed.), *Feminism and science* (pp. 58–68). Bloomington: Indiana University Press.

Jaggar, A. M. (1983). *Feminist politics and human nature.* Totowa, NJ: Rowman & Allanheld.

Jaggar, A. M. (1989). Love and knowledge: Emotion in feminist epistemology. In A. M. Jaggar & S. Bordo (Eds.), *Gender/body/knowledge.* New Brunswick, NJ: Rutgers University Press.

Jaggar, A. M., & Rothenberg, P. (Eds.). (1984). *Feminist frameworks* (2nd ed.). New York: McGraw-Hill.

James, W. (1890). *Principles of psychology.* New York: Holt.

Jenkins, J. M., & Astington, J. W. (1996). Cognitive factors and family structure associated with theory of mind development in young children. *Developmental Psychology, 32*, 70–78.

Jessor, R., Colby, A., & Shweder, R. A. (Eds.). (1996). *Ethnography and human development: Context and meaning in social inquiry.* Chicago: University of Chicago Press.

Johnson, A., & Ames, E. (1994). The influence of gender labelling on preschoolers' gender constancy judgements. *British Journal of Developmental Psychology, 12*, 241–249.

Johnson-Laird, P. N., & Byrne, R. M. J. (1991). *Deduction.* Hove, England: Erlbaum.

Jones, S., & Smith, L. (1993). The place of perception in children's concepts. *Cognitive Development, 8*, 113–139.

Jordan, J. V. (1992). The relational self: A new perspective for understanding women's development. *Contemporary Psychotherapy Review, 7*, 56–71.

Kail, R., & Hagen, J. (1977). *Perspectives on the development of memory and cognition.* Hillsdale, NJ: Erlbaum.

Kantrowitz, B., & Kalb, C. (1998). Boys will be boys. *Newsweek, 131* (No. 19), 54–60.

Katz, P. A. (1986). Modification of children's gender-stereotyped behavior: General issues and research considerations. *Sex Roles, 14*, 591–602.

Katz, P. A. (1996). Raising feminists. *Psychology of Women Quarterly, 20*, 323–340.

Keil, F. C. (1989). *Concepts, kinds, and cognitive development.* Cambridge, MA: MIT Press.

Keil, F. C., & Lockhart, K. L. (1999). Explanatory understanding in conceptual development. In E. K. Scholnick, K. Nelson, S. A. Gelman, & P. H. Miller (Eds.), *Conceptual development: Piaget's legacy* (pp. 103–130). Mahwah, NJ: Erlbaum.

Keller, E. F. (1982). Feminism and science. *Signs, 7*(3), 589–602.

Keller, E. F. (1983). *A feeling for the organism: The life and work of Barbara McClintock.* New York: Freeman.

Keller, E. F. (1985). *Reflections on gender and science.* New Haven, CT: Yale University Press.

Keller, E. F. (1990). Gender and science. In J. M. Nielson (Ed.), *Feminist research methods* (pp. 41–57). Boulder, CO: Westview.

Kerber, L. K., Greeno, C. G., Maccoby, E. E., Luria, Z., Stack, C. B., & Gilligan, C. (1986). On *In a different voice*: An interdisciplinary forum. *Signs, 11*, 304–333.

Kessen, W. (1979). The American child and other cultural inventions. *American Psychologist, 34*, 815–820.

Kessler Shaw, L. (1998). *Conversational uses of know and think by mothers and 2-year-old children.* Unpublished doctoral dissertation, City University of New York Graduate School.

Kim, J. (1994). What is "naturalized epistemology"? In H. Kornblith (Ed.), *Naturalizing epistemology* (2nd ed.). Cambridge, MA: MIT Press.

Kinsbourne, M. (1980). If sex differences in brain lateralization exist, they have yet to be discovered. *Behavioral and Brain Sciences, 3*, 241–242.

Kohlberg, L. (1966). A cognitive-developmental analysis of children's sex-role concepts and attitudes. In E. E. Maccoby (Ed.), *The development of sex differences* (pp. 82–173). Stanford, CA: Stanford University Press.

Kohlberg, L. (1971). From is to ought: How to commit the naturalistic fallacy and get away with it in the study of moral development. In T. Mischel (Ed.), *Cognitive development and epistemology* (pp. 152–232). New York: Academic Press.

Kohlberg, L. (1981). *The philosophy of moral development: Essays on moral development* (Vols. I & II). San Francisco: Harper & Row.

Kornblith, H. (1990). *The naturalistic project in epistemology: A progress report.* Paper presented at a meeting of the American Philosophical Association, Pacific Division.

Kornblith, H. (Ed.). (1994). *Naturalizing epistemology* (2nd ed.). Cambridge, MA: MIT Press.

Kristeva, J. (1984). *The revolution in poetic language.* New York: Columbia University Press.

Kristeva, J. (1987). *Tales of love.* New York: Columbia University Press.

Kuebli, J., Butler, S., & Fivush, R. (1995). Mother-child talk about past emotions: Relations of maternal language and child gender over time. *Cognition and Emotion, 9*, 265–283.

Kuhn, T. (1970). *The structure of scientific revolutions* (2nd ed.). Chicago: University of Chicago Press.

Laboratory for Comparative Human Cognition. (1983). Culture and cognitive development. In P. H. Mussen (Series Ed.) & J. H. Flavell & E. M. Markman (Vol. Eds.), *Handbook of child psychology: Vol. 3. Cognitive development* (4th ed., pp. 295–356). New York: Wiley.

Labouvie-Vief, G. (1994). *Psyche and Eros: Mind and gender in the life course.* Cambridge, England: Cambridge University Press.

Labov, W., & Waletzky, J. (1967). Narrative analysis: Oral versions of personal experiences. In J. Helm (Ed.), *Essays on the verbal and visual arts* (pp. 12–44). Seattle: University of Washington Press.

Lacan, J. (1968). *Language of the self.* Baltimore: Johns Hopkins University Press.

Ladd, G. W. (1983). Social networks of popular, average, and rejected children in school setting. *Merrill-Palmer Quarterly, 29*, 283–307.

Lakoff, G. (1987). *Women, fire, and dangerous things: What categories reveal about the mind.* Chicago: University of Chicago Press.

Lakoff, G., & Johnson, M. (1980). *Metaphors we live by.* Chicago: University of Chicago Press.

Lakoff, R. (1975). *Language and women's place*. New York: Harper & Row.

Lamb, M. F., Hwang, C. P., Frodi, A., & Frodi, M. (1982). Security of mother- and father- attachment and its relation to sociability with strangers in traditional and nontraditional Swedish families. *Infant Behavior and Development, 5*, 355–367.

Leahy, R. L., Shirk, S. R. (1984). The development of classificatory skills and sex-trait stereotypes in children. *Sex Roles, 10*, 281–292.

Leaper, C. (1994). Exploring the consequences of gender segregation on social relationships. In C. Leaper (Ed.), *Childhood gender segregation: Causes and consequences* (New Directions for Child Development, No. 65, pp. 67–86). San Francisco: Jossey-Bass.

Leaper, C., & Anderson, K. J. (1997). Gender development and heterosexual romantic relationships during adolescence. In W. Damon (Series Ed.) & S. Shulman & W. A. Collins (Issue Eds.), *Romantic relationships in adolescence: Developmental perspectives* (New Directions for Child Development, No. 78, pp. 85–103). San Francisco: Jossey-Bass.

Leaper, C., Anderson, K. J., & Sanders, P. (1998). Moderators of gender effects on parents' talk to their children: A meta-analysis. *Developmental Psychology, 34*, 3–27.

Leaper, C., Breed, L., Hoffman, L., & Perlman, C. (1999, April). *Variations in the gender-stereotyped content of children's television cartoons across genres*. Paper presented at the biennial meeting of the Society for Research in Child Development, Albuquerque.

Leaper, C., & Gleason, J. B. (1996). The relation of gender and play activity to parent and child communication. *International Journal of Behavioral Development, 19*, 689–703.

Leaper, C., Leve, L., Strasser, T., & Schwartz, R. (1995). Mother-child communication sequences: Play activity, child gender, and marital status effects. *Merrill-Palmer Quarterly, 41*, 307–327.

Leaper, C., & Valin, D. (1996). Predictors of Mexican-American mothers and fathers attitudes toward gender equality. *Hispanic Journal of Behavioral Sciences, 18*, 343–355.

Lennon, K., & Whitford, M. (Eds.). (1994). *Knowing the difference: Feminist perspectives in epistemology*. London: Routledge.

Lepowsky, M. (1994). Women, men, and aggression in an egalitarian society. *Sex Roles, 30*, 199–211.

Lerner, R. M. (1991). Changing organism-context relations as the basic process of development: A developmental contextual perspective. *Developmental Psychology, 27*, 27–32.

Lerner, R. M. (1998). Theories of human development: Contemporary perspectives. In W. Damon (Series Ed.) & R. M. Lerner (Vol. Ed.), *Handbook of child psychology: Vol. 1. Theoretical models of human development* (5th ed., pp. 1–23). New York: Wiley.

Leslie, A. M. (1988). Some implications of pretence for mechanisms underlying the child's theory of mind. In J. W. Astington, P. L. Harris, & D. R. Olson (Eds.),

Developing theories of mind (pp. 19–46). Cambridge, England: Cambridge University Press.

Levy, G. D., Taylor, M. G., & Gelman, S. A. (1995). Traditional and evaluative aspects of flexibility in gender roles, social conventions, moral rules, and physical laws. *Child Development, 66,* 515–531.

Lewis, C. (1994). Episodes, events, and narratives in the child's understanding of mind. In C. Lewis & P. Mitchell (Eds.), *Children's early understanding of mind: Origins and development* (pp. 457–480). Hillsdale, NJ: Erlbaum.

Lewis, C., & Mitchell, P. (Eds.). (1994). *Children's early understanding of mind: Origins and development.* Hillsdale, NJ: Erlbaum.

Lewis, C., Freeman, N. H., Kyriakidou, C., Maridaki-Kassotaki, K., & Berridge, D. M. (1996). Social influences on false belief access: Specific sibling influences or general apprenticeship. *Child Development, 67,* 2930–2947.

Lewis, M. (1991). Ways of knowing: Objective self-awareness or consciousness. *Developmental Review, 11,* 231–243.

Lewis, M. (1995). Aspects of self: From systems to ideas. In P. Rochat (Ed.), *The self in infancy: Theory and research* (pp. 95–115). Amsterdam: North-Holland-Elsevier.

Lewis, M., & Brooks-Gunn, J. (1979). *Social cognition and the acquisition of self.* New York: Plenum Press.

Lewis, M., Sullivan, M. W., Stanger, C., & Weiss, M. (1989). Self development and self-conscious emotions. *Child Development, 60,* 146–156.

Liben, L. S., & Bigler, R. S. (1987). Reformulating children's gender schemata. In L. S. Liben & M. L. Signorella (Eds.), *Children's gender schemata* (pp. 89–105). San Francisco: Jossey-Bass.

Liben, L. S., & Signorella, M. L. (Eds.). (1987). *Children's gender schemata.* San Francisco: Jossey-Bass.

Lieblich, A. (1994). Introduction. In A. Lieblich & R. Josselson (Eds.), *Exploring identity and gender: The narrative study of lives* (Vol. 2). London: Sage.

Lillard, A. S. (1997). Other folks' theories of mind and behavior. *Psychological Science, 14,* 96–107.

Linton, M. (1982). Transformations of memory in everyday life. In U. Neisser (Ed.), *Memory observed* (pp. 77–91). San Francisco: Jossey-Bass.

Lipman-Blumen, J. (1984). *Gender roles and power.* New York: Prentice-Hall.

Liss, M. B. (1983). Learning gender-related skills through play. In M. B. Liss (Ed.), *Social and cognitive skills: Sex roles and children's play* (pp. 147–166). New York: Academic Press.

Lloyd, G. (1984). *The man of reason: 'Male' and 'female' in Western philosophy.* London: Methuen.

Lloyd, G. (1993a). Maleness, metaphor, and the "crisis" of reason. In L. M. Antony & C. Witt (Eds.), *A mind of one's own: Feminist essays on reason and objectivity* (pp. 69–84). Boulder, CO: Westview Press.

Lloyd, G. (1993b). *The man of reason: "Male" and "female" in Western philosophy* (2nd ed.). Minneapolis: University of Minnesota Press.

Lloyd, G. (1998). Rationality. In. A. M. Jaggar & I. M. Young (Eds.), *A companion to feminist philosophy* (pp. 165–172). Oxford, England: Blackwell.

Locke, J. (1959). *An essay concerning human understanding* (Vol. 2). New York: Dover. (Original work published 1894)

Lockheed, M. E., Harris, A. M., & Nemceff, W. P. (1983). Sex and social influence: Does sex function as a status characteristic in mixed-sex groups of children? *Journal of Educational Psychology, 75*, 877–888.

Lockheed, M. E., & Klein, S. S. (1985). Sex equity in classroom organization and climate. In S. S. Klein (Ed.), *Handbook of achieving sex equity through education* (pp. 189–217). Baltimore: Johns Hopkins University Press.

Longino, H. E. (1990). *Science as social knowledge: Values and objectivity in scientific inquiry.* Princeton, NJ: Princeton University Press.

Longino, H. E. (1993). Subjects, power, and knowledge: Description and prescription in feminist philosophies of science. In L. Alcoff & E. Potter (Eds.), *Feminist epistemologies* (pp. 101–120). New York: Routledge.

Lorde, A. (1984). *Sister outsider.* Trumansburg, NY: Crossing Press.

Lott, B. (1991). Social psychology: Humanist roots and feminist future. *Psychology of Women Quarterly, 15*, 505–519.

Lott, B., & Maluso, D. (1993). The social learning of gender. In A. E. Beall & R. J. Sternberg (Eds.), *The psychology of gender* (pp. 99–123). New York: Guilford Press.

Lovibond, S. (1989). Feminism and postmodernism. *New Left Review, 178*, 5–28.

Luria, A. R. (1976). *Cognitive development: Its cultural and social foundations.* Cambridge, MA: Harvard University Press. (Original work published in 1974.)

Luria, Z. (1986). A methodological critique. *Signs, 11*, 316–321.

Lutz, C. (1992). Culture and consciousness: A problem in the anthropology of knowledge. In F. S. Kessell, P. M. Cole, & D. L. Johnson (Eds.), *Self and consciousness: Multiple perspectives* (pp. 64–87). Hillsdale, NJ: Erlbaum.

Lutz, S. E., & Ruble, D. N. (1995). Children and gender prejudice: Context, motivation, and the development of gender conceptions. In R. Vasta (Ed.), *Annals of child development* (Vol. 10, pp. 131–166). London: Kingsley.

Lyons, J. (1977). *Semantics: Vol. 1.* New York: Cambridge University Press.

Lytton, H., & Romney, D. M. (1991). Parents' differential socialization of boys and girls: A meta-analysis. *Psychological Bulletin, 109*, 267–296.

Maccoby, E. E. (1998). *The two sexes: Growing up apart, coming together.* Cambridge, MA: Harvard University Press.

Maccoby, E. E., & Jacklin, C. N. (1974). *The psychology of sex differences.* Stanford, CA: Stanford University Press.

MacDonald, C. D., & O'Laughlin, E. M. (1997, April). *Relational aggression and risk behaviors in middle school students.* Poster presented at the biennial meeting of the Society for Research in Child Development, Washington, DC.

MacKinnon, C. (1982). Feminism, Marxism, and the state: An agenda for theory. *Signs, 7*(3), 515–544.

MacKinnon, C. (1987). *Feminism unmodified: Discourses on life and law*. Cambridge, MA: Harvard University Press.

MacWhinney, B., & Snow, C. (1990). The Child Language Data Exchange System: An update. *Journal of Child Language, 17*, 457–472.

Main, M., & Weston, D. R. (1981). The quality of toddlers' relationship to mother and to father: Related to conflict behavior and the readiness to establish new relationships. *Child Development, 52*, 932–940.

Marecek, J. (1995). Psychology and feminism: Can this relationship be saved? In D. C. Stanton & A. J. Stewart (Eds.), *Feminisms in the academy*. Ann Arbor: University of Michigan Press.

Marini, M. M. (1978). Sex differences in the determination of adolescent aspirations: A review of research. *Sex Roles, 4*, 723–753.

Markman, E. M. (1989). *Categorization and naming in children: Problems in induction*. Cambridge: MIT Press.

Markus, H. R., & Kitayama, S. (1993). Culture and the self: Implications for cognition, emotion, and motivation. *Psychological Review, 98*, 224–253.

Markus, H. R., Mullally, P. R., & Kitayama, S. (1997). Selfways: Diversity in modes of cultural participation. In U. Neisser & D. A. Jopling (Eds.), *The conceptual self in context: Culture, experience, and self-understanding. The Emory Symposia in Cognition* (pp. 13–61). New York: Cambridge University Press.

Markus, H. R., & Oyserman, D. (1988). Gender and thought: The role of the self concept. In M. Crawford & M. Hamilton (Eds.), *Gender and thought* (pp. 100–127). New York: Springer.

Marler, P. (1991). The instinct to learn. In S. Carey & R. Gelman (Eds.), *The epigenesis of mind: Essays on biology and cognition* (pp. 37–66). Hillsdale, NJ: Erlbaum.

Marsh, H. W., & Byrne, B. M. (1991). Differentiated additive androgyny model: Relations between masculinity, femininity, and multiple dimensions of self-concept. *Journal of Personality and Social Psychology, 61*, 811–828.

Martin, C. L. (1987). A ratio measure of sex stereotyping. *Journal of Personality and Social Psychology, 52*, 489–499.

Martin, C. L. (1989). Children's use of gender-related information in making social judgments. *Developmental Psychology, 25*, 80–88.

Martin, C. L. (1993). New directions for investigating children's gender knowledge. *Developmental Review, 13*, 184–204.

Martin, C. L. (1994). Cognitive influences on the development and maintenance of gender segregation. In C. Leaper (Ed.), *Childhood gender segregation: Causes and consequences* (New Directions for Child Development, No. 65, pp. 35–51). San Francisco: Jossey-Bass.

Martin, C. L., Eisenbud, L., & Rose, H. (1995). Children's gender-based reasoning about toys. *Child Development, 66*, 1453–1471.

Martin, C. L., & Halverson, C. F. (1981). A schematic processing model of sex typing and stereotyping in children. *Child Development, 52*, 1119–1134.

Martin, C. L., & Halverson, C. F. (1983). The effects of sex-typing schemas on young children's memory. *Child Development, 54*, 563–574.

Martin, C. L., & Parker, S. (1995). Folk theories about sex and race differences. *Personality and Social Psychology Bulletin, 21*, 45–57.

Mayr, E. (1982). *The growth of biological thought*. Cambridge, MA: Harvard University Press.

Mayr, E. (1991). *One long argument: Charles Darwin and the genesis of modern evolutionary thought*. Cambridge, MA: Harvard University Press.

McCabe, A., & Peterson, C. (1991). Getting the story: A longitudinal study of parental styles in eliciting narratives and developing narrative skill. In A. McCabe & C. Peterson (Eds.), *Developing narrative structure* (pp. 217–253). Hillsdale, NJ: Erlbaum.

McCarthy, M. (1957). *Memories of a Catholic girlhood*. New York: Harcourt, Brace.

McCawley, J. D. (1981). *Everything that linguists have always wanted to know about logic*. Chicago: University of Chicago Press.

McFadyen-Ketchum, S. A., Bates, J. F., Dodge, K. A., & Pettit, G. S. (1996). Patterns of change in early childhood aggressive-disruptive behavior: Gender differences in predictions from early coercive and affectionate mother-child interactions. *Child Development, 67*, 2417–2433.

McNeilly-Choque, M. K., Hart, C. H., Robinson, C. C., Nelson, L. J., & Olsen, S. F. (1996). Overt and relational aggression on the playground: Correspondence among different informants. *Journal of Research in Childhood Education, 11*, 47–67.

Mead, G. H. (1934). *Mind, self, and society from the standpoint of a social behaviorist*. Chicago: University of Chicago Press.

Medin, D. L. (1989). Concepts and conceptual structure. *American Psychologist, 44*, 1469–1481.

Merchant, C. (1980). *The death of nature: Women, ecology, and the scientific revolution*. San Francisco: Harper & Row.

Mervis, C. B., & Rosch, E. (1981). Categorization of natural objects. *Annual Review of Psychology, 32*, 89–115.

Messick, D. M., & Mackie, D. M. (1989). Intergroup relations. *Annual Review of Psychology, 40*, 45–81.

Messner, M. A. (1992). *Power at play: Sports and the problem of masculinity*. Boston: Beacon Press.

Middleton, D., & Edwards, D. (1990). Conversational remembering: A social psychological approach. In D. Middleton & D. Edwards (Eds.), *Collective remembering* (pp. 23–45). London: Sage.

Mill, H[arriet] T[aylor]. (1970). Enfranchisement of women. In A. S. Rossi (Ed.), *Essays on sex equality* (pp. 89–122). Chicago: University of Chicago Press. (Original work published 1851)

Mill, J[ohn] S[tuart]. (1970). The subjection of women. In A. S. Rossi (Ed.), *Essays on sex equality* (pp. 123–242). Chicago: University of Chicago Press. (Original work published 1869)

Miller, P. H. (1993). *Theories of developmental psychology* (3rd ed.). New York: Freeman.

Miller, P. H., & Aloise, P. A. (1995). Preschoolers' strategic behavior and performance on a same-different task. *Journal of Experimental Child Psychology, 60*, 284–303.

Miller, P. J. (1994). Narrative practices: Their role in socialization and self-construction. In U. Neisser & R. Fivush (Eds.), *The remembering self: Construction and accuracy in the life narrative* (pp. 158–179). New York: Cambridge University Press.

Miller, P. J., Mintz, J. Hoogstra, L., Fung, H., & Potts, R. (1992). The narrated self: Young children's construction of self in relation to others in conversational stories of personal experience. *Merrill-Palmer Quarterly, 38*, 45–67.

Miller, P. J., Potts, R., Fung, H., Hoogstra, L., & Mintz, J. (1990). Narrative practices and the social construction of self in childhood. *American Ethnologist, 17*, 292–311.

Millett, K. (1970). *Sexual politics.* Garden City, NY: Doubleday.

Mohanty, C. (1991). Introduction: Cartographies of struggle. In C. Mohanty, A. Russo, & L. Torres (Eds.), *Third world women and the politics of feminism* (pp. 1–50). Bloomington: Indiana University Press.

Moller, L.C., Hymel, S., & Rubin, K. H. (1992). Sex typing in play and popularity in middle childhood. *Sex Roles, 26*, 331–353.

Monk, R. (1990). *Ludwig Wittgenstein: The duty of genius.* London: Cape.

Montemayor, R., & VanKomen, R. (1985). The development of sex differences in friendship patterns and peer group structure during adolescence. *Journal of Early Adolescence, 5*, 285–294.

Morawski, J. G., & Agronik, G. (1991). A restive legacy: The history of feminist work in experimental and cognitive psychology. *Psychology of Women Quarterly, 15*, 567–579.

Morss, J. R. (1992). Making waves: Deconstruction and developmental psychology. *Theory and Psychology, 2*, 445–465.

Mosak, H. H., & Schneider, S. (1977). Masculine protest, penis envy, women's liberation and sexual equality. *Journal of Individual Psychology, 33*, 193–202.

Mullen, M. K. (1994). Earliest recollections of childhood: A demographic analysis. *Cognition, 52*, 55–79.

Mullen, M. K., & Yi, S. (1995). The cultural context of talk about the past: Implications for the development of autobiographical memory. *Cognitive Development, 10*, 407–419.

Myaskovsky, L., & Wittig, M. A. (1997). Predictors of feminist social identity among college women. *Sex Roles, 37*, 861–883.

Myers, D. G. (1990). *Social psychology*. New York: McGraw-Hill.

Nagel, T. (1986). *The view from nowhere*. New York: Oxford University Press.

Neisser, U., & Winograd, E. (1992). *Affect and accuracy in recall: Studies of flashbulb memories*. New York: Cambridge University Press.

Nelson, K. (1985). *Making sense: The acquisition of shared meaning*. New York: Academic Press.

Nelson, K. (1986). *Event knowledge: Structure and function in development*. Hillsdale, NJ: Erlbaum.

Nelson, K. (Ed.). (1989). *Narratives from the crib*. Cambridge, MA: Harvard University Press.

Nelson, K. (1996). *Language in cognitive development: The emergence of the mediated mind*. New York: Cambridge University Press.

Nelson, K., & Gruendel, J. M. (1981). Generalized event representations: Basic building blocks of cognitive development. In M. E. Lamb & A. L. Brown (Eds.), *Advances in development psychology* (Vol. 1, pp. 131–158). Hillsdale, NJ: Erlbaum.

Nelson, K., Plesa, D., & Henseler, S. (1998). Children's theory of mind: An experiential interpretation. *Human Development, 41*, 17–29.

Nelson, L. H. (1990). *Who knows: From Quine to a feminist empiricism*. Philadelphia: Temple University Press.

Nelson, L. H. (1993). Epistemological communities. In L. Alcoff & E. Potter (Eds.), *Feminist epistemologies* (pp. 121–159). New York: Routledge.

Nelson, L. H. (1998). Empiricism. In. A. M. Jaggar & I. M. Young (Eds.), *A companion to feminist philosophy*. Oxford, England: Blackwell.

Nelson, L. H. (2000). The very idea of a feminist logic. Paper presented at the Engendering Rationalities Conference, University of Oregon, Eugene, OR.

Nelson, M. O. (1991). Another look at masculine protest. *Individual Psychology, 47*, 490–497.

Nicholson, L. (Ed.). (1997). *The second wave: A reader in feminist theory*. New York: Routledge.

Nicolson, P. (1997). Feminist social psychology: A re-view. *Feminism and Psychology, 7*, 248–254.

Nisbett, R. E. (1990). Evolutionary psychology, biology, and cultural evolution. *Motivation and Emotion, 14*, 255–263.

Nisbett, R. E. (1993). *Rules for reasoning*. Hillsdale, NJ: Erlbaum.

Nye, A. (1990). *Words of power*. New York: Routledge.

O'Brien, M. (1981). *The politics of reproduction*. Boston: Routledge & Kegan Paul.

Ogbu, J. U. (1981). Origins of human competence: A cultural-ecological perspective. *Child Development, 52*, 413–429.

Ogbu, J. U. (1993). Differences in cultural frame of reference. *International Journal of Behavioral Development, 16*, 483–506.

Omark, R. R., Omark, M., & Edelman, M. (1975). Formation of dominance hierarchies in young children. In T. R. Williams (Ed.), *Psychological anthropology* (pp. 289–316). Paris: Mouton.

Ortner, S. (1974). Is female to nature as male is to culture? In M. Rosaldo & L. Lamphere (Eds.), *Woman, culture and society* (pp. 67–88). Stanford, CA: Stanford University Press.

Osmond, M. W., & Thorne, B. (1993). Feminist theories: The social construction of gender in families and society. In P. G. Boss, W. J. Doherty, R. LaRossa, W. R. Schumm, & S. K. Steinmetz (Eds.), *Sourcebook of family theories and methods: A contextual approach* (pp. 591–623). New York: Plenum Press.

Overton, W. F. (1971, April). *The active organism in structuralism.* Paper presented at a meeting of the Eastern Psychological Association, Philadelphia.

Overton, W. F. (1995). The arrow of time and the cycle of time: Concepts of change, cognition and embodiment. *Philosophical Inquiry, 5,* 213–237.

Overton, W. F. (1998). Developmental psychology: Philosophy, concepts and methodology. In W. Damon (Series Ed.) & R. M. Lerner (Vol. Ed.), *Handbook of child psychology: Vol. 1. Theoretical models of human development* (5th ed., pp. 107–187). New York: Wiley.

Oyama, S. (1985). *The ontogeny of information: Developmental systems and evolution.* New York: Cambridge University Press.

Pappas, A., & Gelman, S. A. (1998). Generic noun phrases in mother-child conversations. *Journal of Child Language, 25,* 19–33.

Parke, R. D., & Slaby, R. G. (1983). The development of aggression. In P. H. Mussen (Series Ed.) & E. M. Hetherington (Vol. Ed.), *Handbook of child psychology: Vol. 4. Socialization, personality, and social development* (4th ed., pp. 547–641). New York: Wiley.

Parker, J. G., & Asher, S. R. (1993). Friendship and friendship quality in middle childhood: Links with peer group acceptance and feelings of loneliness and social dissatisfaction. *Developmental Psychology, 29,* 611–621.

Parlee, M. B. (1992). Feminism and psychology. In S. R. Zalk & J. Gordon-Kelter (Eds.), *Revolutions in knowledge: Feminism in the social sciences* (pp. 33–55). Boulder, CO: Westview.

Patterson, G. R. (1986). Performance models of antisocial boys. *American Psychologist, 41,* 432–444.

Patterson, G. R., DeBaryshe, B. D., & Ramsey, E. (1989). A developmental perspective on antisocial behavior. *American Psychologist, 44,* 329–335.

Patterson, G. R., Dishion, T. J., & Bank, L. (1984). Family interaction: A process model of deviancy training. *Aggressive Behavior, 10,* 253–267.

Peplau, L. A., R. C., Veniegas, Taylor, P. L., & DeBro, S. C. (1999). Sociocultural perspectives on the lives of women and men. In L. A. Peplau, S. C. DeBro, R. C. Veniegas, & P. L. Taylor (Eds.), *Gender, culture, and ethnicity: Current research about women and men* (pp. 23–37). Mountain View, CA: Mayfield.

Pepper, S. C. (1946). *World hypotheses: A study in evidence.* Berkeley: University of California Press.

Perner, J. (1991). *Understanding the representational mind.* Cambridge, MA: MIT Press.

Perner, J., Ruffman, T., & Leekam, S. R. (1994). Theory of mind is contagious: You catch it from your sibs. *Child Development, 65,* 1228–1238.

Perry, D. G., & Bussey, K. (1979). The social learning theory of sex differences: Imitation is alive and well. *Journal of Personality and Social Psychology, 37,* 1699–1712.

Perry, D. G., White, A. J., & Perry, L. C. (1984). Does early sex typing result from children's attempts to match their behavior to sex role stereotypes? *Child Development, 55,* 2114–2121.

Pettigrew, T. F. (1991). Advancing racial justice: Past lessons for future use. In H. J. Knopke, R. J. Norrell, & R. W. Rogers (Eds.), *Opening doors: Perspectives on race relations in contemporary America* (pp. 165–178). Tuscaloosa: University of Alabama Press.

Piaget, J. (1932). *The moral judgement of the child.* London: Kegan Paul.

Piaget, J. (1970a). Piaget's theory. In P. H. Mussen (Ed.), *Carmichael's manual of child development* (3rd ed., pp. 703–732). New York: Wiley.

Piaget, J. (1970b). *Structuralism.* New York: Norton.

Piaget, J. (1971). *Insights and illusions of philosophy* (W. Mays, Trans.). New York: Meridian Books.

Piaget, J. (1985). *The equilibration of cognitive structures.* Chicago: University of Chicago Press.

Plesa, D. N., Goldman, S., & Edmondson, D. (April 1995). *Negotiation of meaning in a false belief task.* Poster presented at the biennial conference of the Society for Research in Child Development, Indianapolis.

Plumwood, V. (1993). The politics of reason. *Australasian Journal of Philosophy, 71*(4), 436–462.

Povinelli, D. J. (1995). The unduplicated self. In P. Rochat (Ed.), *The self in early infancy* (pp. 161–192). Amsterdam: North-Holland-Elsevier.

Povinelli, D. J., Landau, K. R., & Perilloux, H. K. (1996). Self-recognition in young children using delayed versus life feedback: Evidence of a developmental asynchrony. *Child Development, 67,* 1540–1554.

Powlishta, K. K. (1995). Intergroup processes in childhood: Social categorization and sex role development. *Developmental Psychology, 31,* 781–788.

Premack, D., & Woodruff, G. (1978). Does the chimpanzee have a theory of mind? *Behavioral and Brain Sciences, 1,* 515–526.

Price, H. H. (1933). *Perception.* London: Methuen.

Quine, W. V. O. (1994). Epistemology naturalized. In H. Kornblith (Ed.), *Naturalizing epistemology* (2nd ed.). Cambridge, MA: MIT Press. (Reprinted from *Ontological relativity and other essays,* by W. V. O. Quine, 1969, New York: Columbia University Press)

Raver, C., & Leadbeater, B. J. (1993). The problem of the other in theory of mind and social developmental research. *Human Development, 36,* 350–362.

Reese, E., & Fivush, R. (1993). Parental styles for talking about the past. *Developmental Psychology, 29,* 596–606.

Reese, E., Haden, C. A., & Fivush, R. (1993). Mother-child conversations about the past: Relationships of style and memory over time. *Cognitive Development, 8,* 403–430.

Reese, E., Haden, C. A., & Fivush, R. (1996). Mothers, father, daughters, sons: Gender differences in reminiscing. *Research on Language and Social Interaction, 29,* 27–56.

Reid, P. T. (1985). Sex-role socialization of black children: A review of theory, family, and media influences. *Academic Psychology Bulletin, 7,* 201–212.

Reid, P. T., & Comas-Diaz, L. (1990). Gender and ethnicity: Perspectives on dual status. *Sex Roles, 22,* 397–408.

Rescher, N. (1988). *Rationality: A philosophical inquiry into the nature and the rationale of reason.* Oxford: Clarendon Press.

Rich, A. (1976). *Of woman born: Motherhood as experience.* New York: Norton.

Riger, S. (1992). Epistemological debates, feminist voices. *American Psychologist, 47,* 730–740.

Risman, B. J. (1987). Intimate relationships from a microstructural perspective: Men who mother. *Gender and Society, 1,* 6–32.

Rochat, P. (Ed.). (1995). *The self in early infancy.* Amsterdam: North-Holland-Elsevier.

Rockmore, T. (1992). *Irrationalism: Lukacs and the Marxist view of reason.* Philadelphia: Temple University Press.

Rogoff, B. (1990). *Apprenticeship in thinking.* New York: Oxford University Press.

Rogoff, B. (1997). Evaluating development in the process of participation: Theory, method and practice building on each other. In E. Amsel & K. A. Renninger (Eds.), *Change and development: Issues of theory, method and application* (pp. 265–285). Mahwah, NJ: Erlbaum.

Rogoff, B. (1998). Cognition as a collaborative process. In W. Damon (Series Ed.) & D. Kuhn & R. S. Siegler (Vol. Eds.), *Handbook of child psychology: Vol. 2. Cognition, perception, and language* (5th ed., pp. 679–744). New York: Wiley.

Rorty, R. (1979). *Philosophy and the mirror of nature.* Princeton:, NJ: Princeton University Press.

Rose, A. J., & Asher, S. R. (1999). Children's goals and strategies in response to conflicts within a friendship. *Developmental Psychology, 35,* 69–79.

Rose, A. J., & Montemayor, R. (1994). The relationship between gender role orientation and perceived self-competency in male and female adolescents. *Sex Roles, 31,* 579–596.

Rosch, E. (1978). Principles of categorization. In E. Rosch & B. B. Lloyd (Eds.), *Cognition and categorization* (pp. 27–48). Hillsdale, NJ: Erlbaum.

Ross, M., & Holmberg, D. (1990). Recounting the past: Gender differences in the recall of events in the history of a close relationship. In M. P. Zanna & J. M. Olson (Eds.), *The Ontario Symposium: Vol. 6. Self-inference processes* (pp. 135–152). Hillsdale, NJ: Erlbaum.

Rosser, S. V. (1982). Androgyny and sociobiology. *International Journal of Women's Studies, 5*(5), 435–444.

Rosser, S. V. (1988). *Feminism within the science and health care professions: Overcoming resistance.* New York: Teachers College Press.

Rosser, S. V. (1990). *Female friendly science: Applying women's studies methods and theories to attract students to science.* New York: Pergamon Press.

Rosser, S. V. (1997). *Re-engineering female friendly science.* New York: Teachers College Press.

Rosser, S. V. (in press). *Women's studies and women scientists and physicians: The crucial union for the next millennium.* New York: Teachers College Press.

Rothbart, M., & Taylor, M. (1992). Category labels and social reality: Do we view social categories as natural kinds? In G. R. Semin & K. Fiedler (Eds.), *Language, interaction, and social cognition* (pp. 11–36). London: Sage.

Rothfield, P. (1990). Feminism, subjectivity, and sexual difference. In S. Annew (Ed.), *Feminist knowledge: Critique and construct* (pp. 121–144). New York: Routledge.

Rubin, D. (1989). *Autobiographical memory.* New York: Cambridge University Press.

Rubin, D. (1996). *Reconstructing our past: Studies in autobiographical memory.* New York: Cambridge University Press.

Ruble, D. N., & Martin, C. L. (1998). Gender development. In W. Damon (Series Ed.) & N. Eisenberg (Vol. Ed.), *Handbook of child psychology: Vol. 3. Social, emotional and personality development* (5th ed., pp. 993–1016). New York: Wiley.

Ruddick, S. (1982). Maternal thinking. In B. Thorne & M. Yalom (Eds.), *Rethinking the family: Some feminist questions* (1st ed., pp. 76–94). Reading, MA: Longman.

Russell, B. (1912). *The problems of philosophy.* Oxford, England: Oxford University Press.

Russell, J. (1992). The theory theory: So good they named it twice? *Cognitive Development, 7,* 485–519.

Rys, G. S., & Bear, G. G. (1997). Relational aggression and peer rejection: Gender and developmental issues. *Merrill-Palmer Quarterly, 43,* 87–106.

Sadker, M., & Sadker, D. (1994). *Failing at fairness: How America's schools cheat girls.* New York: Scribner.

Saltz, E., & Medow, M. L. (1971). Concept conservation in children: The dependence of belief systems on semantic representation. *Child Development, 42,* 1533–1542.

Sampson, E. (1989). The deconstruction of the self. In. J. Shotter & K. J. Gergen (Eds.), *Texts of identity* (pp. 1–19). London: Sage.

Sapolsky, R. M. (1997). *The trouble with testosterone: And other essays on the biology of the human predicament.* New York: Scribner.

Scarr, S. (1985). Cultural lenses on mothers and children. In L. Friedrich-Cofer (Ed.), *Human nature and public policy.* New York: Praeger.

Schatten, G., & Schatten, H. (1983). The energetic egg. *The Sciences, 23,* 28–34.

Schmitt, R. (1995). *Beyond separateness: The social nature of human beings—Their autonomy, knowledge and power.* Boulder, CO: Westview Press.

Schofield, J. W. (1981). Complementary and conflicting identities: Images and interaction in an interracial school. In S. R. Asher & J. M. Gottman (Eds.), *The development of children's friendships* (pp. 53–90). New York: Cambridge University Press.

Scholnick. E. K. (1999). Representing logic. In I. E. Sigel (Ed.), *Theoretical perspectives in the development of representational (symbolic) thought* (pp. 113–128). Mahwah, NJ: Erlbaum.

Schott, R. M. (1998). Kant. In. A. M. Jaggar & I. M. Young (Eds.), *A companion to feminist philosophy* (pp. 38–48). Oxford, England: Blackwell.

Schwartz, B., & Reisberg, D. (1991). *Learning and memory.* New York: Norton.

Schwartz, S. P. (Ed.). (1977). *Naming, necessity, and natural kinds.* Ithaca, NY: Cornell University Press.

Scott, J. (1988). *Gender and the politics of history.* New York: Columbia University Press.

Scribner, S. (1997). Modes of thinking and ways of speaking: Culture and logic reconsidered. In E. Tobach, R. J. Falmagne, M. B. Parlee, L. W. Martin, & A. Scribner Kapelman (Eds.), *Mind and social practice: Selected writings by Sylvia Scribner* (pp. 125–144). New York: Cambridge University Press.

Sellars, W. (1973). Does empirical knowledge have a foundation? In R. M. Chisholm & R. J. Schwarz (Eds.), *Empirical knowledge.* Englewood Cliffs, NJ: Prentice Hall.

Seller, A. (1994). Should the feminist philosopher stay at home? In K. Lennon & M. Whitford (Eds.), *Knowing the difference: Feminist perspectives in epistemology* (pp. 230–248). London: Routledge.

Serbin, L. A., Tonick, I. J., & Sternglanz, S. H. (1977). Shaping cooperative cross-sex play. *Child Development, 48,* 924–929.

Sheldon, A. (1992). Conflict talk: Sociolinguistic challenges to self-assertion and how young girls meet them. *Merrill-Palmer Quarterly, 38,* 95–117.

Sherif, C. W. (1987). Bias in psychology. In S. Harding (Ed.), *Feminism and methodology* (pp. 37–56). Bloomington: Indiana University Press.

Shotter, J. (1989). Social accountability and the social construction of the 'You.' In J. Shotter & K. J. Gergen (Eds.), *Texts of identity* (pp. 133–151). London: Sage.

Shweder, R. A.(1996). True ethnography: The lore, the law, and the lure. In R. Jessor, A. Colby, & R. A. Shweder (Eds.), *Ethnography and human development: Context and meaning in social inquiry* (pp. 15–52). Chicago: University of Chicago Press.

Shweder, R. A., Goodnow, J., Hatano, G., LeVine, R. A., Markus, H., & Miller, P. (1998). The cultural psychology of development: One mind, many mentalities. In W. Damon (Series Ed.) & I. E. Sigel & K. A. Renninger (Vol. Eds.), *Handbook of child psychology: Vol. 4. Child psychology in practice* (5th ed., pp. 1145–1207). New York: Wiley.

Siegal, M., & Robinson, J. (1987). Order effects in children's gender-constancy responses. *Developmental Psychology, 23,* 283–286.

Siegler, R. S. (1996). *Emerging minds: The process of change in children's thinking.* New York: Oxford University Press.

Siegler, R. S., & Ellis, S. (1996). Piaget on childhood. *Psychological Science, 7,* 211–215.

Silverstein, L. B. (1996). Evolutionary psychology and the search for sex differences. *American Psychologist, 51,* 160–161.

Smith, D. (1987). *The everyday world as problematic: A feminist sociology.* Boston: Northeastern University Press.

Smith, D. (1990). *Texts, facts and femininity: Exploring the relations of ruling.* New York: Routledge.

Smith, D. (1997). Comment on Hekman's "Truth and method: Feminist standpoint revisited." *Signs, 22*(2), 392–398.

Smith, J., & Russell, G. (1984). Why do males and females differ? Children's beliefs about sex differences. *Sex Roles, 11,* 1111–1120.

Smith, P. A., & Midlarsky, E. (1985). Empirically derived conceptions of femaleness and maleness: A current view. *Sex Roles, 12,* 313–328.

Sober, E. (1994). *From a biological point of view.* New York: Cambridge University Press.

Solomon, G. E. A., Johnson, S. C., Zaitchik, D., & Carey, S. (1996). Like father, like son: Young children's understanding of how and why offspring resemble their parents. *Child Development, 67,* 151–171.

Spanier, B. (1982, April). Toward a balanced curriculum: The study of women at Wheaton College. *Change, 14,* 31–34.

Spelman, E. V. (1988). *Inessential woman: Problems of exclusion in feminist thought.* Boston: Beacon Press.

Spence, J. T. & Helmreich, R. L. (1978). On assessing androgyny. *Sex Roles, 5,* 721–738.

Sperber, D. & Wilson, D. (1986). *Relevance: Communication and cognition.* Cambridge, MA: Harvard University Press.

Sperry, R. W. (1974). Lateral specialization in the surgically separated hemispheres. In F. O. Schmitt & F. G. Wardon (Eds.), *The neurosciences: Third study program.* Cambridge, MA: MIT Press.

Springer, K. (1996). Young children's understanding of a biological basis for parent-offspring relations. *Child Development, 67,* 2841–2856.

Sroufe, L. A. (1979). The ontogenesis of emotion. In J. D. Osofsky (Ed.), *Handbook of infant development* (pp. 462–516). New York: Wiley.

Sroufe, L. A., Bennett, C., Englund, M., & Urban, J. (1993). The significance of gender boundaries in preadolescence: Contemporary correlates and antecedents of boundary violation and maintenance. *Child Development, 64,* 455–466.

Stanback, M. H. (1985). Language and black woman's place: Evidence from the black middle class. In P. A. Treichler, C. Kramarae, & B. Stafford (Eds.), *For alma mater: Theory and practice in feminist scholarship* (pp. 177–193). Urbana: University of Illinois Press.

Stanley, L. (1992). *The auto/biographical I: The theory and practice of feminist auto/biography*. Manchester, England: Manchester University Press.

Stanton, D. C., & A. J. Stewart (Eds.), *Feminisms in the academy*. Ann Arbor: University of Michigan Press.

Steedman, G. (1986). *Landscape for a good woman: A story of two lives*. London: Virago.

Stein, N. L., & Glenn, C. G. (1979). An analysis of story comprehension in elementary school children. In R. O. Freedle (Ed.), *Advances in discourse processes: Vol. 2. New directions in discourse processing* (pp. 53–120). Norwood, NJ: Ablex.

Stein, N. L., & Levine, L. J. (1989). The causal organization of emotional knowledge: A developmental study. *Cognition and Emotion, 3*, 343–378.

Stevenson, M. R., & Black, K. N. (1988). Paternal absence and sex-role development: A meta-analysis. *Child Development, 59*, 793–814.

Stipek, D. J., & Gralinski, J. H. (1991). Gender differences in children's gender-related beliefs and emotional responses to success and failure in mathematics. *Journal of Educational Psychology, 83*, 361–371.

Stoddart, T., & Turiel, E. (1985). Children's concepts of cross-gender activities. *Child Development, 56*, 1241–1252.

Tajfel, H. (1982). Social psychology of intergroup relations. *Annual Review of Psychology, 33*, 1–39.

Tanesini, A. (1999). *An introduction to feminist epistemologies*. Oxford, England: Blackwell.

Tannen, D. (1993). *Gender and conversational interaction*. Oxford, England: Oxford University Press.

Tavris, C. (1992). *The mismeasure of woman*. New York: Simon & Schuster.

Taylor, M. C., & Hall, J. A. (1982). Psychological androgyny: A review and reformulation of theories, methods, and conclusions. *Psychological Bulletin, 92*, 347–366.

Taylor, M. G. (1996). The development of children's beliefs about social and biological aspects of gender differences. *Child Development, 67*, 1555–1571.

Taylor, M. G. (1997, April). *Boys will be boys, cows will be cows: Children's causal reasoning about human and animal development*. Poster presented at the biennial meeting of the Society for Research in Child Development, Washington, DC.

Taylor, M. G., & Gelman, S. A. (1993). Children's gender and age-based categorization in similarity and induction tasks. *Social Development, 2*, 104–121.

Taylor, M. G., & Gelman, S. A. (1999). *Children's beliefs about animal and human development: The role of category-membership and environment.* Unpublished manuscript, University of Puget Sound.

Tenney, Y. J. (1989). Predicting conversational reports of a personal event. *Cognitive Science, 13,* 213–233.

Tessler, M., & Nelson, K. (1994). Making memories: The influence of joint encoding on later recall by young children. *Consciousness and Cognition, 3,* 307–326.

Thelen, E., & Smith, L. B. (1998). Dynamic systems theory. In W. Damon (Series Ed.) & R. M. Lerner (Vol. Ed.), *Handbook of child psychology, Vol. 1. Theoretical models of human development* (5th ed., pp. 563–634). New York: Wiley.

Thompson, R. A. (1998). Early sociopersonality development. In W. Damon (Series Ed.) & N. Eisenberg (Vol. Ed.), *Handbook of child psychology: Vol. 3. Social, emotional and personality development* (5th ed., pp. 25–104). New York: Wiley.

Thorne, B. (1986). Girls and boys together...but mostly apart: Gender arrangements in elementary schools. In W. W. Hartup & Z. Rubin (Eds.), *Relationships and development* (pp. 167–184). Hillsdale, NJ: Erlbaum.

Thorne, B., & Luria, Z. (1986). Sexuality and gender in children's daily worlds. *Social Problems, 33,* 176–190.

Tirrell, L. (1998). Language and power. In. A. M. Jaggar & I. M. Young (Eds.), *A companion to feminist philosophy* (pp. 139–152). Oxford, England: Blackwell.

Tomasello, M., Kruger, A. C., & Ratner, H. H. (1993). Cultural learning. *Behavioral and Brain Sciences, 16,* 495–552.

Tong, R. (1989). *Feminist thought: A comprehensive introduction.* Boulder, CO: Westview Press.

Tong, R. (1998). *Feminist thought* (2nd ed.). Boulder, CO: Westview Press.

Trepagnier, B. (1994). The politics of white and black bodies. *Feminism and Psychology, 4,* 199–205.

Triandis, H. C. (1989). Cross-cultural studies of individualism and collectivism. *Nebraska Symposium on Motivation: Vol. 37* (pp. 41–133). Lincoln: University of Nebraska Press.

Trivers, R. L. (1972). Parental investment and sexual selection. In B. Campbell (Ed.), *Sexual selection and the descent of man* (pp. 136–179). Chicago: Aldine.

Turkle, S., & Papert, S. (1991). Epistemological pluralism and the revaluation of the concrete. In I. Harel & S. Papert (Eds.), *Constructionism* (pp. 161–191). Norwood, NJ: Ablex.

Turner, J. C., Hogg, M. A., Oakes, P. J., Richer, S. D., & Wetherell, M. S. (1987). *Rediscovering the social group: A self-categorization theory.* New York: Basil Blackwell.

Ullian, D. (1976). The development of conceptions of masculinity and femininity. In B. Lloyd & J. Archer (Eds.), *Exploring sex differences.* London: Academic Press.

Unger, R. K., & Crawford, M. E. (1992). *Women and gender: A feminist psychology*. Philadelphia: Temple University Press.

Urwin, C. (1984). Power relations and the emergence of language. In J. Henriques, W. Holloway, C. Urwin, C. Venn, & U. V. Walkerdine (Eds.), *Changing the subject: Psychology, social regulation and subjectivity*. London: Methuen.

Valsiner, J. (1998a). The development of the concept of development: Historical and epistemological perspectives. In W. Damon (Series Ed.) & R. M. Lerner (Vol. Ed.), *Handbook of child psychology: Vol. 1. Theoretical models of human development* (5th ed., pp. 189–232). New York: Wiley.

Valsiner, J. (1998b). *The guided mind*. Cambridge, MA: Harvard University Press.

Vander Zanden, J. W. (1993). *Human development*. New York: McGraw-Hill.

Vinden, P. G. (1996). Junin Quechua children's understanding of mind. *Child Development, 67*, 1707–1716.

Vygotsky, L.S. (1962). *Thought and language*. Cambridge, MA: MIT Press.

Vygotsky, L. S. (1978*). Mind in society: The development of higher psychological processes*. Cambridge, MA: Harvard University Press.

Wagenaar, W. (1986). My memory: A study of autobiographical memory over 6 years. *Cognitive Psychology, 18*, 225–252.

Waldfogel, S. (1948). The frequency and affective character of childhood memories. *Psychological Monographs, 62*.

Walkerdine, V. (1984). Developmental psychology and the child-centred pedagogy: the insertion of Piaget into early education. In J. Henriques et al. (Eds.), *Changing the subject: Psychology, social regulation and subjectivity*. London: Methuen.

Walkerdine, V. (1988). *The mastery of reason: Cognitive development and the production of rationality*. London: Routledge.

Weisner, T. S. (1979). Some cross-cultural perspectives on becoming female. In C. B. Kopp (Ed.), *Becoming female: Perspectives on development* (pp. 313–332). New York: Plenum Press.

Weisner, T. S. (1996). Why ethnography should be the most important method in the study of human development. In R. Jessor, A. Colby, & R. A. Shweder (Eds.), *Ethnography and human development: Context and meaning in social inquiry* (pp. 305–324). Chicago: University of Chicago Press.

Weisstein, N. (1971). Psychology constructs the female. In V. Gornick & B. K. Moran (Eds.), *Woman in sexist society*. New York: Basic Books.

Weisstein, N. (1993). Psychology constructs the female, or, The fantasy life of the male psychologist (with some attention to the fantasies of his friends, the male biologist and the male anthropologist). *Feminism and Psychology, 3*, 195–210.

Welch-Ross, M. K., Fasig, L., & Farrar, M. J. (1999). Predictors of preschoolers' self-knowledge: References to emotion and mental states in mother-child conversation about past events. *Cognitive Development, 14*.

Wellman, H. M. (1988). First steps in the child's theorizing about the mind. In J. W. Astington, P. Harris, & D. Olson (Eds.), *Developing theories of mind*. New York: Cambridge University Press.

Wellman, H. M. (1990). *The child's theory of mind.* Cambridge, MA: MIT Press.

Wellman, H. M., & Gelman, S. A. (1998). Knowledge acquisition in foundational domains. In W. Damon (Series Ed.) & D. Kuhn and R. S. Siegler (Vol. Eds.), *Handbook of child psychology: Vol. 2. Cognition, perception, and language* (5th ed., pp. 523–573). New York: Wiley.

Werner, N. E., & Crick, N. R. (in press). Relational aggression and social-psychological adjustment in a college sample. *Journal of Abnormal Psychology.*

Wertsch, J. V. (1991). *Voices of the mind.* Cambridge, MA: Harvard University Press.

Wertsch, J. V., & Tulviste, P. (1992). L. S. Vygotsky and contemporary developmental psychology. *Developmental Psychology, 28,* 548–557.

West, C., & Zimmerman, D. H. (1987). Doing gender. *Gender and Society, 1,* 125–151.

White, J. W. (1993). Feminist contributions to social psychology. *Contemporary Social Psychology, 17,* 74–78.

Whitford, M. (1988). Luce Irigaray's critique of rationality. In M. Griffith & M. Whitford (Eds.), *Feminist perspectives in philosophy* (pp. 109–130). London: Macmillan.

Whiting, B. B. (1986). The effect of experience on peer relationships. In E. C. Mueller & C. R. Cooper (Eds.), *Process and outcome in peer relationships* (pp. 79–99). Orlando, FL: Academic Press.

Whitley, B. E. (1983). Sex role orientation and self-esteem: A critical meta-analytic review. *Journal of Personality and Social Psychology, 44,* 765–778.

Wiley, A. R., Rose, A. J., Burger, L. K., & Miller, P. J. (1998). Constructing autonomous selves through narrative practices: A comparative study of working-class and middle-class families. *Child Development, 69,* 833–847.

Wilkinson, S. (1997). Feminist psychology. In D. Fox & I. Prilleltensky (Eds.), *Critical psychology: An introduction* (pp. 247–264). London, England: Sage.

Willett, C. (1995). *Maternal ethics and other slave moralities.* New York: Routledge.

Wilson, E. A. (1998). *Neural geographies: Feminism and the microstructure of cognition.* New York: Routledge.

Wilson, E. O. (1975). *Sociobiology: The new synthesis.* Cambridge, MA: Harvard University Press.

Wimmer, H., & Perner, J. (1983). Beliefs about beliefs: Representation and constraining function of wrong beliefs in young children's understanding of deception. *Cognition, 13,* 103–128.

Wittgenstein, L. (1968). *Philosophical investigations* (G. E. M. Anscombe, Trans.). Oxford: Basil Blackwell.

Wittgenstein, L. (1971). *On certainty* (G. E. M. Anscombe & G. H. von Wright, Eds., D. Paul & G. E. M. Anscombe, Trans.). New York: Harper Torchbooks.

Wollstonecraft, M. (1975). *A vindication of the rights of woman* (C. Poston, Ed.). New York: Norton. (Original work published 1891)

Wong, J. (1996). Adventures in socio-historical meta-epistemology: The idea of the normal child. *Explorations in knowledge, 14,* 1–24.

Wood, J. T. (1999). *Gendered lives: Communication, gender, and culture* (3rd ed.). Belmont, CA: Wadsworth.

Wyer, R. S., & Srull, T. K. (1983). *Memory and cognition in its social context.* Hillsdale, NJ: Erlbaum.

Contributors

Lorraine Code is Distinguished Professor of Philosophy at York University in Toronto. She is the author of Epistemic Responsibility (1987), What Can She Know? Feminist Theory and the Construction of Knowledge (1991), and Rhetorical Spaces: Essays on (Gendered) Locations (1995). She is General Editor of a one-volume Encyclopedia of Feminist Theories forthcoming from Routledge UK, and has edited five other books. Her areas of expertise are theory of knowledge, feminist epistemology and the politics of knowledge, theories of subjectivity, and agency. Her next book, written with a Killam Research Fellowship from the Canada Council, will develop an ecological model for knowledge and subjectivity.

Nicki R. Crick is Associate Professor of Child Development in the Institute of Child Development at the University of Minnesota. She has received the Boyd R. McCandless Young Scientist Award from the American Psychological Association (Division 7), a Faculty Scholar Award from the William T. Grant Foundation, and a FIRST award from the National Institute of Mental Health. She currently is an associate editor for Merrill-Palmer Quarterly. Dr. Crick publishes in the areas of social adjustment, peer victimization, social information processing, and social development, especially regarding relational aggression and gender.

Rachel Joffe Falmagne is Professor of Psychology and former Director of the Women's Studies program at Clark University. She is coeditor of Mind and Social Practice: Selected Writings of Sylvia Scribner. She has published on cognitive development, logic, language and mind, and epistemology. Her current research is on reasoning and inference, the interplay of cultural discourses and counter-discourses in the construction of reasoning processes, and the feminist critique of rationalism. She currently is co-editing a collection, Feminist Perspectives on Logic.

Robyn Fivush is Professor of Psychology at Emory University and recently was Director of Emory Institute for Women's Studies (1996-1999). She is so-author of Gender Development and co-editor of Knowing and Remembering in Young Children and The Remembering Self: Construction and Accuracy in the Self Narrative. She publishes articles and chapters on cognitive development, including autobiographical memory in social context, gender differences, emotions, and self.

Susan A. Gelman is Professor of Psychology at the University of Michigan. She publishes in the area of cognitive development, particularly conceptual representation and knowledge acquisition, including gender concepts. Dr. Gelman has received the Boyd R. McCandless Young Scientist Award (Division 7), the Distinguished Scientific Award, and Fellow status from the American Psychological Association; the American Psychological Foundation Robert L. Fantz Award; the Chase Memorial Award (biennial award for a young scientist) from Carnegie-Mellon University; and a Guggenheim Fellowship.

Sarah Henseler is a Ph. D. candidate in the Developmental Psychology program at the City University of New York Graduate School and University Center. Her work is concerned with the development of understanding of self and other.

Campbell Leaper is Associate Professor of Psychology at the University of California, Santa Cruz. He is editor of Childhood Gender Segregation: Causes and Consequences. Dr. Leaper has published articles on gender and communication in families, peer groups, friendships, and romantic relationships; self concept and social identity; the influence of activity settings on social and cognitive development; gender bias in schools; and images of gender in the media.

Patricia H. Miller is Professor of Psychology and an affiliate faculty member in Women's Studies at the University of Florida. She is the author of Theories of Developmental Psychology, co-author of Cognitive Development, and co-editor of Conceptual Development: Piaget's Legacy. She publishes research articles in the areas of cognitive development, social cognition, and gender. She is a Fellow in two divisions of the American Psychological Association and serves on the Editorial Boards of Psychological Bulletin and the Journal of Experimental Child Psychology.

Katherine Nelson is Distinguished Professor of Psychology at the Graduate School and University Center of the City University of New York. Her recent books include Language in Cognitive Development: Emergence of the Mediated Mind, Narratives from the Crib, and co-edited volumes, Socio-Cultural Psychology: Theory and Practice of Doing and Knowing, and Conceptual Development: Piaget's Legacy. Professor Nelson has published widely on the development of memory, cognition and language. She is a former Editor of Cognitive Development and serves on several other editorial boards. She is a Fellow of APA and APS, and a 1999 recipient of an Award for Distinguished Contribution to Research in Child Development from the Society for Research in Child Development.

Daniela Plesa is a Ph. D. candidate in the Developmental Psychology program at the City University of New York Graduate School and University Center. Her published work concerns children's understanding of narrative texts and genres, and children's theory of mind. Her current research focuses on the development of the understanding of perspectival conflict.

Amanda J. Rose is Assistant Professor of Psychology at the University of Missouri, Columbia. She received several research and teaching awards while a graduate student at the University of Illinois. She publishes on the social competencies necessary for children to be successful in their friendships, gender differences in peer relationships in childhood and adolescence, and gender role development.

Sue V. Rosser is Dean of Ivan Allen College at Georgia Institute of Technology and Professor of History, Technology, and Science. She was Director of the Center for Women's Studies and Gender Research at the University of Florida (1995-1999) and Senior Program Officer for Women's Programs at the National Science Foundation (1995). She has published 7 books, including Female-Friendly Science, Re-engineering Female-Friendly Science, Feminism and Biology: A Dynamic Interaction, Women's Health: Missing from U. S. Medicine, and Teaching the Majority. She publishes on women and science, women's health, and pedagogy based on women's studies' research.

Ellin Kofsky Scholnick is Associate Provost for Faculty Affairs, Professor of Psychology, and an affiliate faculty member in Women's Studies at the University of Maryland, College Park. She formerly was Special Assistant to the President on Women's Issues at Maryland. She has edited four books and published empirical articles on cognitive development, specifically, conceptual representation, logic, and planning in children. Dr. Scholnick has been associate editor of Child Development and Developmental Psychology, and President of the Jean Piaget Society. She is a Fellow of the American Psychological Association and the American Psychological Society.

Marianne G. Taylor is Assistant Professor of Psychology at the University of Puget Sound. Her research examines children's understanding of social categories. She has published articles on children's gender-related beliefs and concepts, as well as gender salience and flexibility. Her current work focuses on the role of parent-child conversations in shaping children's beliefs about gender and race.

Melissa K. Welch-Ross is Assistant Professor of Psychology at Georgia State University. She has published articles on the development of memory, on suggestibility, and on the relation between memory and knowledge of gender-roles. Her area of expertise is the interrelations among autobiographical memory, self-understanding, and theory of mind. Professor Welch-Ross holds a FIRST award from NIMH.

Index